Unaffected
by the Gospel

Fig. 1. *Cler-mónt, First Chief of the Tribe.* This is actually Clermont II, leader of the Arkansas Osage in the 1830s. His father, Clermont I, permitted the first Protestant missionaries to move into Osage Country in 1820, and Clermont II allowed the missionaries to remain. (George Catlin, Smithsonian American Art Museum, Gift of Mrs. Joseph Harrison Jr., 1834.)

Unaffected
by the Gospel

Osage Resistance to the Christian Invasion
(1673–1906): A Cultural Victory

Willard Hughes Rollings

University of New Mexico Press **❙** Albuquerque

Library of Congress Cataloging-in-Publication Data

Rollings, Willard H.
Unaffected by the Gospel : the Osage resistance to the Christian
invasion (1673–1906) : a cultural victory / Willard Hughes Rollings.
     p. cm.
Includes bibliographical references and index.
ISBN 0-8263-3557-8 (cloth : alk. paper) —
ISBN 0-8263-3558-6 (pbk. : alk. paper)
1. Osage Indians—Religion. 2. Osage Indians—Missions. 3. Osage Indians—
Social conditions. 4. Catholic Church—Missions—Great Plains—History.
5. Presbyterian Church—Missions—Great Plains—History. 6. Christianity and
culture—Great Plains—History. 7. Racism—Religious aspects—Christianity.
I. Title.
 E99.O8R65 2004
 200'.89'975254—dc22
                                        2004011809

Design and composition by Maya Allen-Gallegos
Typeset in Minion 11/13.5
Display type set in Frutiger

To mi alma, Barbara

Contents

Illustrations

Acknowledgments

When I began this project, I had no idea that it would take so long to complete. I began this endeavor soon after I finished my first book about the Osage people. Thinking, since I was so familiar with the people and the topic, that with a bit more research, I could soon write a book about Osage interaction with the United Foreign Missionary Society and the American Board of Commissioners for Foreign Missions missionaries.

Thus inspired, I traveled to the Houghton Library at Harvard where the UFMS and ABCFM materials are stored and searched through the missionary board's records and correspondence. I copied all of the relevant material from the American Missionary Register and the America Missionary Herald in the Harvard-Andover Seminary Library and returned to Las Vegas where the university kindly awarded me a year's leave to complete the research and write the book.

The book was not written that year, for we discovered that the frequent dizzy spells that had plagued me that spring were caused by an oligodendroglioma—a brain tumor—that was deemed inoperable. A year of experimental chemotherapy directed by two life-saving neuro-oncologists stopped the growth of the glioma, but I spent most of my energies that year fighting fatigue and nausea, instead of writing the book.

As I recovered and returned to the project, I turned to friends who provided me with the much needed encouragement and direction. I dashed off an e-mail to my friend, Richard White, whose counsel has always been helpful. Richard thought the topic was sound, but he posed thel question: "Where are the Jesuits? Willard, you have to include the Jesuits and examine their role in the process." Richard has this remarkable ability to point out the obvious, that is never obvious until he points it out. To deal with the Jesuit's role I turned to another friend, Jackie Peterson, an expert on the western Jesuits, who provided information, great insights, and a kind introduction to the Jesuit archivists in St. Louis.

With Jackie and Richard's direction, I launched a new round of research at the Midwest Jesuit Archives and began reshaping my examination of the Christian missionary efforts among the Osage in a new and broader context. I incorporated the new material in several papers that I gave at academic conferences where my friends: Terry Austrin, Colin Calloway, Denys Delâge, David Edmunds, John Finger, Mike

Green, Rayna Green, Markku Henriksson, Fred Hoxie, Ritva Levo-Henriksson, Theda Perdue, Helen Tanner, and others too numerous to recount, provided direction and advice. Phil Deloria and Neal Salisbury, who were editing an article of mine about Indians and Christianity, also provided invaluable help in shaping the book.

Other friends and colleagues provided help with the project. I want to thank Gussie Tanenhaus for translating Father Ponzigliones' two hundred and thirty-eight page Latin journal into English, Tina Stergios for drawing the maps, and Margaret Connell-Szasz for sending me to UNM Press. I would also like to thank my dear friend and forever mentor, John Wunder, who provided help and encouragement.

I wish to express my gratitude to Father William B. Faherty, S.J. and Nancy Merz at the Midwest Jesuit Archives in St. Louis, who opened up their archives to a stranger and provided valuable advice and information about the Jesuit Fathers. Thanks also to my two good friends, Julie and Kenny Sturma, who welcomed me into their home while I conducted research that summer. My thanks to Cindy Stewart at the Western Historical Manuscript Collection at the State Historical Society of Missouri and Mary Jane Warde at the Oklahoma Historical Society for their help. Chris Wiatrowski and Maria White at the University of Nevada, Las Vegas Library were especially helpful, and I am grateful for their support. My thanks to the University of Nevada, Las Vegas for supporting my research trips to Cambridge and St. Louis and granting me a sabbatical to complete the book. My thanks also go to the staff of the Newberry Library where I began this project so many years ago, and to those who helped me at the Houghton Library. I would also like to thank everyone at the University of New Mexico Press, with special thanks to David Holtby, Jill Root, Kathy Sparkes, and Maya Allen-Gallegos.

Members of my family were especially supportive. Although my mother, Luella Rollings, and my sister, Davetta Chavez Fry, did not survive to see the completion of the book, they both provided the inspiration necessary to finish it. Aunt Clara and Uncle Bill Cunningham were also helpful, and I am grateful for their love and support. Friends and colleagues provided help and friendship through this endless project, and I want to express my special thanks to Michael W. Bowers; Earline and James Braddy; Jim Escalante; Michele Litsey; Joe Martinic, Linda Martinic, and Alice Martinic; Sharon Braddy-McKoy, James McKoy; Joyce Neitling; Lea Sexton; Jen Stenfors; Allen Svec; David and

Ginger Tanenhaus, and Susan Unger. I also want to acknowledge the help my two cats, Socorro and KC, provided, napping on my desk and occasionally demanding attention, thus providing me with needed breaks from the nineteenth-century prairie-plains.

I want to extend my special thanks to David R. Miller whose help was priceless. More importantly, David introduced me to the wonderful Assiniboine people of Montana and Saskatchewan who welcomed me into their Medicine Lodge. I want to thank all my Lodge brothers and sisters for their powerful songs and prayers that provide strength and hope, and I especially want to thank Jim Shanley, Larry Wetsit, Edna Wetsit, Kate Shanley, David Moore, Rosella Archdale, George Redstone, Joe "Jo Jo" Miller, Harold Bailey, Kenneth Ryan, and the late Oliver Archdale for their friendship and guidance.

I would especially like to thank three fine physicians: Dr. William Shapiro, Dr. Luis Diaz, and Dr. Clark Haskins for providing the diagnosis and treatment that saved my life. Any funds I receive from this book will be given to the Barrows Neurological Institute in Phoenix to assist them in their vital research. While these fine doctors treated my body, my dear amigo, David Lanehart, who, with his late night calls and whitewater rafting trips, provided needed support for my frightened spirit. Without these skilled and caring people, I would not have survived to write this book.

Many kind and brilliant people made this book possible, but their efforts pale in comparison with those of my beloved and amazing wife, Barbara. She was a tremendous help with the book, traveling with me on research trips, typing notes, making countless copies, and retrieving the chapters when the computer crashed. She read chapters repeatedly and provided needed insight and perspective while catching my careless mistakes. Barbara graciously and generously provided all this help while attending law school and studying for and passing the bar. Her steadfast support and keen intelligence are responsible for any contribution this book might make. All mistakes are mine and mine alone.

I would like to extend my special thanks to the Osage people. They are truly an extraordinary people with a rich and remarkable history. The Wah-zha-zhe entered my life twenty-three years ago and will forever remain a part of my life. Although they were once the fierce enemies of my people when we were forced into their prairie homelands, I hold them in highest regard and greatest respect. Thi-ku´-tha, Mânî Mniha.

Fig. 2. *Wa-másh-ee-sheek, He Who Takes Away; Wa-chésh-uk, War; Mink-chésk, Three Distinguished Young Men.* These three are members of the Arkansas Band Osage. (George Catlin, Smithsonian American Art Museum, Gift of Mrs. Joseph Harrison Jr., 1834.)

1

The Osage:
Unaffected by the Gospel

I must tell you I am not without my trials. I sometimes
feel great discouragement, while I look around upon this
people [Osage] and behold them sinking into their
graves, entirely unaffected by the gospel.
—Reverend Nathaniel Dodge, *Missionary Herald*[1]

The Osage Indians are vicious and lazy, having no desire
to be made Christians or to become good. . . . What our
Fathers do in this mission apart from the schools
amounts to very little. . . .
—Father John Druyts,
The Jesuits of the Middle United States[2]

These sad epistles from missionaries on the Osage prairies
might be seen as cries of despair from failed missions, or
as vivid evidence of Osage victories as they held fast to
their way of life and fought to retain their culture. Perspective is so
important in viewing the past. History is interpretive, as cultural and
temporal contexts shape all accounts. Historical interpretation depends
upon the interpreter, and, until recently, Native history was written by
non-Natives relying solely on the records and perspectives of outsiders.
I am one of those outsiders trying to interpret the history of Native
peoples, and although I am linked genetically with those peoples, I
remain a creature of the twentieth century. Born in the late 1940s, I am
also a product of Cold War American culture.

This Cold War context, which grows colder by the hour, provides
us with an appropriate and hopefully revealing metaphor for Native

history. Just imagine the quality of U.S. history written in the Soviet Union from 1946 to 1989. Such history was limited in sources, and those limited sources were misunderstood and misinterpreted, because the Soviets lacked an understanding of Americans. They could not truly understand America, nor the cultural diversity of the United States. This misunderstanding was exacerbated because the Soviets were engaged in a bitter and often violent competition with the United States for the hearts, minds, and resources of the world. This bitter competition, combined with the limited sources and lack of a shared culture, produced questionable accounts of history. Such is the history that, until recently, has been written about Native Americans.

Tragically, the shared history of Native Americans and Euro-Americans was filled with violence. The Europeans, who would in time become Euro-Americans and eventually Americans, fought to gain control of the land and resources of North America. Also tragic has been historians' and scholars' narrow focus on the violence and the violent. This focus is unfortunate, for the history of Native Americans and Euro-Americans, while often violent, was much more complex and much more significant than mere accounts of the Pequot War or the general accounts of nineteenth-century violence on the Great Plains.[3]

Many Native groups did not engage in violent confrontation with the Euro-American invaders, but resisted in other ways, and their history has unfortunately lagged behind that of those who did violently resist invasion. This lag is disappearing, for scholars are now examining the complex and incredibly diverse history of all Native peoples of North America. The history of those peoples was shaped by the context of the great invasion, with resistance, both violent and nonviolent, playing a vital role in that history.

This book is an attempt to examine such nonviolent resistance to the Euro-American invasion, specifically the nonviolent resistance of the Osage to the invasion of their lives and culture. The nonviolent nature of their resistance is ironic, for the Osage were renown for their martial skills. The Osage were fierce warriors who went out onto the plains in the eighteenth century, seized control of the central and southern prairie-plains, and maintained hegemony over the region for at least one hundred years.[4]

Osage hegemony was created and maintained by violent conflict with other Native peoples. This eighteenth-century warfare continued well into the nineteenth century, as the Osage continued to fight their

Native rivals until the 1870s. This eighteenth- and nineteenth-century conflict, however, was focused exclusively on Native American rivals. The Osage, although engaged in occasional threats of violence against the French, the Spanish, and the people of the United States, never once conducted any large-scale attacks on Euro-Americans.

The Osage were able to avoid war with the invaders because of a fortuitous combination of location in place and time, and a keen and clear understanding of those circumstances. The Osage seemed able to understand their ever-changing realities and were able to combine a cultural tenacity with cleverness and pragmatism to survive the ongoing invasions. They were able to pick their battles and to maintain some control over the shape and nature of the conflicts. Some might argue that the Osage had little control of their conflicts, that circumstance and events shaped Osage decisions, and that the thoughtful pragmatism I attribute to them was merely a reaction to the changing realities of the nineteenth-century prairie-plains. I would counter that the Osage retained a great deal of control of their lives and were never mere victims to the invasion of their lands and lives; this book will examine such invasions and try to reveal their partial victory.

The ever-changing realities of the prairie-plains indeed shaped their responses, but if one carefully examines the Osage history, they will discover a unique history. Other Native American people, such as my people, the Cherokee, fought Europeans and the United States, and with defeat struck compromises to retain some control of their lives and culture. The Iroquois Confederation, Shawnee, Creek, and Lakota all fought similar battles and were defeated, and their subsequent compromises were shaped by their battlefield defeats.

The Osage, challenged by those same French, Spanish, English, and American conquerors, took another approach and skillfully avoided military defeat. By avoiding military defeat they were better able to control the compromises forced upon them. While they challenged the French and Spanish, the Osage never attacked a French or Spanish settlement. They remained friendly with the British, who were never immediate threats, and they balanced threat with compromise when dealing with the Americans. Living among the competing colonial frontiers, the Osage skillfully manipulated the imperial competition. They used the fears and jealousies of the French, Spanish, British, and Americans to obtain power and to maintain the accompanying autonomy throughout the eighteenth century and the first years of the nineteenth century.[5]

With the departure of the Europeans, Osage manipulation was severely limited, because the source of their power on the plains was the firearms and ammunition that they had acquired from the competing Europeans. The very items that created their power had also created a serious dependency upon European trade. When world political changes rearranged the Osage market in 1814 and left them with only one trading partner, the United States, the Osage compromised and made the changes necessary to keep trade open without surrendering complete control of their lives.

The essential change was a call for continued peace with the United States, and that peace was easily maintained in the early nineteenth century, for the United States presented no immediate or visible threat to the Osage. The number of whites in the region, although growing, was still small, and almost all of them were either hunters who could be intimidated without any large-scale violence or traders who were providing the Osage with desired goods.

Although peace with the United States was easily maintained, peace in the region, however, would be more difficult to sustain, for the Osage were being confronted with an increasing number of dangerous invasions in the region. In the late eighteenth century eastern tribes, forced from their homelands by the growing invasion of white settlers, began hunting in the Osage hunting territory. The eastern invasion only increased in the nineteenth century, as hundreds of Potawatomi, Sauk, Mesquakie, Delaware, Kickapoo, Shawnee, Choctaw, and Cherokee moved into the Osage forests and prairies and challenged them for control of the region. The eastern threats were soon exacerbated by growing new threats in the West.

The Comanche, Wichita, Kiowa, and other plains tribes, long restrained by Osage power, began to forge alliances in the late eighteenth century, and united they were able to challenge the Osage for control of the western plains.[6] Unfortunately for the Osage these growing threats in the eastern forests and the western plains came about just as their trade became restricted to only the United States. The growing threats, combined with the U.S. trade monopoly, severely limited Osage options and forced them to come up with new compromises to fight the Native invaders while maintaining good relations with the United States.

Those good relations would be sharply challenged by a newly created U.S. Indian policy (see chapter 2). President Jefferson was creating the ambitious new policy to end the costly warfare on the frontier and to bring about the peaceful union of all American peoples. Jefferson's plan called for the eastern tribes to surrender their lands east of the Mississippi in exchange for lands west of the Mississippi in the newly acquired French Louisiana. Removing the Indians to the West would open the rich lands in the East and end Indian-white frontier violence. Jefferson also planned to send teachers, missionaries, and other agents of American culture out among the Indians to transform them into white Americans. Jefferson realized that such cultural changes would require time, but he believed that the newly emptied eastern lands would sate the white demands for land, and while they settled the eastern forests, the American agents would have enough time to bring about the transformation of the Indian people. Once transformed into white—at least culturally white—yeomen farming families, the Indians would be assimilated into the American population, and Americans could harvest their country's bountiful resources unencumbered by racial violence.

This ambitious national removal plan would inescapably involve the Osage, for they occupied much of the prime western lands immediately west of the Mississippi where the United States wanted to relocate the eastern tribes. Soon after the United States "acquired" these western lands, they began badgering the Osage to vacate the land to make room for the eastern tribes. In 1808, they coerced the Osage into ceding most of their forest hunting territory to make room for the forced arrival of the eastern tribes. This pressure for the removal of the eastern tribes would continue to grow as whites spread into eastern tribal lands.

The removal policy created tremendous problems for the Osage, for even before it became U.S. policy the eastern tribes had been moving into Osage lands. With the creation of a formal removal policy the trickle of invaders became a flood, and the Osage were soon surrounded by the eastern peoples. The Indian invasion of Osage territory began to multiply the Osage's problems. The eastern invaders were skilled hunters and experienced traders; their growing presence in the region created serious competition for the game and trade in the West. A declining share of the game and trade brought about a decline in the amount of arms and ammunition, which were vital to the Osage in controlling their western plains. Further, the United States, their sole trading partner, wanted peace in the region. Not just peace with the Osage, but also with the eastern tribes moving west onto Osage lands, for any warfare in the region would only discourage eastern tribes already reluctant to surrender their homelands and move across the Mississippi.

Osage dependence on U.S. trade guaranteed peace with the United States and imposed a dangerous limit on the violence they could take against eastern tribes. The United States used Osage dependency to establish some means of controlling them. The Americans used a trade embargo to coerce the first land cession, and thereafter they established forts in Osage territory. The United States combined its military presence with the increased opportunity for trade to gain some control over the Osage and to maintain the peace necessary for removal.

The Americans also took advantage of this forced peace to support cultural agents who volunteered to go among the Osage and prepare them for assimilation into American culture. The United States funded and encouraged Christian missionaries to go among the Native peoples to persuade them to abandon their cultures and to embrace the American way of life, to become "civilized." Nineteenth-century Americans, however, defined civilization according to their own mandates, and to nineteenth-century white Americans "civilized" meant people living in individual, nuclear families engaged in small-scale subsistence farming, with the men cultivating the soil and the women tending to the household chores. The missionaries' idea of civilization, moreover, also required the Indians to abandon their native religions and convert to Christianity.[7]

Protestant Christian churches became deeply involved in the "civilizing" program, and missionaries surged onto Indian lands to convert and civilize the "heathen savages." The fervor of the Second Great Awakening (see chapter 3), combined with the U.S. funding and support of the missionaries, created a Protestant missionary rush into Indian country. The Osage, located between the two expanding Indian frontiers and with their desperate need for United States trade, were unable to attack and drive these cultural agents away, and were therefore forced to tolerate their presence.

The Osage were, however, able to shape and control their contacts with missionaries and were thus able to maintain control of their cultural lives. Unwilling to attack the agents of assimilation, the Osage often tolerated them and simply ignored their message. They sometimes feigned interest in order to use the missionaries to their advantage, devised a variety of nonviolent techniques to resist the unwanted cultural invasion, and in time learned to co-opt the messengers and discard the message.

New England Protestant missionaries from the United Foreign Missionary Society (UFMS), filled with the energy and spirit of the Second Great Awakening, arrived in Osage country in 1820 and established mission stations among them. For seventeen years they worked to convert the Osage to Protestant Christianity and American civilization with little success, and then decided their spiritual energies and financial support would best be applied elsewhere. In 1837 they surrendered, closed their Osage stations, and moved on to attempt to convert other tribes.

The Osage first encountered Catholic missionaries in the eighteenth century, but the contacts were brief and of little consequence. In the nineteenth century, however, priests from the reestablished Jesuit order returned to the Osage to convert them to Roman Catholicism. Jesuits visited the northern band villages throughout the 1820s and 1830s, and in 1847 established a mission among them. Jesuit fathers worked diligently to convert the Osage until they were forced from the region in 1872.

Earlier scholars have chronicled the efforts of the Protestant and Catholic missionaries among the Osage. The general interpretation of these endeavors was that the Protestants were abject failures at converting the Osage, while the Jesuits were successful champions. This is a common interpretation among many scholars examining Christian missionary efforts among Indian people. In the case of the Osage it is a mistaken one, for upon close examination it is clear neither the New England Protestants nor the Roman Catholics succeeded in converting the Osage to Euro-American Christianity.[8]

Both groups failed in their missions among the Osage because the Osage, subjected to fifty-two years of ardent and zealous missionary efforts by both New England Protestants and Roman Catholic Jesuits, remained Osage—with their culture and cultural adaptations firmly in their control. While the Osage indeed changed from 1820 to 1872, their spiritual lives remained largely traditional. They were able to sustain their own self-defined, cultural-spiritual framework and to withstand the enormous challenges that confronted them in the nineteenth century. Their durable framework would be forced to bend and change, but the necessary changes were shaped by the Osage themselves. The Osage used familiar forms and patterns that retained enough of their earlier patterns to remain distinct and familiar. This book will relate how the Osage were able to resist the colonial spiritual invasion of Christianity and to hold on to their traditional religious beliefs in the years of concentrated missionary efforts.

In the summer of 1819 Reverend Epaphras Chapman, a missionary of the UFMS, came up the Arkansas River to meet with the western Cherokee to secure their permission to establish a mission among them. Upon discovering that the Cherokee were already "taken" by the American Board of Commissioners for Foreign Missions (ABCFM), Chapman traveled on to the newly established Fort Smith, where he met with a group of Osage leaders who had come to the fort to speak with the Cherokee. Chapman spoke with Gra-to-moh-se, or Clermont, one of the southern bands' leaders, who agreed to give land to the UFMS for a mission among his people. After securing a location for the southern bands' mission, Chapman traveled north, visiting northern Osage villages on his return home.

Upon Chapman's return to New York, the UFMS gathered together twenty-one people to go among the Osage, to save their souls and transform them into civilized members of the American-Christian community (see chapter 3). The UFMS missionaries left their homes in April, making their way down the Ohio to the Mississippi and slowly up the Arkansas River. Bouts with illness took the lives of two of the young teachers and continued illnesses, combined with the low water of the Arkansas, stranded them in the newly formed community of Little Rock. While they waited to recover and for the river to rise, Chapman, five of the male missionaries, and three "hired men" continued on to the mission site to begin construction of the mission.

They arrived in mid-November 1820, and the eight began construction of their mission "on a fine prairie" along the west bank of the Neosho River. They believed the site ideal; it was located near a large spring, close to the river, with sufficient timber to build their mission; the surrounding prairie was ideal for the farming necessary to feed the missionaries and their livestock. They would later note that perhaps they should have chosen a site a bit farther west, closer to the Osage villages and above the damp river bottom.

In February 1821 the mission family arrived at the station, which they named Union in honor of the union of the three denominations—Presbyterians, Dutch Reform, and Associated Reform—who made up the UFMS. The mission site was only twenty miles from a small group of trading posts located where the Verdigris and Neosho Rivers joined the Arkansas River, known as the Three Forks. More importantly the mission was only about twenty-five miles from the large towns of the southern Osage bands led by Gra-to-moh-se and Tah-hah-ka-he, or Tally.

While the Union missionaries were stranded in Little Rock, a group of northern-band Osage led by Sans-Nerf, alerted to the proposed mission by Chapman's visit, traveled to Washington and requested a mission among their bands to get their share of whatever was being offered to the southern bands. Sans-Nerf's visit was prompted by factional jealousies, not by the desire for words of the Christian God. Sans-Nerf called on Thomas McKenney, superintendent of Indian Trade, who quickly relayed the message to the UFMS in New York. The UFMS sent a representative to meet with the northern band leaders and agreed to send another mission family to the northern villages.[9]

The UFMS immediately assembled another missionary family, who departed in March 1821 for the northern Osage villages.[10] This large mission family, composed of forty-one people, made their way up the Osage River. On August 13, 1821, they established their mission station along the prairie marshes of the Marais des Cygnes River near a U.S. trading factory.[11] This mission, named Harmony for the harmonious relations they intended to establish with the Osage, was about fifteen miles from the two large northern band communities led by Pawhuska, or White Hair, and Nez-ah-mo-nee, or Walk in the Rain.[12] From these two mission bases the missionaries would establish other mission stations among the Osage. In 1823 Union missionaries established their first station, a mission farming community made up of a few Osage and mixed-blood families, which they named Hopefield, a few miles north of Union on the east bank of the Neosho.

In the summer of 1822, just one year after the Harmony Mission had been established, the federal government closed its trading factory near the mission. This closure forced the northern bands to leave their old town sites on the forks of the Osage River and move south to establish villages near the Chouteau trading post on the Neosho River. These bands would return north in 1825, but not to their traditional village sites near the mission. Instead they established their villages along the upper Neosho River some eighty miles southwest of the Harmony station, near another Chouteau trading post. To remain near the Osage, the Harmony Mission sent a missionary to the Neosho River in September 1824, where he established their Neosho station.[13]

The missions, despite the sincere and concentrated efforts of the missionaries, did not have much success in converting the Osage into civilized Christians (see chapters 4 and 5). The missionary at Neosho angered the U.S. agent there, charging him with fraud and corruption. In 1830 the agent, with the support of the Chouteaus and some of the northern bands leaders, had the missionary expelled from the region. The missionaries, undeterred, regrouped, moved a few miles to the south, and established a new mission community, named Boudinot in honor of Elais Boudinot, an ABCFM supporter.

In 1825 the Osage were coerced into ceding more lands for the resettlement of the removed eastern tribes, and in 1828 the Cherokee bought the land where Union and Hopefield were located. As the Cherokee began moving into the region, they insisted the Osage farmers leave, so in 1830 the Hopefield settlers moved fifty miles north, where they reestablished their mission farms at a site they named New Hopefield.

Despite Cherokee claims on the land, the original mission school at Union remained in operation, but Cherokee, Choctaw, and other immigrant tribes soon surrounded it, and only a few Osage children attended. With the ever-declining enrollment, most of the Union missionaries relocated to the remaining mission stations at Harmony, Boudinot, or New Hopefield. The New Hopefield mission was short-lived, for the Cherokee also claimed that site, and their claim along with repeated attacks of cholera drove most of the Osage from the community.

In 1836 Harmony was also abandoned because only a few Osage lived near the mission. It was now in Missouri, and whites settling the region demanded the Osage leave the land they had ceded in 1808. William Requa, the single remaining Protestant missionary among the Osage, moved his New Hopefield followers north to merge with the Boudinot Mission, and by the spring of 1836, his was the only Protestant Osage mission that remained. This outpost lasted for less than a year, for in 1837 Requa, realizing the futility of his task, closed the mission. This closing thereby ended the Protestants' seventeen-year effort to convert the Osage.

The Roman Catholic Church was also concerned about the souls of the Indians (see chapters 7 and 8), and as early as the seventeenth century they began sending priests into Osage country. Father Marquette's visit to the region resulted in the earliest recorded appearance of the Osage, for in 1673 Father Marquette placed them on his crudely drawn map. Later, in the 1720s, the Roman Catholic Church established missions at Arkansas Post near the mouth of the Arkansas River and at Cahokia and Kaskaskia along the east bank of the Mississippi where the Osage came to trade. These brief, limited contacts provided no spiritual changes among the Osage. With the expulsion of the Jesuits from Louisiana in 1764, the Osage had no further contact with Catholic missionaries until 1818, when Bishop Du Bourg moved his See to the fur-trade city of St. Louis.

This move would be the prelude to their spiritual invasion of the Osage. In 1820 Osage leaders from the northern bands were visiting General William Clark in St. Louis when Sans-Nerf, the same Osage spokesman who had traveled to Washington to ask the UFMS for missionaries, called on Bishop Du Bourg and asked him to visit their villages. Bishop Du Bourg never made a visit, but he sent another priest, Father Charles de la Croix, to visit the northern Osage villages. In 1821 de la Croix made a brief visit to one village where "[h]e was very well received and baptized a great many children."[14] He returned in the summer of 1822 to visit the Osage River villages with Auguste Pierre Chouteau, the Osage subagent, where he again baptized several people and conducted Masses.[15] With the success of de la Croix's visits, Bishop Du Bourg, in hopes of Christianizing the Indians of the West, traveled to Washington, where he secured federal funding for Catholic missions among the Indians. In the fall of 1823 Bishop Du Bourg visited the Novitiate of Jesuits at White Marsh, Maryland, to enlist more Jesuits for these Indian missions.[16]

Bishop Du Bourg, a Sulpician, owned a farm at Florissant, a French farming community fifteen miles northwest of St. Louis. To support the Jesuits' efforts he gave them his farm.[17] By June 1824 the Jesuit fathers had constructed a boarding school for Indian children on this land and now needed students. The leader of the Jesuit novices, Father Van Quickenborne, visited the northern Osage villages on several occasions and was able to solicit a few full-blood Osage and métis children for the Jesuits' school.[18] Van Quickenborne's plan of separating the children who attended the school from their people and culture in hopes of converting them failed. The boarding school never attracted many students, for the Osage were unhappy about having their children separated from them, and the students were not willing "to bend under the yoke of discipline."[19]

With the failure of the Florissant school, Van Quickenborne returned to older Jesuit traditions and began to plant Jesuit missionary centers among the Indians' homelands in an effort to convert them. In June 1836 Jesuits established a mission at the Kickapoo reservation just north of Fort Leavenworth, and in March 1839 they established another mission among the Potawatomi along Sugar Creek, a small tributary of the Marais des Cygnes.[20]

By 1839 all of the Osage bands had been forced north, and most of their villages were near the Sugar Creek Mission. Jesuits from the Potawatomi mission frequently visited the nearby Osage villages where they celebrated Mass and baptized Osage and métis. In 1847 the Catholics received funding for an Osage mission, and in April Jesuit Father John Schoenmakers arrived at Flat Rock Creek and began constructing the Osage Mission two miles from the Neosho River. The site was ideal, for it was near the American Fur Company and other trading posts, and it was only a few miles from several northern Osage villages. The Jesuits brought out the Sisters of Loretto and together they established a boarding school for the Osage and the métis children of the traders.

Kansas in the 1850s, however, became a scene of great violence as proslavery and antislavery mobs flocked to eastern Kansas and fought to determine the future of the territory. The violence grew with the outbreak of the Civil War and threatened the very survival of the mission. Kansas became filled with Native American refugees of Indian Territory violence, and guerilla warfare raged across the region. Some members of the southern bands supported the Confederate efforts, while members of northern bands fought for the Union. Southern rebels threatened to burn the mission because of the northern sympathies of the Jesuits, but the priests were persuaded to leave the mission and the mission buildings survived the war. The mission, however, would not survive the postwar peace, for soon white settlers flooded the region and clamored for the Osage to leave Kansas.

In 1865 the Osage ceded a portion of their Kansas lands, and this cession placed the Osage Mission and almost all of the Osage villages on federal land. The Osage, however, remained in their villages along the Neosho and Verdigris Rivers, and the Catholic brothers and sisters continued to administer to the Indian and mixed-blood children. Kansans continued their demands for Osage land, and in 1870 the Osage surrendered all their land in Kansas, agreeing to move south to a new reservation. Confusion surrounding the boundaries of their new homeland delayed the move south, but by 1872 the Osage had left Kansas and were settled on their new lands in Indian Territory. With the expulsion of the Osage from Kansas, the former Roman Catholic mission for the Osage became a Catholic boarding school for white children.[21] Although the Jesuit fathers continued to visit the Osage periodically, they directed their energies to the growing white Catholic communities of southern Kansas, never reestablishing their Osage Mission.

Neither the Catholics nor the Protestants ever had much success converting the Osage to Christianity. It is clear from the records that the first efforts of the Protestant missionaries among the Osage were a failure. This failure is acknowledged in a report written in anticipation of the abandonment of their last Osage mission station in 1836.[22]

A retrospect of the history of this mission cannot be taken without awakening many painful emotions. Very few, if any, of the adults of the tribe have been induced to exchange their savage and migratory habits for a civilized and industrious life; or to substitute the Christian doctrines and practices for the ridiculous and absurd superstitions; or have been in any other manner benefitted as to the condition of their character. . . . The amount of funds expended on the mission has been great; and so also has been the number of laborers who have engaged in promoting it. Not a few of these, after going through a course of arduous service, have gone down to the grave, the victims of disease and hardship; others, worn down by toil and disheartened by opposing difficulties, have retired from the field with broken constitutions; while the remnant, after having labored with much fidelity and patience nearly fifteen years, have felt themselves compelled to abandon the work, leaving the Osages, with scarcely an exception, more miserable and hopeless, both as to condition and character, than they were when the mission was commenced among them.[23]

Nineteenth-century ethnocentrism, racism, and cultural arrogance aside, it is clear from this account, by one of the participating Protestant missionaries, that the Protestant Osage missions were a grand and expensive debacle.

These missions failed because the missionaries never understood their challenge. They were asking a people to give up a successful and satisfying way of life, to adopt an alien way of life ill-adapted for the prairies. The Protestants demanded they substitute a life of community for one of individualism and loneliness, a life of generosity for one of miserliness. They asked the Osage to give up their diverse and successful hunting, gathering, and farming economy to become yeoman farmers. The Protestant mission farms' livestock, tools, and experienced farmers were never able to support the missionaries' stations. They would have collapsed entirely if not for the ongoing support of their missionary societies, yet these same unsuccessful farmers expected the Osage to stop hunting and adopt farming without any such support.

The grim struggles of the Hopefield communities offered ample proof of a flawed system. Despite growing pressures from the east and west, the Osage economy remained strong, and they saw no need to abandon success for failure. Osage life in the 1820s and 30s remained soundly based despite the influx of newcomers to the region, the increased exposure to diseases, and violence. With a familiar and successful life pattern, they had no impetus to make the dramatic cultural changes demanded by the Protestants.

While the Protestant missions were clearly accepted as failures, everyone who has examined the Catholic efforts to convert the Osage has pronounced their efforts a resounding success. It is noted that Osage children attended the Osage Mission school in Kansas and that they only left when the Osage moved to their new reservation in Indian Territory; this is not entirely true. An examination of the Osage Mission lists that record Osage baptisms, marriages, and interments does show hundreds of Osage Catholic "converts," in striking contrast to the few, if any, recorded Osage Protestants.[24] From these records it appears that the Jesuits converted many more Osage than did the Protestants; however, I am dubious of the sincerity of those conversions, for the nature of conversion is different for the Protestant than it is for the Roman Catholic. I am convinced that most of the Osage politely ignored Catholic theology, while those who claimed to convert still retained much of their traditional religion beneath a thin veneer of Catholicism.

The Osage practiced an elaborate religion, with a complex theology containing a rich and elaborate liturgy. Osage bands possessed lengthy and detailed cosmologies. They maintained an active ritual calendar that called for public and private rituals for the good of the people to be performed at various times throughout the year. They held ceremonies to welcome the new year, to ensure good planting, to guarantee successful hunts, and even to control the weather. Their *Tsi Wa-kon-da-gi,* or House of Mystery, rituals prepared them for war or sanctified peace. The *Non-hon-zhin-ga,* or Little Old Men, were the clan priests who presided over tattooing rituals, naming ceremonies, and healing ceremonies to cure their people. They conducted burial and mourning rituals when the healing ceremonies failed. Clans and individuals created and maintained their *wa-xo-be,* or sacred bundles, that contained powerful spiritual items.[25]

The Jesuits seemingly had success among the Osage for a variety of reasons. It helped that the Jesuits' mission was established in the midst of the métis fur trading community settled along the Neosho. The French traders were nominal Catholics, and many wanted religious sanction for their unions with Osage women and wanted their métis children to be baptized and educated by the Church. These same individuals were bilingual, speaking Osage and French. All of the early Jesuits spoke French, and thus they could communicate with the community more easily than the Protestants, who could speak only English. Only three Protestants learned Osage, and two of them would depart the missions shortly after they acquired the language, one dying of cholera and the other so disliked that the Osage formally asked him to be withdrawn from their villages.[26]

The Jesuits were also better trained and educated than most of the Protestants. Although led by seminary-trained pastors, many of the Protestants possessed more enthusiasm than religious education, this in striking contrast to the Jesuits' years of religious training. The Jesuits all came from Europe, eager to cross the Atlantic to work abroad among the Indians. Most of the Protestant missionaries also wanted to go abroad to save the souls of natives, but often those deemed less qualified were sent to the domestic charges, the Indians of the West.[27]

Jesuits, unlike the Protestants, went among the Osage as unattached single men. Initially this might have caused some concern because of their celibacy, but it allowed them to travel freely with the semi-nomadic Osage, unencumbered by families. The Jesuits were free of any family responsibilities and could focus their attention solely on the Osage. Almost all of the Protestant missionaries were married with families, and these families were a responsibility added to their task of converting the Natives. Although occasionally a few

Protestants went on hunting trips with the Osage, they could never stay long, for they had to return to care for their families back at the mission station.[28]

The Osage could also more easily accept an allegiance to Catholicism, for they shared many superficial spiritual traits with the Catholics. Both Roman Catholics and Osage believe that objects can possess spiritual significance. Catholics believe that sacramentals (religious objects), when properly used, can bring about the grace of God. The Osage instead believe objects possess a spiritual power that can bring good fortune. These are two distinct and different ideological interpretations of religious objects, but the differences are subtle and can be easily overlooked. When Sans-Nerf visited Bishop Du Bourg, the bishop gave him crucifixes and medals of the saints. While the two did not share an understanding of what the objects meant, they agreed they were objects possessing spiritual significance.[29] The Protestants, however, did not share those beliefs. Their spirituality was largely an intellectual exercise devoid of sacred objects possessing any spiritual powers. Crosses were merely symbols of faith, not actual sacramentals. The New England Protestants never handed out crosses to the Osage, nor erected them at their missions; instead they constructed sawmills and grist mills.[30]

The Osage practiced a complex religion filled with lengthy and elaborate rituals, conducted by a spiritual elite attired in elaborate clothing. Chanting and the recitation of lengthy sacred stories accompanied these rituals. The Roman Catholic Mass, conducted by priests wearing sacred vestments and accompanied with songs and chants, was perhaps misunderstood by the Osage, but again was superficially familiar enough to be recognized as a sacred and respected ceremony.

Both Osage and Catholic ceremonies were unlike the Protestant religious services, which were conducted by preachers dressed in plain clothing and consisted of lengthy sermons with little ritual and only limited singing. Although the Osage sometimes attended the lengthy services and repeatedly were told that the ceremonies were holy, the Protestant ceremonies never followed any of the Osage's familiar sacred forms, and their drab Sunday services were in striking contrast to the more elaborate Osage and Catholic rituals (see chapter 8).

The Jesuits tried to use any similarity between their faith and that of the Osage to make their faith more acceptable to the Osage. The Osage were polytheistic, and, while ascribing the highest power to the sun, moon, earth, and thunder, they believed that the world was filled with spirits and that plants and animals possessed a spirituality that must be acknowledged and respected. While the Roman Catholics did not ascribe souls to plants and animals, the fact that they revered a variety of saints could be easily employed by the Jesuits to seek a spiritual commonality with the Osage.

These shared elements all contributed to the apparent Roman Catholic success, but the Roman Catholics also had an another advantage. Catholic liturgy and ritual were more focused on the sacraments than were those of the Protestants. Protestants focused on the words; to them the holy sacraments existed only as symbols. Thus the sacraments would always remain mere symbols and not true acts of grace. Symbols only succeed when all agree on what they represent, and cultural differences make it very difficult to understand abstract symbolism.

Both Protestants and Catholics performed the sacraments as reminders of the earlier acts of Christ. The command to "Do this in memory of me" was the core of Protestant sacraments. For Protestants, Communion was an act in which bread symbolized the body of Christ and wine symbolized his blood. Protestants would eat the bread and drink the wine to remind them of the sacrifice that Christ made to save them. Further, nineteenth-century Presbyterians would only share Communion with those who had had a spiritual conversion experience accepted by the congregation and with those who had also passed an examination on church doctrine.[31] Thus Communion, one of the few dramatic rituals the Protestant missions conducted and that might have had an impact on the Osage, was conducted privately, seldom, if ever, in the presence of the Osage.[32]

In striking contrast, the Jesuit missionaries frequently conducted their seven sacraments before the converted and nonconverted alike, for all to see and share. While the Jesuits were also concerned with the Osage's doctrinal understanding, this understanding was not a prerequisite to sharing their sacramental rituals with them. They believed that the sacraments were more than mere symbolic reminiscences, that they were in fact the acts of worship created by Christ, and that by participating and performing the sacraments one could achieve grace.[33] There is an immediacy to the Catholic sacraments that is missing from the Protestants' beliefs. For the Catholics, the sacraments are spiritual in and of themselves, and the very act of performing the ritual properly goes well beyond symbol, becoming a real act of spirituality conveying Christ's grace.

Communion, although an act shared by both Protestants and Roman Catholics, is therefore substantially different in form and substance. Catholics perform the ritual every day in public, and it is much more than a symbolic reminder of Christ's sacrifice. Their daily celebration of the Mass, which serves to remind them of Christ's ultimate sacrifice, goes beyond mere memory. The bread and wine are not merely symbols, because in the very act of Mass they become the body and blood of Christ through the process of transubstantiation. Through this daily ritual a physical Christ, not a symbolic memory of him, comes among them. The Mass is conducted by sacred individuals clothed in ornate gowns, and it is a dramatic act filled with song, incense, and grandiose gestures. This elaborate ritual was understandably more attractive to the Osage than the Protestant services, which contained lengthy sermons on the true nature of sin and attempted to convince the Osage they were in a wretched state.

In addition, the Jesuits were willing to baptize infants who knew nothing of the Christian faith and to consider them saved. They would also marry couples who could not understand the words of the ceremony, convinced that the sacrament conducted by a priest made it a holy union. They would perform extreme unction for dying people, believing the sacrament was enough to achieve salvation. They would anoint the head of the sick with blessed oil, praying for them to be healed. To the Jesuits their worship was inseparable from their sacraments.[34]

The real nature of the Osage conversions is suspect, however. Although the Osage Mission records contain hundreds of names of Osages and mixed-bloods who participated in the Roman Catholic ritual, it does not reveal the true nature of their conversion. The Roman Catholics were indeed successful in converting the Osage from their theological standpoint; that is not questioned. The question, however, is the exact nature and extent of the Osage's acceptance of the Roman Catholic faith. It is more likely that the Osage, only because of the superficial similarities with the Catholic faith, were willing to accept a Catholic veneer, while they actually continued to believe and practice their own religion.

Some Osage were willing to attend Mass because it was filled with music and ritual; some may even have sent their children to the mission school because it made their friendly neighbors, the Jesuits, happy and more willing to share food, shelter, blankets, pots, pans, and tools. The Osage were also willing to accept Catholic baptism and prayers for their dead, because their faith was one of inclusion, not exclusion. They would occasionally participate in Catholic services, in the hopes that participation would contribute to their success in hunting and in wars against their enemies. The Osage did not abandon their traditional faith and become Roman Catholics; they simply added the Catholic rituals and sacramentals to their spiritual lives.

The Osage in nineteenth-century Kansas and Oklahoma became neither Presbyterians nor Roman Catholics; they remained Osage. Despite the differences in Roman Catholic and Protestant theology, both were Christian and shared a common European-inspired worldview. Both preached of sin, a concept truly alien to the Osage. Protestants preached that man was filled with sin and degradation and that only conversion would save them from eternal damnation. Protestant conversion of the Osage, particularly among the Presbyterians who operated the Osage missions, was especially difficult. They insisted that the Osage demonstrate both spiritual conversion and intellectual understanding of their faith before they would be deemed converted. Few if any Osage ever experienced the call for spiritual conversion, and fewer still were ever able to pass the congregation leaders' lengthy and detailed examination. While the Catholics provided an easier means for forgiveness of sins, one still had to understand and believe in sin to be forgiven. While their religious practices differed greatly in detail, emphasis, and practice, they shared a common view of a theological construct based on a single Christian God whose only son, Christ, was born, died, and resurrected to save the souls of humankind.

The Osage, on the other hand, believed that they were only one of many spiritual creatures inhabiting the universe. Their universe was shared with all things, human and nonhuman. The Osage's shared place within the universe's space was maintained by acts of reciprocity. Religious ritual was required to maintain the reciprocal relationship between humans and nonhumans, for this relationship required balance of the universe. Osage religion called for the exchange of goods and social interaction with humans and nonhumans, and they took the steps necessary to keep themselves and their universe in balance. This was in striking contrast to the Protestants and Catholics, who saw themselves as the single most important inhabitants of the planet. Christianity called for the conquest and harnessing of the elements of nature. Its practitioners never saw themselves as only one of the many participants in a much larger world.

The Christians believed that only humans possessed spiritual value, and they arranged their universe according to a linear hierarchical construct with their God reigning supreme over the universe he had created. In the Book of Genesis the Supreme Being, God, or Yahweh, gives Adam (mankind) the power to name all of the animals. In that same first book of the Bible, Noah is given the power to choose which animals to save from the great flood. Christians did not believe in an equality of existence and a sharing of space with the elements of nature. They insisted on seizing, controlling, and consuming nature. Euro-American ideologies of domination and submission were not understood by the Osage, for the Osage's ethos was one in which the social, natural, and supernatural worlds were defined and shaped by reciprocity rather than by domination and submission.[35]

Christians preached that the followers of Christ made individual decisions regarding their beliefs, and that they chose Christian moral behaviors; thus at death Christians were separated from sinners by a judgmental God. Notions of heaven, hell, and purgatory were the very antithesis of Osage beliefs, The Osage maintained they were certain to reach the other world after death, regardless of their earthly behavior. The Osage paid little attention to the afterlife, although they believed it was much like their present-day life on the prairies, only with an abundance of game and ever-bountiful gardens.

The Osage prayed, but not to be saved from eternal damnation. They sent their prayers to Wa-kon-da, their all-pervasive holy spirit, in the sacred smoke of their pipes to ask his help to find bison, bear, and deer to feed their people. They prayed for successful raids against the Pawnee, but never for salvation. The Christian faith was simply too alien. Neither Catholicism, with all its seeming similarities, nor Protestantism, with its sharp differences, was attractive or believable enough to tempt the Osage to abandon their traditional beliefs.

During more than fifty years of interaction with these aggressive Christian missionaries committed to converting them, the Osage continually resisted. As long as the Osage men were able to hunt and raid on the plains, and their women and children were free to farm on the prairies, they remained Osage. Throughout their resistance they were able to maintain, adapt, and change their ceremonies and rituals based on their beliefs—Osage beliefs.

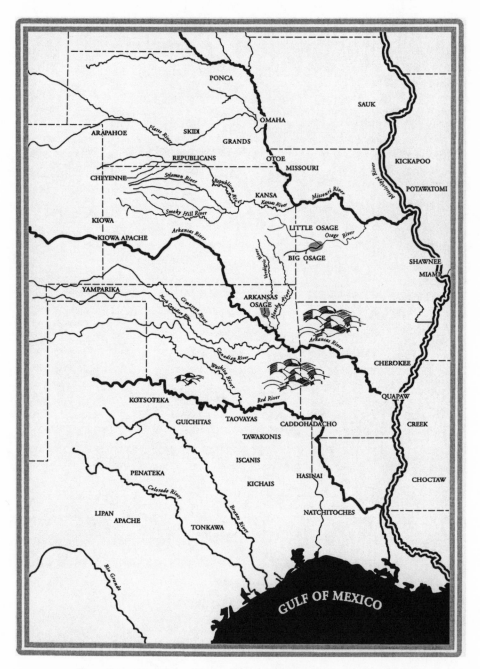

Fig. 3. Location of the Osage villages and the tribes surrounding them ca. 1800. (Artist, Christine Stergios, 2003.)

2

Osage Hegemony on the Prairie-Plains

You see the Arkansas [Quapaw], who cannot go hunting
on the prairies without having their throats cut by the
Osages. They as well as we are obliged to hunt roebuck
on the Mississippi, while the Osages make themselves
masters of all the hunting country. The Osages, my
Father, are at war with all men, white and red, steal the
horses, and kill all the white men they find. The white
men of Illinois carry goods to them, Ah! my father, if the
Osages had only their arrows and they were not given any
merchandise, we could soon finish them.
                                   —Thomas, Chickasaw Chieftain, 1793[1]

Neither the Protestants nor the Roman Catholic missionaries who ventured onto the Osage prairies in the
1820s knew of such charges made against the Osage;
indeed they knew little of the people they sought to save. The leaders
of their societies heard a brief description presented by the superintendent of Trade, Thomas McKenney, but it is not clear whether that
brief bit of information was shared with the missionaries out in the
field. Both the New England Protestants and the Flemish Catholics
thought the Osage were heathen savages who possessed little worth-
while culture or history. Hence they never really knew whom they were
trying to convert. That ignorance, combined with a general lack of
interest, hindered their pursuits to bring about any meaningful conversions in Osage lives.[2]

When the UFMS missionaries arrived in 1820, the Osage were confronting enormous challenges to their lives. The missionaries' presence was only peripheral, and although sometimes annoying, it was

of little consequence to them. For the first time since they had moved onto the western prairies-plains they were facing a growing threat from two rapidly advancing Native American frontiers. This was a new and uncomfortable position for the Osage, who had dominated the region since their migration there two hundred years before.

In the early seventeenth century a large group of Dhegian-Siouan speakers composed of Quapaw, Osage, Kansa, Omaha, and Ponca people, pressed by the violence of the Beaver Wars, left the eastern forests of the Ohio Valley, migrated across the Mississippi River, and moved north along the Missouri River Valley.[3] The Osage broke away from this larger group and established villages along the Great Plains prairies near the headwaters of the Osage River, where Father Marquette encountered them.[4] Living along the prairies, the Osage created a new way of life that incorporated their older woodland cultural traits with new elements that better suited their prairie life. They planted familiar crops on the forest edges, and after planting their gardens they left to hunt buffalo out on the shortgrass plains along the Arkansas, Cimarron, and Smoky Hill Rivers.

Caddoan-speaking peoples, however, occupied these shortgrass plains. North of the Arkansas along the Platte, Republican, and Loup Rivers were the four bands of Pawnee: Republican, Skidi, Tapage, and Grand. Along the Arkansas Valley and south to the Red River were the Pawnee's Caddoan kin: the Guichitas, Taovayas, Tawakonis, Iscanis, and Kichais collectively known as the Wichita.[5] South of the Red River were the Caddoan Hasinai, Caddohadacho, and Natchitoches tribes often referred to collectively as the Caddo. The Pawnee, Wichita, and Caddo were large groups and posed a potential barrier to any Osage expansion west. They also, however, provided great raiding opportunities for the Osage, for the Pawnee, Wichita, and Caddo villages were occupied by thousands of women and children and were filled with Spanish horses and agricultural products from the village gardens.

In the seventeenth century the Osage maintained a brief peace with the western Caddoans.[6] This harmony ended, however, when French traders from Canada came among the Osage in the late seventeenth century, and the prairie-dwelling Osage became eager participants in the growing trade. When they acquired metal tools and muskets, the seventeenth-century peace between the Osage and the Caddoans quickly gave way to forceful Osage expansion, fueled by their new acquisitions.

By the 1680s the Osage were mounted on horses; with the advent of French settlements in Illinois, Missouri, and Louisiana they became better armed and began hunting and raiding in the south and west for goods to trade to the French.[7] Henry Tonty, traveling among the Caddo along the lower Red River, reported Osage raiding for horses in 1698.[8] They began hunting buffalo on the Wichita hunting grounds along the Arkansas and deer in the southern Ozark and Ouachita forests. They raided the Natchitoches, Caddohadacho, and Hasinai villages in the south, stealing horses and capturing people to trade to the French.[9]

The Osage, unwilling to see their western Caddoan rivals armed, sought to block French traders from traveling to the Pawnee, Taovaya, Iscani, Tawkoni, Kichai, and Wichita. French traders, traveling alone or in small groups, were easily barred from traveling west by the Osage. Eighteenth-century French records are filled with accounts of confrontations between French traders and the Osage warriors as they sought to block any western trade with the Wichita.[10] One of these confrontations in 1719, described by a French soldier-trader, provides a glimpse into their eighteenth-century embargo. Claude-Charles DuTisné, an agent of the Mississippi Company en route west to establish peace and trade with the Wichita, passed through an Osage village. DuTisné described the scene: "When I reached the Osages I was well received at my arrival. I explained to them your [Bienville's] plans [for trade] which they accepted very well as far as it concerns them; but when I mentioned to them that I wanted to go to the Pani [Wichita], they were opposed to it."[11] The Osage reluctantly allowed DuTisné to continue on, but not before taking all of his trade goods save three muskets and sending word ahead to the Wichita that DuTisné was a slave trader.[12] DuTisné narrowly avoided attack by quickly convincing the Wichita he was not a slaver, merely a trader without trade goods. Living along the Arkansas, Missouri, Osage, and Red Rivers allowed the Osage to severely obstruct French trade into the West and to seriously limit their western rivals' access to the guns and ammunition necessary to counter Osage raids.[13]

Massive herds of buffalo roamed the shortgrass plains to the west, and large Wichita, Taovaya, Iscanis, Kichai, and Tawakoni villages filled with horses, women, and children were strung along the Arkansas and Red River valleys. The Osage, armed with French muskets, were able to attack the villages, steal the horses, and capture the women and children, whom they traded to the French. This pattern of western raids and eastern trade grew throughout the eighteenth century, and French and Spanish records have abundant accounts of the constant western violence.

Just as the Pawnee, Wichita, and Caddo faced attacks from the French-armed Osage, the Osage faced potential attacks from eastern tribes who had greater access to French and British traders. In the early eighteenth century, however, the Osage were protected from eastern tribe attacks by distance. Forest tribes such as the Shawnee, Potawatomi, Kickapoo, Ho-chunk, Sauk, and Mesquakie were facing more immediate threats in their eastern forest homelands, and in the early eighteenth century they seldom traveled far enough to the west to attack the Osage. This pattern would change in the later part of the eighteenth century, but for most of the century the Osage's northern frontier was protected by distance and by the presence of Missouri, Oto, and Iowa villages that absorbed most northeastern attacks and buffered the Osage villages from these raids.

The Osage villages were also sheltered by distance from the large southeastern tribes. The Choctaw, Chickasaw, Creek, and Cherokee were too engaged with their immediate neighbors and with European colonial conflicts to travel to the distant prairies to attack the Osage. In addition, the presence of their Dhegian kin, the Quapaw, living east of them along the Mississippi and the lower Arkansas Rivers buffered most southeastern attacks. With distance and substantial buffer villages to the east, the Osage turned west and expanded onto the plains, mounted on Spanish horses and armed with French muskets, and by the mid-eighteenth century they dominated the prairie-plains from the Arkansas south to the Red River.

Denied ready access to the French, the Wichita and Caddo could not turn to their western European neighbors, the Spanish, for arms, for the Spanish were more intent on acquiring and holding territory than the French. Spanish colonials, intent on converting the Southern Plains tribes into Spanish peasants, were loath to arm people they intended to conquer; thus they provided the Osage with weak opponents. The Republican and other Pawnee who lived north of the Osage maintained access to French trade, but had to deal with the constant onslaught of Lakota attacks from the north.[14] Although hammered by the Lakota and challenged by the Kansa, the Pawnee remained strong enough to shape Osage expansion, directing the Osage south and west to the country of the poorly armed tribes.[15]

The immediate targets of the Osage were the Wichita bands who inhabited the central plains from the Smoky Hill River south to the Red River. In 1719, when Jean-Baptise Bénard, sieur de la Harpe, visited the Wichita along the Arkansas (near present-day Tulsa, Oklahoma), he described a village of six thousand people gathered from the surrounding Wichita villages to celebrate the summer hunt and trade with the French.[16] By the 1740s most of the Wichita villages along the Arkansas were abandoned, victims of Osage raids. The few remaining villages along the Arkansas were casualties of blistering Osage attacks throughout the 1740s, and by 1750 the Osage had driven all the Wichita tribes from the Arkansas Valley. The two Wichita villages remaining on the Red River in 1750 were heavily fortified and surrounded by large earthen walls.[17]

These successful conquests in the region created a growing population and a new prosperity among the Osage. In 1719, when Claude-Charles DuTisné visited, he estimated that there were two hundred Osage warriors living with their families in two hundred lodges along the Osage River. Later, in the 1750s, the Spanish claimed that there were at least 950 Osage warriors, and in the 1770s the Spanish reported at least twelve hundred Osage.[18] The population growth, combined with the growing economy, created internal political and social stress. Mounted, armed, and with a growing population, the Osage no longer had to live and hunt in a single group. To cope with the new economic, social, and political conditions that horses and guns had created, the Osage separated into three autonomous divisions. About 1713 a group known as the Little Osage left the villages on the Osage headwaters and moved north to the Missouri River to gain better access to Missouri River trade. Those remaining on the Osage River were called the Big Osage. The Big Osage split further in the 1770s when a group moved south to take advantage of the southern trade and proximity to the Wichita villages. These Arkansas Osage, as they were called, moved south to the Three Forks region where the Neosho and Verdigris join the Arkansas River. The three groups would maintain separate polities and identities, but the two northern bands, bound by culture and location, usually acted in concert, while the Arkansas Osage remained separate and distinct from the Big and Little Osage. Despite the division and ongoing factional disputes, all three groups maintained their tribal identity and shared their forest and plains hunting grounds.[19]

The Osage were able to dominate the region because of the market for the animal resources in the area they controlled. The French traders desired bear tallow, deerskins, buffalo hides, mules, horses, and Indian slaves, and the Osage were able to secure those items in their ever-expanding homelands. The French also wanted to maintain friendly ties with the most powerful tribe in order to deny the Spanish and British entry into the region, so they continued to trade with the Osage even when they had no real need or desire for Osage goods.[20]

Beginning in the late seventeenth century, the Osage villages were between the French and the Spanish colonial settlements. The Osage were fortunate that their western prairie homelands lay between competing European frontiers, although that situation changed somewhat in the late 1760s with the French cession of North America to the British and Spanish. Despite the departure of the French colonial officials, the Spanish in Louisiana continued French trade patterns and brought goods to the Arkansas Post, Cape Girardeau, and St. Louis to exchange with the Osage. Familiar French Canadian traders continued to visit the Osage, joined frequently by outlaw traders from America. Combined, they kept the Osage supplied with ample trade, muskets, and powder.[21] With the end of the American Revolution in 1783, American traders flocked to the West to compete with those same French Canadian and British traders who continued, despite the treaty restrictions, to trade with the Osage and to compete with the Spanish for their trade.

Throughout the eighteenth century the Osage skillfully manipulated European rivalries to ensure consistent trade, good prices, guns and ammunition, and other desirable goods for themselves. If European traders denied them trade goods or made unreasonable demands, the Osage would threaten to go to their rival's traders. Such threats were easily carried out because of the flood of competing traders traveling along the Mississippi, Missouri, and Arkansas River valleys. Those same threats allowed them to limit trade to the Wichita and Caddo.[22]

Living near but not directly on the Missouri, Arkansas, and Mississippi Rivers, the Osage had access to the river-based trade. Yet their distance from the major rivers and the limited summer flow of the Osage River kept them out of the mainstream river trade traffic and provided them with some protection from the diseases that accompanied that traffic. This distance from the "epidemic corridor" apparently allowed the Osage to survive the massive population losses of the eighteenth-century epidemics that devastated the Quapaw,

Missouri, Kansa, Omaha, Ponca, and other river tribes.[23] Their immediate departure from the Plains expedition of Etienne de Véniard, sieur de Bourgmont, in 1724 when signs of disease first appeared is evidence the Osage were well aware of the danger of the new diseases and their consequences.[24] This isolation ended with the 1801 smallpox epidemic.[25]

Eighteenth-century epidemics, however, had an immediate impact on their relations with their northern kin, the Kansa. The Kansa living near the mouth of the Kansas River had ready access to the French and hunted the Arkansas and Smoky Hill valleys for buffalo, competing with the Osage for control of the rich region. The Kansa became infected with smallpox in the 1750s, and the outbreak devastated the tribe.[26] Weakened by smallpox, the Kansa made peace with the Osage around 1763 and thereafter peacefully shared the hunting territory between the Kansa and Smoky Hill Rivers; together they fought the Pawnee for control of the Smoky Hill, Saline, and Solomon River valleys.[27] This new peace along the lower Missouri enabled more traders to come among the Osage, further enabling their expansion west into the Pawnee and Wichita plains.

The Wichita, under attack from the Osage, were also threatened by the Apache, who had migrated into the Southern Plains in the seventeenth century. The Apache were composed of several groups. In the early eighteenth century the Carlana, Jicarilla, Faron, and Lipan Apache were occupying the region between the Pecos River and the Cross Timbers. Apache bands continued to move south and to deny the Wichita unobstructed access to the Spanish trade in the Rio Grande Valley of New Mexico and to the missions of south Texas. Osage raids had driven the Wichita southwest, where they fought the Apache for land and trade.[28]

Pressed by the Osage and Apache, the Wichita faced still another challenge at the beginning of the eighteenth century when the Comanche entered the Southern Plains. The Comanche were members of a large group of Northern Shoshone people living in the mountains of Colorado. In the late seventeenth century several bands—the Penateka, Yamparika, and Kotsoteka—broke away and migrated south. By 1705 the Penateka Comanche were living along the headwaters of the Arkansas and Cimarron Rivers, drawn south by the buffalo and horses of the Southern Plains. The farming villages of the Wichita, along with the Pueblo and Spanish communities of the northern Rio

Grande Valley and south Texas, lured the Comanche south. The Comanche invasion of the Southern Plains grew stronger throughout the eighteenth century; with the Osage to the northeast, Apache to the south, and Comanche to the north, the Wichita struggled to survive.[29]

Although the Comanche occasionally attacked the Wichita, they directed most of their attacks to the south where, along with their Ute allies, they raided the Apache *rancherias* filled with horses and potential slaves for the Spanish markets in nearby New Mexico. As French traders moved onto the plains in the 1740s, some detoured south and made their way west up the Red River, avoiding the Osage embargo along the Arkansas. In the mid 1740s French traders had established trade with the Wichita and began using the two large Taovaya villages on the Red River as a base for Southern Plains Indian trade.[30]

This French trading post on the Red River would shape new political patterns on the Southern Plains. After a series of Comanche attacks on the Rio Grande pueblos in the 1740s, the Spanish suspended trade with the Comanche. In search of trade and allies to fight the Apache, the Comanche turned to the beleaguered Wichita. Sometime around 1747 the Comanche made peace with the Wichita and joined them to share the French trade and to drive the Apache from the Southern Plains.[31] Together they also launched a series of attacks on the Osage hunting out on the plains in the 1750s.[32]

French trade with North America was disrupted during the Seven Years' War (1756–63), depriving the Osage of needed guns and ammunition, and the war, combined with the recent Comanche-Wichita alliance, temporarily stalled Osage westward expansion. Only temporarily, because with the end of the war in 1763 both British and French Canadian traders returned to the Osage villages with muskets and ammunition. Rearmed, the Osage renewed their attacks against the Pawnee, Wichita, and Comanche. By the 1770s the Wichita had abandoned their fortified villages on the Red River and had fled south to the Brazos.[33]

Osage expansion into the region continued despite the entry of still another invader from the north. The Kiowa and Kiowa-Apache, driven south from the Platte by Lakota attacks, first appeared along the headwaters of the Arkansas in the 1790s.[34] Challenged by the Pawnee, the Kiowa and Kiowa-Apache moved south to the upper Cimarron, where they fought the Comanche for buffalo and horses. Sometime in the late eighteenth century the Kiowa and Comanche began a process toward peaceful relations. This peace gradually came about as both decided that they faced greater threats from the newly arrived Cheyenne and Arapahoe than from each other; they gradually stopped fighting one another and began to share that region south of the Cimarron along the upper Canadian River.[35] The Kiowa-Comanche peace was preceded by the peace the Comanche had forged with the Spanish in 1786.[36] Peaceful trade with the Spanish, combined with this newly created peace, empowered the Comanche, Kiowa, and Wichita to drive the Apache from the region and to mount real challenges to the Osage raiders for control of the upper regions of the Arkansas, Cimarron, Canadian, and Red Rivers.[37]

The Osage were able to withstand these growing western challenges in the late eighteenth and early nineteenth centuries. They had driven the Wichita from the Red River and severely limited European access to the western tribes, while at the same time increasing their trade with the British and Spanish. This trade continued throughout the eighteenth century while the Osage remained between imperial frontiers. In the 1770s the Osage were between the Spanish and the British; after the American Revolution, despite the treaty-directed removal of the British traders, they maintained an illegal trade with the British and remained amidst the competing frontiers of the Spanish, American, and British. Canadian traders, both French and British, continued to visit Osage villages after 1783, seeking potential allies and the products of the forests and prairie-plains. Spanish traders living in the former French Louisiana maintained trade with the Osage reluctantly but out of necessity, because the Spanish feared that by denying them trade the powerful Osage would establish trade with the Americans just across the Mississippi.[38] Indeed, outlaw traders from the United States traveled among the Osage to trade firearms and ammunition for horses, mules, and buffalo robes.[39] With their greater and more immediate contact with competing traders, the Osage remained better armed than their western rivals and were able to confront the challenges of the Pawnee and the increased challenges created by the Wichita, Comanche, Kiowa, and Kiowa-Apache peace in the West.

The remainder of the eighteenth century saw constant conflict in the central and Southern Plains as the Osage contested with the Pawnee, Wichita, Caddo, and Comanche for control of the region and its resources. The late eighteenth-century Spanish records from San Antonio, Natchitoches, and St. Louis are filled with never-ending complaints of Osage attacks.[40] Lieutenant Governor Athanase de Mézières, in a letter from Natchitoches, in 1770 provides a typical tirade against the Osage:

> The Osages, living on the river of the same name, which empties into the Missuris [sic], have from time immemorial been hostile to the Indians of this jurisdiction; . . . But that river of the Akansa [Arkansas] having become infested by the concourse of malefactors of which I have spoken, they soon came to know the Osages, and incited them with powder, balls, fusils, and other munitions. . . . Thus all at once this district has become a pitiful theater of outrageous robberies and bloody encounters.[41]

Throughout the 1770s, 1780s, and 1790s the Osage sustained their control of the central prairie-plains region, and the bloody encounters continued into the nineteenth century as the Osage maintained their control. Such was the power of the Osage when Jefferson wrote of Osage domination in 1803. They remained powerful throughout the first three decades of the nineteenth century and would begin to weaken only when a unique combination of circumstances gradually coalesced to destroy the elements of Osage power.

The Osage had grown to dominate the central prairie-plains due to a unique set of factors primarily based on their location. Living near three major western rivers that were a gateway to the West gave them unlimited access to the region, while at the same time allowing them to control this gateway and limit European access to the West. Living between the competing European frontiers provided them with autonomy and power. By manipulating the European rivalries, the Osage ensured their ready access to trade and control over that trade. This control ensured both an immediate market for their goods and ample guns and ammunition for their warriors. With only weak or distant rivals in the east, the Osage were able to focus their energies westward where there were only a few rivals, who could, because of the Osage control of the western gate, be denied the gun trade that supported Osage expansion.

All of the Osage eighteenth-century advantages gradually began to disappear in the nineteenth century, as their eighteenth-century gateway became a nineteenth-century highway for American westward expansion. The movement west was spearheaded by Native American emigrants fleeing the American expansion and was soon followed by thousands of Indians forced into the region by American removal policies. These native invasions were closely followed by American traders who brought disease to the Osage and guns to their western rivals. Combined, these invasions would eventually overwhelm the Osage and bring an unexpected end to their prairie-plains power.

As the eighteenth century ended, the first of a series of dramatic changes came about when the distances that had protected the Osage from their northeastern enemies in the eighteenth century shrank dramatically. The Kickapoo, Potawatomi, Delaware, and other eastern tribes who had formerly lived too far to be a serious threat moved closer, driven west by U.S. expansion, and began making frequent attacks on the northern bands. Buffer tribes like the Iowa, Oto, and Missouri who had taken the brunt of the earlier attacks were by the 1790s too weakened by disease and war to be a barrier to the growing assaults, and the Osage became more vulnerable to the northeastern attacks. In 1799 a group of Kickapoo attacked an Osage hunting camp near the Missouri River and killed forty-five Osage. In 1804 Sauk leader Paunblanche ambushed and killed a group of Osage on their way to St. Louis. Main Poche, a prominent Potawatomi war chief, began a series of devastating raids on the northern bands, and in November 1805 he attacked and destroyed a Little Osage village on the Missouri River, killing thirty-four and taking sixty captives back to Illinois.[42] These attacks only increased in intensity as more and more Potawatomi, Kickapoo, Sauk, Mesquakie, Delaware, and Shawnee were driven west.[43]

Conditions in the southeast were similar as Choctaw, Chickasaw, and Cherokee hunters made their way up the Arkansas and White Rivers. Throughout the eighteenth century southeastern tribes had occasionally crossed the Mississippi to hunt in the forest east of the Osage villages, but the Quapaw, living along the lower Arkansas, had been the primary victims of these eighteenth-century raids. By the 1790s the Quapaw, assailed by disease and the escalating eastern raids, were no longer able to absorb the assaults, so that Osage hunters increasingly became the targets of southeastern attacks.

The Spanish welcomed the eastern invasion, for they saw the eastern tribes as allies and potential barriers to both Osage and British aggression.[44] In the late eighteenth century, refugees from the southeastern tribes were welcomed by the Spanish, and they began establishing settlements on the lower Arkansas River and eastern Ozarks.[45]

In 1782 a group of Cherokee established a small community along the White River, which grew steadily as Cherokee emigrants fled the Tennessee Valley.[46] In 1788 Shawnee and Miami bands also crossed the Mississippi to the west bank and established several villages near Cape Girardeau.[47] The Osage attacked the eastern tribes when they crossed into their territory, and their heretofore peaceful east became the scene of increased violence.

The increased raiding in the northeast made Osage life along the Missouri dangerous as well, and in 1794 the Little Osage abandoned their Missouri River villages and returned to the safety of the Big Osage villages along the Osage River.[48] While they moved the villages away from the increasingly dangerous northeast, they continued to cross the Missouri to hunt and trade along the Chariton and Grand Rivers. Despite the new threats in the east the Osage remained powerful and were determined to protect their homelands. In 1806 Zebulon Pike visited the northern Osage on his way west to return some Osage prisoners taken by Main Poche and described the new situation for the northern bands: "they [the Big and Little Osage] have become a nation of Quakers, as it respects the nations to the north and east of them; at the same time that they continue to make war on the naked and defenceless [sic] savages of the west."[49]

Their power, however, remained dependent on the arms and ammunition, supplied by American, Canadian, and Spanish traders, that enabled them to withstand the growing threat in the east and maintain their power in the west.

Those traders continued to flock to the Osage country to acquire forest, prairie, and plains products, and the American Revolution provided only a temporary halt to British trade. Trading resumed after the war despite British promises to close their western forts. The British remained at Prairie du Chien, and Canadian traders continued to visit the Osage to exchange guns and ammunition for furs, horses, and friendship. At the same time Spanish and French traders in St. Louis and New Orleans, along with American traders who began crossing into Spanish Louisiana, continued the lucrative Osage trade. The combination of Canadian, Spanish, and American traders fueled Osage expansion.

The Osage were largely unaffected by the Louisiana Purchase in 1803, for although they now lived and hunted in territory claimed by the United States, the Osage ignored any international trade sanctions and continued their eighteenth-century patterns of raiding in the west for trade in the east. The United States tried to bring about changes in their newly acquired territory by officially banning other countries' hunters and traders from the region, but the bans were ignored and never enforced. Canadian traders continued to come among the Osage, and the Louisiana Purchase only increased the number of American traders who provided competition for the Canadians and better trade for the Osage.

The acquisition of Louisiana introduced potential changes, for the United States brought to the region an Indian policy. Initially the policy had no impact on the Osage, but it would eventually change their lives. President Thomas Jefferson wanted all American Indians to abandon their cultures and become small-scale subsistence farmers. Jefferson realized that such dramatic changes would require time, energy, and a bit of coercion to bring about, but he was convinced that such changes were preferable to the unpleasant and expensive bloodshed that the country had recently experienced.

Assimilating Indians into the American culture was not Jefferson's original plan. The assimilation plan was urged by President Washington and former secretary of war Henry Knox. Jefferson, however, subsequently made a significant contribution to this plan, for he proposed a means of avoiding the earlier violence that had marred the earlier assimilation programs. Jefferson realized that people are never willing to abandon their way of life, and he also knew that until the people involved made the necessary cultural changes, conflict was inevitable. Therefore, Jefferson proposed a plan that he was convinced would end the violence and provide the time necessary for the cultural transformation of the American Indians. Jefferson proposed to move all of the Indians living east of the Mississippi to the newly acquired Louisiana Territory where they would be out of the way of Anglo settlement and have the time to become acculturated. He believed that the removal of the eastern Indians would end the unpleasant and expensive Indian-white violence in the trans-Appalachian West. With the Indians removed, white settlers could peacefully cross the Appalachians and settle America, creating the agrarian-based democracy of Jefferson's dreams. While America was being settled peacefully by democratic American farmers, the United States would send missionaries, teachers, and other American cultural agents among the removed tribes and convert them into small-scale subsistence farmers, thus gradually assimilating them into American culture.[50]

Jefferson's Indian policy plans were an important part of Lewis and Clark's mission. They were to make peace with the western tribes to lay the groundwork for the proposed removal. In order to secure peace and trade with the native peoples, and to prepare them for land cessions, Jefferson urged Lewis and Clark to send representatives from the important tribes back to Washington, D.C., to impress them with the size and power of the United States. The Osage were the first western tribe sent to Washington by Lewis and Clark because they occupied and controlled that region just across the Mississippi between the Missouri and the Red Rivers that was to be the new homeland for the eastern tribes. The Osage power and their central role in the proposed new policy are revealed in the letter sent to Lewis in January 1804 confirming the transfer of Louisiana to the United States, for in that same letter Jefferson enjoined Lewis to arrange a trip for the very important southern Siouan group, the Osage, to visit Washington.[51]

Therefore, along with the final preparations for their Pacific expedition, both Lewis and Clark worked to organize the Osage's visit to Washington. Arranging the Osage trip occupied so much of their time that the planned April departure was delayed until May so Lewis could finalize the Osage's trip.[52] Finally, on May 19, 1804, fourteen Osage from the northern bands, accompanied by Pierre Chouteau, left for Washington to meet with Jefferson. Three days later Lewis and Clark began their journey up the Missouri.

The Osage arrived in Washington in July 1804 and met with President Jefferson on the twelfth. Jefferson was impressed with the Osage, and the next day he shared his thoughts about them in a letter to his secretary of the navy, Robert Smith: "The truth is, they [Osage] are the great nation South of the Missouri, their possession extending from thence to the Red river, as the Sioux are great North of that river. With these two powerful nations we must stand well, because in their quarter we are miserably weak."[53]

To accelerate the removal policy Jefferson modified an already existing element of the U.S. Indian policy, the federally funded Indian trading factories begun under President Washington. The government had originally created government Indian trading posts, called factories, in 1795 in hopes of bringing order to the Indian frontier.[54] These federally subsidized trading factories were to provide quality trade goods at prices private traders could not match. The factories' goods and prices would drive private traders out of the trading system, thus bringing an end to corrupt trading practices, and would also stop the flood of alcohol into the Indian communities. Together these would end the violence that liquor and corrupt traders created on the frontier. Again, Jefferson did not create the trading factories, but he included them in his removal plans. Jefferson urged factory expansion and encouraged the factories to provide abundant credit to create large Indian debts that the United States could later use to acquire Indian land. Jefferson explained this plan in a letter to Indiana governor William Henry Harrison in 1803:

> To promote this disposition to exchange land, which they have to spare and we want, for necessaries, which we have to spare and they want, we shall push our trading uses, and be glad to see the good and influential individuals among them run in debt, because we observe that when these debts get beyond what the individuals can pay, they become willing to lop them off by a cession of lands.[55]

The government constructed a factory near the southern Osage band villages in order to bring peace to the frontier and to forge new ties with the Osage. In 1805 they established the factory at the Arkansas Post near the mouth of the Arkansas River. The United States tried to use this factory to lure the Osage away from the Canadian and American free traders, but instead of limiting trade, the factory only provided more trade opportunities for the Osage. The government therefore was unsuccessful at using these factories as a weapon to control the Osage.

Eager to remove the eastern tribes to the west, the government needed to stop attacks on immigrants and to remove the Arkansas Osage from the Arkansas Valley to make room for the southeastern tribes. In 1805, immediately after the Arkansas Post trading factory was opened, territorial governor James Wilkinson closed it and banned all trade with the Osage on the Arkansas River. Wilkinson wanted to remove the Osage from the region to open it up for eastern tribes, and he threatened to end all trade with the Arkansas band until they returned north to the Osage River and rejoined the Big Osage.[56] The ban failed, because it only closed the federal trading factory. Private traders ignored Wilkinson's ban and continued to transact business with the Arkansas Osage who remained in the south.

In 1808 the United States tried again to control the Osage by means of trade. In August, secretary of war Henry Dearborn ordered the construction of a trading factory at the Big Osage villages in hopes of creating friendlier and closer ties with the Osage, and perhaps of luring the Arkansas Osage back to the north. At the same time, and unknown to Dearborn, newly appointed territorial governor Meriwether Lewis tried to force the Osage to behave by banning all trade with their three bands. Lewis ordered the Osage to abandon their villages on the Arkansas and Osage Rivers and to move to a site on the Missouri River. Only the Big and Little Osage complied with Lewis's order, and when they arrived at the designated Fire Prairie site they were met by General William Clark. Clark, threatening war and an end to all trade, forced them to sign a treaty providing them peace, a trading factory at Fire Prairie, and an annual annuity of $1,200 in exchange for a cession of fifty thousand square miles of land.[57] The Osage, however, soon abandoned their Fire Prairie villages on the Missouri. The river sites were too exposed to Potawatomi, Sauk, Mesquakie, and Shawnee attacks, so the Osage returned to their Osage River sites.

Sauk and Mesquakie bands moved across the Mississippi in 1813 and began hunting along the lower Chariton, Grand, and Missouri Rivers. Kickapoos also crossed the Mississippi and began hunting south of the Missouri in Osage hunting lands, and in 1814 a small band of Kickapoo established a village along the lower Gasconade just south of the Missouri. With their continued access to Canadian and American traders, however, the Osage were able to meet the challenges posed by these northeastern invasions.

Challenges grew in the south. Eight hundred Cherokee, promised land and support by the federal government in 1810, left their eastern homes and moved four hundred miles up the Arkansas River to join the Cherokee settlements at Dardanelles Rock.[58] Again, traders competing for Osage trade provided ample arms for Osage warriors, and their competition provided the Osage with power and autonomy. This competition, however, would gradually vanish. With the conclusion of the War of 1812, the British finally closed their trading post at Prairie du Chien and stopped sending traders into American territory. Although Canadian traders occasionally visited the northern bands after 1814, the Osage could no longer rely on Canadian traders to provide trade goods and were forced to deal solely with American-based traders. Although competition among the various American trading companies provided good trade for Osage products, the Osage were forced to remain at peace with the United States, for after 1814 the United States controlled all trade with the Osage.

This was a critical turning point for the Osage in 1814, for soon after all three bands were compelled to surrender some of their autonomy. By now the Osage were completely dependent on trade, for without guns and ammunition they could not defend their eastern homelands nor retain control of the western plains. Any trade stoppage would destroy them, and the Osage were keenly aware of their dependency. They remained at peace with the Americans, becoming one of the few western tribes who never fought the United States. Even the independent southern band that had consistently defied French, Spanish, and American demands understood their new status and grudgingly began to cooperate with the United States. Although aware of their weakened position, the Osage continued to contest all outside control and to shape that necessary peace with occasional threats and frequent nonviolent resistance. When forced to give up something, they agreed reluctantly and often immediately repudiated or ignored any concessions, as witnessed by their refusal to consolidate all three bands in the north or to vacate any lands ceded in the 1808, 1818, 1825, and 1839 treaties.[59]

The Osage maintained their peace with the Americans because peace was essential for their continued survival. They used that American peace to fight their Native American foes, who grew larger and stronger in the nineteenth century. Eastern tribes were encouraged, and often coerced, to cede their lands east of the Mississippi and move to the Indian Territory west of the river, to land that the Osage had ceded in 1808.

The "status quo ante bellum" provisions of the Treaty of Ghent devastated the eastern tribes who had fought alongside the British in the War of 1812, for they could never return to their prewar state and the British abandoned them after the war. Any hopes of the Shawnee, Sauk, and other northeastern tribes to resist the American invasion with force and to keep the white settlers from their lands dissipated, as Black Hawk and his people would discover in 1831. After the war the United States negotiated a series of peace and land cession treaties with the northeastern tribes that were forerunners to the eventual treaties for removal.[60]

The War of 1812 also destroyed any possible military resistance by the southeastern tribes. Andrew Jackson's devastating defeat of the

Creeks at Horseshoe Bend crushed any possible southeastern tribal resistance, and his successful raids into West Florida during the later days of the war had driven the British from the region. His later Florida raids also ended any possible Spanish assistance to the southeastern tribes already weakened by the war. In 1818 the Spanish ceded Florida to the United States, further weakening the southeastern tribes' ability to resist U.S. land seizures. Conditions in the region shaped by the growing invasion by white settlers on tribal lands, destruction of game, and in many instances the outright attacks on Choctaw, Chickasaw, Creek, and Cherokee communities by white settlers convinced many of these people to voluntarily migrate to the western lands to escape the deteriorating conditions.

In 1817 events would create more pressure on the Osage and heighten tension and violence in the south. In hopes of removing the Cherokee in the east, General Andrew Jackson went to the Cherokee Agency in Tennessee in July 1817 and urged them to leave Tennessee and move to Arkansas. Jackson promised them land in Arkansas in exchange for their eastern lands and guaranteed them provisions and boats to help them move to Arkansas.[61] The Cherokee agreed and signed a treaty providing for the exchange of lands and their removal. The treaty's promises and the deteriorating conditions in the east convinced many Cherokee to flee to Arkansas. Soon there were six thousand Cherokee in central Arkansas.[62]

Shortly after the treaty was signed, Secretary of War Richard Graham ordered Jackson to begin the construction of a fort on the Arkansas River "to take all proper measure for the restoration of peace, and the preservation of harmony between the Osage and Cherokee tribes."[63] Troops would not arrive until late December. Before they arrived to restore the peace, a war party made up of Arkansas Cherokee and kinsmen recruited from the eastern Cherokee towns attacked the southern Osage. Their fall attack would destroy any possible peace between the Cherokee and the Osage.

The war party struck a southern band village filled with food stored for the winter and protected only by those too young or too old to go out onto the plains. While the Osage hunters were out on the plains on their winter hunt, the Cherokee raiders burned the village, killing about eighty Osage. They seized over one hundred women and children, and returned to their Arkansas homes with their captives to celebrate their victory.[64] Fort Smith, erected just after the Cherokee attack, failed to establish peace between the warring tribes because the Osage sought revenge for the 1817 massacre; their revenge attacks triggered Cherokee reprisals, and the violence escalated.

In the 1820s over six thousand Cherokee moved to settlements along the White and Arkansas Rivers. Creek and Choctaw people had moved into the Ouachita Mountains south of the Arkansas River, and their growing invasion of the southern mountains and the Arkansas Valley triggered more Osage attacks. Throughout the 1820s the entire region from the Missouri to the Red River became a battleground between the Native invaders and the Osage.

At the same time changes were taking place in the west. In the late eighteenth century the Comanche, who had earlier established peaceful relations with the Wichita tribes to gain access to eastern trade, made gestures of peace towards the Kiowa and their close allies, the Kiowa-Apache. By the 1820s the Comanche, Kiowa, and Wichita had stopped fighting one another, and united they began to challenge the Osage for the hunting grounds on the western plains, especially the region between the Smoky Hill and Red Rivers.

The western tribes had long challenged Osage in the west, but their challenges grew stronger after Mexican independence from Spain in 1821. Mexico opened its previously closed borders and welcomed American traders into the northern Mexican markets.[65] The Arkansas Valley became a busy thoroughfare for Mexican and American traders, whose livestock overgrazed the valley and disturbed the game, particularly the massive herds of buffalo along the river. The new chaos in the west, through some of the prime hunting territory of the Osage, disrupted their summer hunts and threatened their livelihood. The flood of American traders crossing the prairie-plains to Santa Fe and Chihuahua became an even greater threat when they began providing the western tribes with guns and ammunition. The Osage could not stop the nineteenth-century Santa Fe Trail traffic as they had the eighteenth-century French and Spanish, for the trade was on a much larger scale, and, more importantly, it was primarily American. Trade dependency prevented any Osage attacks on their only trading partner, and for the first time the western tribes began to mount a serious challenge to Osage control of the central and southern prairie-plains.

In 1822 Comanche leader Cordero went to Santa Fe to complain of Osage attacks. "They steal our horses and murder our people," he said

Fig. 4. *Comanche Warrior Lancing an Osage, at Full Speed.* This painting depicts a Comanche warrior chasing an Osage warrior in the 1830s. (George Catlin, Smithsonian American Art Museum, Gift of Mrs. Joseph Harrison Jr., 1837–39.)

"and the Americans sell them the arms and ammunition they use in war on us."[66] In 1823 a group of Comanche attacked the Osage and killed twenty-five hunters. Another Comanche attack on Osage hunters in 1824 was foiled when the Osage ambushed the scouting party, but such attacks became much more common.[67] By the 1820s the area along the Upper Red, Cimarron, and Canadian Forks, long controlled by the Osage, was being contested by the Comanche, Kiowa, Kiowa-Apache, Wichita, and two newcomers, the Cheyenne and the Arapahoe.[68]

Throughout the 1820s the Osage therefore came under serious attacks in both the east and west as more tribes fleeing American expansion invaded the Osage forests and prairies, and as better armed western tribes launched attacks on the Osage plains. The strategic location that had once provided the Osage with power and wealth had become a dangerous position by the late 1820s, when they found themselves caught between two expanding Indian frontiers.

It was in this tense environment that Epaphras Chapman first met the Osage in the summer of 1819 when they were at Fort Smith seeking the return of prisoners taken by the Cherokee in 1817.[69] The United States, eager to end the regional violence and to civilize the Osage, supported the UFMS's efforts to move among the Osage, and Major William Bradford, the commander of Fort Smith, welcomed Chapman. The Osage at the fort were trying to secure the return of their families from the Cherokee and to secure protection for the upcoming fall. The southern Osage were in a very sensitive position, for the Cherokee threat along the Arkansas was growing, so that the Osage were forced to maintain friendly relations with the soldiers and traders at Fort Smith. Chapman, quick to take advantage of the situation, somehow wrangled consent to move his mission to the Osage.

Despite the challenges posed by the Comanche-Wichita-Kiowa alliance on the plains and by the growing threat from the Cherokee and other eastern invading tribes, the Osage remained powerful, confident, and content with their spiritual lives. We will never know why Clermont, leader of one of the Osage southern bands, granted Chapman permission to move onto his land. Clermont was not seeking Christian spiritual help in 1819. Clermont met with Chapman in the midst of the Osage's tense and serious negotiations with the Cherokee, and he may have allowed Chapman to accompany him upriver to gain the goodwill of Major Bradford. His "invitation" to Chapman may have been nothing more than a gesture of hospitality to a potential and much needed white friend. Clermont was extremely shrewd, and perhaps he was gathering new friends around him to buffer Cherokee attacks and to take his side in future negotiations with white authorities. He might have agreed to Chapman's offer of help believing the promised help to be food, clothing, and livestock, rather than the spiritual assistance Chapman was really offering. Whatever prompted Clermont's consent for Chapman's planned settlement, it was enough to send Chapman rushing back to New York, where he quickly convinced the UFMS Board to launch a spiritual invasion of the Osage's prairie homelands.

3

The Protestants Prepare
for the Osage

The object of your Mission is not merely to improve the
temporal state of the Indians, but to save their souls; not
merely, therefore, to civilize, but also to christianize them.
—Reverend Philip Milledoler,
Address delivered to the Union Mission Family,
April 17, 1820[1]

Ever keep in view the great objects of your mission,
which are to evangelize the Indians; and to teach them
the arts of civilized life. In respect to the latter, it will not
be enough to give them the knowledge of agriculture and
of the mechanic arts; you must labour effectually to wean
them from the hunter's life, and to bring them into habits
of patient industry. . . .
    . . . —and never think, that the object of your mis-
sion is accomplished, till you see them brought into the
fold of the son of God, and walking in the faith and order
of the gospel.
—Board of Managers,
Instructions to the Missionaries who are about
proceeding to the Station on the Grand River,
to be denominated Union, April 18, 1820[2]

I n November 1820 five missionaries of the UFMS crossed
into the prairie homelands of the Osage. These five men had
come a long way from their New England homes to bring
the word and wisdom of their god to the Osage people. On November
15 they located the site for their mission on a sloping hillside along the

west bank of the Neosho River (Six Bulls or the Grand). They believed the site was ideal, for it was near water and timber with open land for farming along the river bottom. The mission station, called Union, was only twenty miles from the trading posts at the Three Forks, where the Verdigris and the Neosho joined the Arkansas River, and more importantly it was only twenty-eight miles from the large southern Osage town led by Gra-to-moh-se and Tah-hah-ka-he. The missionaries, with the help of three men they had hired in Little Rock, worked to build cabins for the mission family stranded in Little Rock, but bad weather and chronic illness severely limited their efforts. In February, when the rest of the mission family finally arrived, there was only one cabin to house the fifteen. Their arrival to begin their work to Christianize and civilize the Osage was the end of an exhausting ten-month journey filled with death and hardship.

Just six months later, 150 miles to the north, another band of missionaries from the UFMS completed their arduous journey and began working on their mission near the northern Osage bands. This mission, named Harmony, was located near the Big Osage under the leadership of Pawhuska and the Little Osage led by Nez-ah-mo-nee along the prairie marshes where the Marais des Cygnes and Marmaton (Little Osage) came together to form the Osage River.

These two 1821 settlements marked the beginning of Protestant missionary efforts to convert the American Indians west of the Mississippi. This effort would later be joined by other missionary societies and expanded all the way to the Pacific Coast, but the Union and Harmony missions were the first to venture into the trans-Mississippi West. What could have prompted these forty-two New England Protestants to leave the comfort and security of their New England homes and travel fifteen hundred miles to the prairie's edge to bring the word of their Christian God to a people uninterested in the Christian gospel?[3]

In the late eighteenth and early nineteenth centuries, the United States experienced an outburst of zealous, emotional, and very public spirituality. This outburst of public piety, called the Second Great Awakening, spread across the nation and became a national evangelical movement inspiring thousands of Americans to flock to churches and outdoor gatherings to hear a new message of Christian salvation. Pastors, particularly among the growing Methodist and Baptist churches, had begun preaching a new and welcome spiritual message that rejected the old Calvinist-based faiths that demanded lengthy instruction and examination by the congregation before people were admitted to the church, and perhaps to salvation. They replaced the harsh, formal Calvinism that restricted salvation to the "elect" with a message that offered eternal salvation for any and all who believed in Christ and asked for his salvation.

The Methodist and Baptist clergy, drawn not from the New England seminaries but from the growing community of inspired laity, traveled throughout the rural South sharing this new message of salvation. Discarding the intellectual and formal sermons of the older and traditional churches, these lay preachers spoke in the regional vernacular and couched their messages about sin and salvation in familiar context. They preached a simple and emotional message to their communities in words that their audiences understood. The new message became so popular that church buildings could not hold the crowds flocking to the services. Evangelists held week-long revival meetings outdoors, and thousands camped out to hear the word of God.[4]

This Second Great Awakening, similar to earlier breakout spiritual fervor in the early eighteenth century called the First Great Awakening, was triggered by a variety of circumstances. It was perhaps a revival of religious feelings that had been set aside during the Revolution. The new, personal, and emotional message may have been a rejection of the eighteenth century's reason and rationality. It was perhaps a reaction against the distant and uninvolved Deist god that some had embraced in the eighteenth century. It was also in part a rejection of the strict Calvinism that reserved salvation for only the select few, the "elect."[5]

This new and growing religious enthusiasm was also fueled by the belief that the Millennium, the return of Christ for his thousand-year reign, was at hand. Many clergymen, believing that Christ's return was imminent, urged their followers to prepare for his return by accepting his offer of eternal salvation. These Millennium beliefs increased the spiritual enthusiasm of the period and brought thousand to revivals and camp meetings to prepare for Christ's return.

With the Millennium fast approaching, good Christians believed that they should go to the great uninformed, the heathen of the world, and prepare them for Christ's return. They believed that it was their Christian duty to take the word of their god to the heathen before Christ returned. In their fervor they became convinced that once the heathens were exposed to the words of Christ they would drop their heathen ways, accept Christ as their savior, and welcome his return.

This sense of Christian obligation was enhanced by feelings of guilt. Good Christians believed that they were guilty for not sharing their wonderful beliefs and quality of life with the less fortunate of the world, and the combination of Christian guilt and sense of duty caused many to support missionary efforts. Some provided financial support, while others, urged on by the fast-approaching Millennium and the thrill and adventure of visiting foreign lands, volunteered to become Christian missionaries to the foreign pagans.[6]

These missionary impulses had already been fueled by the activities of The London Missionary Society that had established Christian missions in India, China, and Africa in the eighteenth century. English missionaries had been corresponding with Americans, sharing sermons and accounts of conversions with the American congregations. Religious publishers contributed to the growing enthusiasm by collecting their missionary sermons, letters, and accounts of their missions and publishing them in the form of missionary magazines. Magazines such as the celebrated *Church Missionary Register* were circulated in America and inspired Americans to launch their own missionary efforts.[7]

The combination of the Second Great Awakening, the approaching Millennium, and the English example led a number of Protestant denominations to create missionary societies to sponsor foreign missions. The Society for Propagating the Gospel Among the Indians and Others in North America, The Society of the United Brethren for Propagating the Gospel Among the Heathen, The New York Missionary Society, and others were begun to propagate the gospel.[8] Two important ones were the American Board of Commissioners for Foreign Missions (ABCFM) established in 1810 and the United Foreign Missionary Society (UFMS) established in 1817.

These early American missionary societies were united by the common cause of spreading the word of their Christian gospel to the heathen. There were, however, conflicting opinions on which heathens to save. Some believed that American churches should focus on the American heathen and create and support missions among the Native American communities in the West. Most of these early missionary societies were centered in New England, the scene of earlier failed Indian missions. By the early nineteenth century, Indian communities in the region, attacked by repeated epidemics and the violence of the earlier frontier, had declined dramatically. Thus many New England Protestants believed that with the declining population of American Indians and the general lack of success in earlier missionary efforts, they should direct their attention to Asia, where there were millions of heathen to convert. They contrasted the potential of hundreds of millions of eastern pagans with the scattered Indians in the West and argued that their limited resources should be directed where they would enjoy better returns.[9] Some, however, such as the ABCFM, decided to support missions both at home and abroad, while others, such as the UFMS, despite its name, sponsored missions only within the United States.

Another pressing concern among the early missionary societies centered on the method of conversion. They all insisted that missionaries must convey a religious message, and they agreed that the Indians needed to hear the Christian gospel, but there was little agreement as to the means of bringing about the Indians' conversion. Some believed that in order for the faith to be truly understood and accepted, the Indians would have to learn and adopt American culture. They defined American culture as "civilization" and argued that in order to become real Christians the Indians had first to become civilized. They argued that the Indians could not remain semi-nomadic hunters living communally and become Christians. They argued that Indians, although eventually capable of grasping the tenets of Christianity, were ignorant, savage heathens, and that they had to be educated and civilized before they could be converted. They argued that the Indians had to be educated and made literate before they could truly understand the scriptures. Others argued that the miracles of the gospel were powerful enough to save the Indians' souls. They insisted that hearing the words of Christ was enough to bring about conversion, and that after accepting Christ they could proceed to civilization. This argument raged throughout the entire nineteenth century and never was resolved. Despite this ongoing and often bitter dispute, Protestant missionaries in the field were never able to separate Christianity from civilization, for to them the two were completely intertwined: religion divorced from culture made little sense.[10] Religions are cultural creations, and true conversion would demand cultural change.

Such cultural changes were also supported by secular institutions. U.S. leaders such as George Washington, Henry Knox, Thomas Jefferson, Thomas McKenney, and John C. Calhoun supported efforts to convert the Indians, if not to Christianity then at least to American culture. All agreed that Indian people could not exist as separate and autonomous nations within the United States, and that they had to join with the Americans on their march to success or face extermination. While some indeed called for the extermination of the Indian people, most early American leaders sought only the extermination of their cultures.

President Washington and his secretary of war, Henry Knox, sought to avoid war with the Indians. Early conflicts had been largely unsuccessful because of America's small army and were terribly expensive in terms of lives and dollars. Eighteenth-century America could ill afford such wars of conquest, so Knox proposed to avoid war and deal humanely with the Indians. Knox believed that westward expansion was inevitable, but hoped that the Indians would be willing to exchange their lands for civilization and to become equal partners in American growth.[11] He called for Americans to go among the Indians, to educate them in the ways of white culture, and to bring them, once acculturated, into America as full and equal members.

In 1793 Washington convinced Congress to fund programs to bring civilization to the Indians, and Washington and Knox's national policy of civilization and assimilation was followed by subsequent presidents and secretaries of war. In 1819, Congress created a Civilization Fund that provided $10,000 annually to further the civilization of Indian tribes, to be used at the president's discretion. President Monroe and his secretary of war, John C. Calhoun, both committed to the assimilation program, decided to use the fund to support independent agencies that would establish schools for the education of Indians.[12]

This federal expansion of civilization funding coincided with the creation and expansion of the Protestant missionaries' societies intent on civilizing and Christianizing the American Indians. Ignoring the constitutional separation of church and state, the federal government began funding Christian missionary efforts to convert the American Indians. One such society that sought federal funding was the newly formed UFMS. The UFMS had been created when three Protestant churches— the Presbyterian, Reformed Dutch, and Associate Reformed Church— joined together in 1817 "to spread the Gospel among the Indians of North America, the Inhabitants of Mexico and South America, and in other portions of the heathen and anti-christian [sic] world."[13]

The UFMS, in an effort to spread the gospel beyond the New England frontier, sent two pastors on an exploratory trip to the West in the spring of 1819 to see if the western Cherokee, settled along the Arkansas River, would allow them to establish a mission among them.

Connecticut pastor Reverend Epaphras Chapman and Job P. Vinall were to visit the eastern Cherokee along the Tennessee, to get advice about potential missions and secure introductions to the western Cherokee. While on their journey to the Arkansas they were also instructed to examine the general state of Indian affairs in the region. Passing through Washington, Chapman and Vinall met with Thomas McKenney, superintendent of Indian Trade (precursor of the Indian Office), who secured letters of introduction and promises of assistance. Leaving Washington, they proceeded south to the Cherokee nation, where the ABCFM had established the Brainard Mission (present-day Chattanooga). There they met with Cherokee leaders and took letters from several, including Charles Hicks and "a young chief, by the name of Ross, addressed to one of the principal chiefs at the Arkansas, replete with argument and good sense, and which is supposed to have had great influence."[14]

Leaving Brainard, they made their way along the Tennessee River via Chickasaw Bluffs (modern-day Memphis) to the Arkansas River, which they traveled up 160 miles to the Dardanelle, a western Cherokee community established in the early nineteenth century. Shortly after their arrival at the Cherokee settlement they were stricken by a "bilious fever" that confined them to their beds for four weeks and prevented them from holding a meeting with the Cherokee. The local federal agent, Reuben Lewis, eager to civilize the Cherokee, met with the leaders and secured Cherokee permission for their proposed mission.[15] Having secured Cherokee permission for a UFMS mission and having recovered from their bout with the fever, Chapman and Vinall decided to take advantage of a meeting planned between the Cherokee and their western rivals, the Osage, to learn more about the Indian situation in the region. They traveled upriver with Agent Lewis to newly established Fort Smith, where the meeting was taking place.

Chapman took the opportunity of the Fort Smith meeting to introduce himself to the Osage leaders present at the conference. He broached the topic of a mission among the Osage, and those present agreed. It is not clear that what Chapman proposed and what the Osage agreed to were the same. Chapman reported that after speaking with nine of the Osage leaders they

> expressed their thanks to their great father at Washington for
> sending his white children to instruct them, signified their

desire that their young men might be initiated in the mechanic arts, their young women in domestic economy, and that all their young people might be taught to read and write, they concluded with saying, "I shall consider the house which our great father will build for the education of our children our home, as we do this place. I wish our great father would send us the teachers as soon as he can, with the necessary equipments."[16]

Later Chapman noted, "[t]hey are very desirous of adopting the dress and manner of living of the whites, and say, if good white people will come among them, and show them how to live like the whites, they may occupy as much land as they want."[17] The Osage leaders never included a call for spiritual help in their conversations with Chapman, for in 1819 the Osage were quite satisfied with their spiritual beliefs and were not seeking spiritual guidance from the visiting strangers. They were for asking secular schools to teach them new basic skills to survive in the changing world. Instead, they would of course receive religious schools where the missionaries tried to convert them into Christians.[18]

Vinall, weak from the fever, remained at Fort Smith when Chapman decided to explore upriver.[19] Chapman traveled up the Arkansas with the Osage leaders, accompanied by well-known trader Nathaniel Pryor, one of the members of Lewis and Clark's expedition who had moved to the Three Forks region in 1815. Pryor had become a friend and advisor to the southern Osage, and he helped Chapman select a site for a potential mission station, about twenty miles up the Neosho River just east of the Osage village on the Verdigris.

Having selected a possible mission site among the southern Osage, Chapman began his journey home. Traveling north, he visited the Big and Little Osage villages, where they fed him and directed him to the Missouri River, from which he made his way to St. Louis. Chapman then returned to New York, where he met with the UFMS Board, who informed him that the ABCFM had already begun plans for a mission among the Arkansas Cherokee. Since they shared a common goal with ABCFM and wanted to maintain good relations with their "sister institution," they relinquished their Cherokee mission and began making plans for an "establishment among the Osages."[20]

With promises of support from President Monroe and Secretary of War John C. Calhoun, the UFMS resolved "to promote amongst the

Indians, not only the knowledge of christianity [sic], but also of the arts of civilized life," and decided to send a Christian community of missionaries to the Osage, a community containing not only ordained ministers but also schoolteachers, farmers, blacksmiths, carpenters, mechanics, and a doctor to serve as examples of a Christian community and to provide the services that would help the mission succeed. [21] In honor of the union of the three denominations that made up the UFMS, the Board decided to name their mission among the Arkansas Osage "Union."

When UFMS called for volunteers from the three denominations, hundreds applied to go to the Osage mission on the Arkansas. In early 1820, after carefully reading the letters of application and the accompanying testimonials that the applicants were members of good standing and in full communion of the church, the Committee of Missions recommended that the UFMS Board of Managers appoint seventeen church members and their children to go among the Osage.

The seventeen-member missionary family was made up of nine men and eight women, and was led by two ordained ministers from Connecticut: Reverend William Vaill, who brought his wife, Asenath, and four children, and Reverend Epaphras Chapman and his wife, Hannah. The missionary family also included a physician, Dr. Marcus Palmer, from Connecticut; a carpenter, Abraham Redfield, from New York; a blacksmith, Alexander Woodruff, from New Jersey; a mechanic, George Requa, from New York; and three farmers: William C. Requa, the brother of George, and Stephen Fuller and John Spalding from Connecticut. In addition, there were six schoolteachers: Susan Lines, Eliza Cleaver, Clarissa Johnson, and Dolly Hoyt from Connecticut, and Phoebe Beache and Mary Foster from New York. Eleven members came from Connecticut, five from upstate New York, and one from New Jersey. Four were married, and the remaining thirteen were composed of six single women and seven single men. Records are incomplete, but six were in their mid-twenties and two were in their mid-thirties. [22] The two leaders were experienced pastors: Vaill, educated at Yale, had been a pastor of the North Guilford, Connecticut, church for over eleven years; and Chapman, the UFMS explorer, was a veteran pastor from East Haddam, Connecticut.

As the mission family gathered in New York City, the word went out to collect needed goods for the proposed mission. Supplies valued at $8,000 and cash contributions amounting to $2,500 poured in.

Services were held in the Presbyterian and Dutch Reform churches, where sermons were delivered by invited clergy accompanied by prayers and hymns. Typical of the sermons were the words of Reverend Philip Milledoler, the secretary for foreign correspondence for the UFMS Board:

> Never, perhaps, since the discovery of the American conti-
> nent, has so fair an opportunity been presented of introduc-
> ing the Gospel, with the arts of civilized life, among the
> Heathen of our wilderness. Our Agents in their exploring tour
> were very much encouraged. They found those Tribes which
> had lately been engaged in all the horrors of Savage warfare,
> hushed into tranquility; the war whoop had ceased among
> their mountains; the blood-stained tomahawk they had
> washed and buried; their fierce and raging passions, like the
> ocean waves, were subsiding into a calm. . . .
>
> *There are* peculiar, and very powerful reasons, why the
> American church should enter with deep and lively interest
> into their welfare. We must not forget that God in his
> Providence has placed them at our door—that the soil we now
> occupy was once theirs—that as the prodigious tide of our
> population rolls onward towards the west, they are like, unless
> some mighty revolution be speedily effected in their habits
> and manners, to be carried before it, until we lose sight of
> them forever. . . .
>
> I will notice, first of all, your general intercourse with
> Indians.
>
> To teach children in heavenly knowledge, you will have to
> become children yourselves; and to bear with their weakness,
> their ignorance, their petulence [*sic*], their frowardness [*sic*],
> and slowness of apprehension. . . . As to the matter of your
> communication, we charge you before God, that you know
> nothing among them, but Jesus Christ, and him crucified.
> This is the sharp two-edged sword that will pierce even to the
> dividing asunder of soul and spirit, the joints and the marrow,
> and prove a discerner of the thoughts and intents of the heart.
> This is the mighty engine, which, not withstanding all the
> sneers of ungodly sinners, is to pull down and demolish the
> strong holds of Satan and of Sin. . . . Dear Brethren,—You

stand before God and this assembly, to-night, in a most interesting attitude. You are about to leave Fathers, and Mothers,
Sisters, and Brothers, Companions, and Friends, Ministers
and Altars, and places endeared to you by a thousand tender
recollections, to take up your abode with the savages of the
wilderness, and perhaps never to return. . . .

. . . We have a reasonable prospect that our Master's name
will soon be honoured in another section of the Heathen
world, and that his glory will appear in yon vast desolate
moral wilderness. There the glad tidings of great joy will soon
be proclaimed—there the savage breast will be divested of its
ferocity—there the cry for Mercy will pierce Heaven's mighty
arch, and reach the throne of him that showeth mercy. . . .

. . . There is yet much work to be done, and many hands
to be employed. The ravages of death are rapid and tremendous. Sinners are perishing—judgment is approaching—and
the time for action is short.[23]

Filled with such spiritual inspiration, the mission family gathered in
the Reform Dutch Church on the morning of April 20, 1820, where the
UFMS Board presented them with their final instructions, formal
commissions, and a speech to be delivered to the Osage upon arrival.
After another round of prayers and hymns, the family made their way
to Battery Park, where they departed the city on board the steamboat
Olive Branch, bound for Philadelphia.

At Philadelphia they were warmly received by the congregations of
the three faiths, and after a series of religious services with prayer,
praise, hymns, and collections gathered to support the mission, they
left for Pittsburgh. While they journeyed to Pittsburgh, Chapman traveled to Washington, where he met with President Monroe, Secretary
of War Calhoun, and the superintendent of Indian Trade, Thomas
McKenney. He received last-minute instructions and $700 as a portion
of the funds promised for the Osage school. McKenney also provided
him with a letter containing his recollections of the Osage. This letter
would be the sole source of information about the people the UFMS
missionaries were about to meet and to transform into model
Christian citizens. It is not clear that the letter ever reached the mission family, for it was mailed instead to the UFMS secretary, Reverend
Philip Milledoler in New York.[24]

Chapman rejoined the group in Pittsburgh, where they purchased two keelboats, attended services, gathered donations ("to the amount of about twelve hundred dollars"), and made their way down the Ohio.[25] All along the journey they made stops at Ohio River communities where the ever-present spirit of the Great Awakening inspired local congregations to praise and pray for them and to contribute cash and supplies for their mission among the Osage. On June 21, the missionaries reached the Mississippi River, which they descended to the mouth of the White River and then carefully made their way to the Arkansas River, which they reached on July 1.

While the Union mission family was making its way down the Mississippi, a small group of Osage from the northern bands, led by Sans-Nerf, had arrived in Washington to speak with Thomas McKenney. Sans-Nerf complained that he and his northern-band people had heard, apparently from Chapman's visit, that the government was sending help to the southern band. He could not understand why the United States would ignore the northern bands whose "hands are white" and help the Arkansas Osage whose "hands are bloody."[26]

Sans-Nerf had a good point, for the Big and Little Osage bands in the north had been much more obliging to the United States than the Arkansas band. In 1808 the northern bands had dutifully gathered at Fire Prairie when Governor Lewis ordered their appearance. They had also willingly signed the treaty that William Clark presented them. The Arkansas band had ignored Lewis's orders to come to the treaty negotiations, and only signed the treaty three years later to secure a share of the treaty annuities. Both the Big and Little Osage had supported the United States during the War of 1812 and had gathered with Pierre Chouteau to attack the British at Prairie du Chien.[27] The northern bands, tied closely with the Chouteau family in St. Louis, were indeed much more cooperative with the United States than the Arkansas band. The violence of the Arkansas band against the Cherokee and other eastern tribes had caused the United States to erect a fort between the Indian frontiers to maintain the peace. Yet who received the bounty of the United States? The fiercely independent and often hostile southern band. The truth of the matter is that the southern band got the mission by happenstance. Chapman had simply met the southern band leaders before he visited the northern bands. Having been warmly received by the Arkansas Osage, Chapman and the Board decided to send their missionaries to their town.

McKenney, fully aware of the southern band's obstinacy and the northern bands' cooperation, quickly sent word to the UFMS Board in New York in hopes of providing some answers for Sans-Nerf. The Board promptly sent Reverend Philip Milledoler to Washington to meet with the northern Osage. Milledoler, reading the speech prepared by the Board, told Sans-Nerf:

> Brothers—We have heard that you wish our great Father at Washington to send good men into your nation, to teach your young men how to plough, and sow, and reap, and raise bread out of the ground as the white people do—and how to work in iron, to make ploughs and harrows, to build houses, mills to grind our corn, and saw your wood, and to weave and make clothing for you and your children—and that you wish him to send out good women, to teach your young women how to sew, and knit, and spin, and to prepare your food to eat as the white people eat it—and that you want good men and women to teach your children how to read and write, and number like the white people, so that your children may be like our children . . .[28]

Milledoler graciously offered to send another mission family to the "Great Osage of the Missouri" to teach them all they requested and to teach them the will of the Great Spirit. Sans-Nerf accepted their offer, and he and the Osage accompanying him promised to receive them as friends.[29]

Milledoler admitted that, "[j]udging from their manners, there appeared to be some misapprehension on the part of the Chiefs, as to our real object."[30] Some of that misunderstanding might have been because the conversations took place through interpreters with the words making their way from Osage to French to English, and back from English to French to Osage. Other misunderstandings came about because of cultural differences.

Sans-Nerf was not seeking spiritual guidance; the Non-hon-zhin-ga already provided that for their people. Its is clear from his remarks what he wanted. When he first approached McKenney, he requested a school system to help them become civilized. When they met, Sans-Nerf told Milledoler: "—I told my brother, the Superintendent of Indian Trade, that I did not come on here for my pleasure, nor to see the country. I came to do business."[31] That business was to get their fair share of any help offered the Osage.

Milledoler returned to New York, where the UFMS Board decided to send another mission family to the Osage. They sent out another call to their congregation for missionaries to the heathen and again were answered with hundreds of applications. While the Committee of Missions began examining the applications for another mission family, the first mission family became stalled on the Arkansas.

Traveling down the Mississippi, several members had become ill with a fever, and shortly after entering the Arkansas one of their hired hands died of the fever, possibly typhus. His death was soon followed by the deaths of two of their young schoolteachers, Dolly Hoyt and Susan Lines.[32] Shocked by the deaths, they buried their missionary family members along the banks of the river and moved slowly upriver, reaching Little Rock on July 24. By the time they reached Little Rock almost all were ill, and with the river dropping in level, they decided to stay there until enough had recovered to continue their journey.

They remained in Little Rock for months trying to regain their strength and recover from their illness. The illness continued as described in an August entry: "And were it not for paroxisms [sic] of intermittent, or ague and fever, with which most of us are visited, some every day and others every other day, which are distressing and debilitating, the general health of the family would be much better than for several weeks past."[33] Those healthy enough conducted religious services in Little Rock and nearby communities as the others struggled to recover.

In October, they decided to send ahead those well enough to begin construction of the mission buildings. The Arkansas was still low so they made a pirogue, and William Requa, Abraham Redfield, and Mr. Ranson, a man they had hired to construct their mill, loaded their tools and supplies into the pirogue and started upriver. Reverend Epaphras Chapman and Alexander Woodruff set out overland for the mission site. They soon met up with the three in the pirogue at the Cherokee settlement, and since the river was so low and their journey so difficult, they abandoned the boat, purchased two additional horses to carry the supplies, and made their way to Fort Smith, where they borrowed more horses. They continued west and Chapman wrote, "We arrived, on the 15th [November], at Union, having struggled through many difficulties which the craggy cliffs, and the steep slippery banks had occasioned."[34] When they arrived the Osage were out on the plains for their winter hunt, but Clermont, the leader of the southern band, came later in December to welcome the missionaries. He greeted them warmly and said, "I am glad in my heart that I ever lived to see this day. Now my children will be taught to read, and to live like white people. We want to learn your religion—it is better than ours."[35] They began cutting timber and constructing cabins to have ready for the family's expected arrival.

On December 12, after four months at Little Rock, the missionaries had recovered enough to continue their journey to Union. Some were still weak with fevers and the Arkansas was still low, but the river had risen enough for them to travel. Poling and pulling their two flatboats, they made slow progress, reaching Fort Smith on January 31. They reached the Neosho on February 10, where a sudden storm almost capsized one of the boats. With the Neosho in flood they were unable to pole their way upriver, and they had to pull their way along the shore until they finally reached Union on the morning of February 18, 1821, a journey that had taken ten months to complete. The men who had gone to prepare the cabins had been hampered by snow and illness, and although they had begun five cabins, they had only completed one cabin by the time the family arrived. With only one cabin completed, they crowded into the one and began to complete the other four.

Within a few days of their arrival they were visited by Tah-hah-ka-he, one of the southern band leaders, who welcomed them and invited them to their town to hold a council. In early March, four of the men—Chapman, Vaill, Palmer, and William Requa—went to Clermont's town about twenty-eight miles west of the mission along the Verdigris River, where they were greeted warmly by the Osage. Dr. Palmer describes their greeting: "Having entered the lodge, and had our horses turned out, we took a humble seat around the fire. Presently there was brought to us a wooden bowl, filled with food made of corn. In a short time we were invited to eat at another lodge, and before we had finished at another, and another. In the same manner we were treated, during all the time we remained in the village."[36] The next morning the Osage gathered around the missionaries, who presented them with their letters and speeches from the secretary of war and the UFMS Board. Clermont welcomed them and promised to "send their children as soon as they should be able to settle the war with the Cherokees."[37]

While the Union family began its mission along the Neosho, the UFMS board selected a mission family for the Big and Little Osage. This second mission was a bit larger, but it was organized along the same lines: to establish a Christian community among the Osage in order to teach them useful skills and the word of their Christian God.

The UFMS Board chose twenty-five Christians for the Great Osage mission that they would name Harmony, to remind the community to maintain harmonious relations among themselves and their Indian charges. The twenty-five included three ordained missionaries— Reverends Nathaniel Dodge, Benton Pixley, and William Montgomery, and their wives, Sally Dodge, Lucia Pixley, and Jane Montgomery; a physician, Dr. William Belcher; a blacksmith who was also capable of teaching sacred music; a carpenter and millwright, Daniel Austin; a shoemaker, Amasa Jones; a wagon maker; and two farmers, Samuel Bright and Samuel Newton.[38] Five female schoolteachers who were "qualified to teach all the branches of industry pursued by that sex in this country," Susan Comstock, Harriet Woolley, Mary Weller, Mary Etris, and Eliza Howell, completed the family.[39] Of the twenty-five, ten were males and fifteen were females. Again New England was well represented as six came from Vermont, five from Connecticut, two from New Hampshire, and two from Massachusetts, as well as five from Pennsylvania, three from New Jersey, one from New York, and another from Maryland. All were married save the five female schoolteachers, and the couples were accompanied by their sixteen children.[40] Although incomplete, records show that two members were in their late teens (eighteen and nineteen), five were in their twenties, another five in their thirties, and one was forty-two.[41] Again the leaders were experienced Protestant clergy. Benton Pixley, educated at Middlebury College, was an ordained minister who had been preaching for seven years. Nathaniel Dodge, although he had no seminary education, had been leading a congregation in Vermont for four years before becoming a missionary, and William Montgomery was an experienced minister from Danville, Pennsylvania.

Again the mission family gathered in New York to receive instructions, which included the following:

II. The matter and manner of your preaching.
    As to the matter, let it be the great and distinguishing doc-
trines of divine revelation; such as the sin and misery of man

by the fall; the eternal counsel of God, revealed in time to save sinners by Jesus Christ his own eternal and coequal Son; the incarnation, obedience, suffering, and death of the Son of God in the room of sinners; his resurrection, ascension, intercession in Heaven; his being head over all things to the Church, and the Final Judgement; the application of the Redemption of Christ by God the Holy Spirit; and the absolute necessity of his agency to change the hearts of men, and bring them faith and repentance ... Affect not subtleties and deep points of controversy. Wave as much as possible what would lead to questions, rather than godly edifying. Adhere to the simplicity which is in Christ ...[42]

After receiving their instructions accompanied by the familiar church services of prayer and praise, they departed for the Osage prairies on March 7, 1821, the very day their Union brothers were meeting with Clermont and Tally on the Verdigris.

The Harmony Mission family traced the earlier family's route, traveling to Philadelphia, where they garnered "nearly eighteen hundred dollars," and then overland to Pittsburgh, where they boarded keelboats on April 10 and headed down the Ohio, stopping at the riverside communities, where they led church services and gathered donations for the Osage mission. They collected $95 in cash and $116 worth of provisions in Cincinnati, and $38 in Louisville along with several barrels of flour and bales of clothing. On April 29 Betsy Newton, the wife of mission farmer Samuel Newton, gave birth to a daughter, but within the week both mother and child became ill and died. The mission family buried them along the banks of the river and continued on their way, reaching the Mississippi two days later. They fought driftwood, mosquitoes, and a strong current, but they reached St. Louis on June 6. While resting in St. Louis, Reverends Nathaniel Dodge and Benton Pixley delivered sermons in two Protestant churches where a collection was taken in support of the proposed mission. They only collected $25, in striking contrast to the $1,800 collected in Philadelphia and the $700 collected in Pittsburgh.

While in St. Louis Dodge and Pixley met with William Clark, territorial governor of Missouri and the superintendent of Indians for the Western Territory. He introduced them to Pierre Chouteau and his son, Paul Liguest Chouteau. The Chouteau family was the first family of St. Louis, having founded it in 1763. The Chouteaus had been deeply involved with the Osage, trading with them since the 1760s. Pierre and his brother, Auguste, who had homes and families in St. Louis, had also lived among the northern bands and had married into prominent Osage families.[43] Paul was the federal subagent for the Osage and had been in Washington with Sans-Nerf when he had called for his bands' share of missionary assistance. Paul had just returned from the Chouteau trading post along the upper Osage River when the missionaries arrived, and he and his father welcomed the missionaries and provided advice and information for them. They recommended a possible site for their mission near their trading post where the Marais des Cygnes and Marmaton Rivers joined to form the Osage River. They explained that the site was near both the Big and Little Osage villages, located on rich soil, surrounded by abundant timber, and near several good millsites.

After a few days of rest in St. Louis, the men took the boats up the Mississippi and into the Missouri River. To provide the women and children a break from the uncomfortable and confining boats, Reverend Benton Pixley took the women and children overland to St. Charles, where they rejoined the men. They then traveled up the Missouri, stopping to hold services and passing out Bibles, religious tracts, and hymnals to settlers along the way, reaching the Osage River on the evening of June 29. Low water and sandbars slowed their travel, and they were forced to pole and pull their way up the river; it took them a month to travel the 150 miles to the Chouteaus' trading post near the forks of the river. When they arrived at the Chouteaus', a small group of Osage who were at the post told the missionaries that the leaders and most of the people were out hunting. The missionaries persuaded one of the young Osage to seek out the leaders to tell them they had arrived to fulfill Milledoler's promise.

Leaving the Chouteau settlement they made their way upriver to the river fork, where the Marmaton and Marais des Cygnes joined to form the Osage River. Relying on the Chouteaus' advice, they went up the Marais des Cygnes, but were able to travel only a few miles, for the water became too shallow for them to proceed. Discovering they were near a U.S. trading factory (present-day Papinville, Missouri), they walked to the factory, where they met and consulted with the government factor, George Sibley, and his interpreter, Bill Williams. On the eighth of August the men left the grounded boats and began searching for a suitable site for the mission, which they found a few miles upriver from the trading factory on the north bank of the Marais des Cygnes. They began construction of their mission the next day and worked for three days, cutting logs for their cabins and bringing their supplies from the stranded boats.[44]

On the evening of the third day they returned to the boats to find seventy Osage waiting for them, anxious to begin the business of the mission. The next morning the Osage wanted to visit the proposed site and conduct their business with the missionaries; however, it was a Sunday, and the missionaries explained that the Sabbath was a holy time, and that they could not attend to business on that day. They invited the Osage to participate in their holy services and to wait until the following day for the necessary formalities. The Osage agreed to wait until Monday and attended the Sabbath services. Although the Osage did not understand English and therefore the meaning of the messages, they willingly sat through two lengthy morning and afternoon services followed by a Sabbath school lesson for the children.

The following morning the Osage, accompanied by the men of the mission family, made their way to the mission site, where Dodge and Pixley read their formal messages from the secretary of war and the managers of the UFMS. The Osage leaders listened to the greetings from the Americans and gave their approval of the site. With their approval given that hot August morning, the forty missionaries could officially begin their mission to Christianize and civilize their gracious prairie hosts.[45]

Both missionary families had made long and difficult journeys to get to the Osage to bring them Christ and civilization. They would labor for seventeen years to bring about Osage conversion, and that journey to conversion and civilization would be longer and much more difficult than the one they had just completed. For the Osage were content with their life and culture, and they would cling to their way of life with a resourceful tenacity, resisting the well-intentioned and zealous efforts of the Protestants to take away their way of life.

4

The Protestants Arrive: 1821

For reasons well known to you the gospel has not been
preached to the Indians, and as a natural result little or
no improvement is visible. They remain the same dark
and bewildered race, clinging to their idols, and ignorant
of the Lord who hath bought [*sic*] them. This mission has
been established at great expense of money and at the
expense of some valuable lives. Many prayers have been
offered for its success, and little very little to human view,
either for the want of proper instruments, a lack of faith,
or the imperfection of its plan, has been accomplished.

—Mr. Dodge,
Superintendent of Harmony Station, 1831[1]

In 1821, the Osage were a tribe of six thousand people with at
least one thousand warriors. Living in three groups stretched
from the Osage River to the Arkansas, this powerful tribe was
confronting ever-growing challenges in the early nineteenth century, the
least of which were the thirty-nine New England Protestants who had
just made their way to their prairie neighborhood.[2]

In 1821, when the Protestants arrived, the three groups of Osage
were confronting serious and growing challenges. In the west the
Comanche, Kiowa, and Wichita had made peace among themselves,
and united were challenging Osage control of the central plains. That
western challenge would grow with the opening of the Santa Fe-
Chihuahua Trail in 1821, for the increased access to U.S. trade was
arming these Southern Plains tribes. Now united and armed, they
began for the first time to pose a serious challenge to Osage control of
the region between the Arkansas and the Red River. In the 1820s the
Lakota were pressing the long-time enemies of the Osage in the north,

the Pawnee, which in turn drove them south to increase their threat to that territory north of the Arkansas.

These growing western threats were joined by the increasing invasion of the eastern forests and prairies by well-armed eastern tribes, seasoned veterans of war and diplomacy with the United States. Their martial skills combined with their experience in the east would make them powerful rivals to the Osage.

Potawatomi, Shawnee, Kickapoo, Sauk, and other northeastern tribes, forced across the Mississippi by white settlement, began hunting in the Osage forests and prairies along the Chariton, Missouri, and Osage Rivers. The Cherokee, Chickasaw, Creek, and large southeastern tribes, pushed by white settlement and federal Indian policy, continued to flock to the Arkansas and White Rivers and challenged the Osage for control of the southern forests and western prairies. These surrounding threats would grow in the 1820s and 30s, and make the Protestant cultural invasion only a minor annoyance that could sometimes be used to Osage advantage.

The Osage have a long and successful history of dealing with such external challenges. When the Beaver Wars of the seventeenth century compelled them to leave the eastern forests and move to the forest edges of the prairie-plains of western Missouri, the Osage successfully met the external threats posed by their journey to a new environment. Living along the prairie marshlands, they exploited the forest, plains, and prairie edges and thrived in their new homeland.

The dramatic changes brought about by their seventeenth-century move created internal stress, which the Osage rose to meet. The Osage were a resourceful people, both externally and internally. They had created a successful woodland culture that they were able to modify to their new forest/prairie/plains environment. Their cultural resourcefulness served them well in the eighteenth and nineteenth centuries, allowing them to shape forced changes into a familiar cultural context and to retain control of their culture and their lives.

The Osage preserved their history in the memories of their clan elders, the Non-hon-zhin-ga. These clan elders preserved their history in long oral accounts of their history that they call *wi-gi-e*. The wi-gi-e recorded their history, and the surviving wi-gi-e reveal the resourceful character of the Osage. These accounts are Osage creations created to satisfy Osage needs; hence their functions and meaning remain obscure. The surviving wi-gi-e are so cloaked in seventeenth-, eighteenth-, and nineteenth-century Osage symbolism and metaphor that they are difficult to understand; however, they provide enough clues to reveal instances of cultural adaptation.

Those adaptations are revealed as reactions to what they deemed chaos, which they call *Ga-ni-tha*. In times of chaos the Osage would "move to a new country." These metaphorical "moves to a new country" signaled cultural changes made to deal with the new realities confronting the Osage. Such changes are seen in their changing clan structure.

The Osage created a complex social, political, and spiritual organization based on twenty-four patrilineal clans. These twenty-four clans were organized into earth and sky moieties, which were divided further into four phratries. Each clan was led by a small group of clan elders who had achieved their position by performing acts of skill and bravery and by memorizing the lengthy clan wi-gi-e. Too old to hunt and fight, these wise and experienced clan elders, the Non-hon-zhin-ga, met to provide direction for their people. When confronted with Ga-ni-tha, the Non-hon-zhin-ga met the new challenges and shaped and directed any necessary "moves to a new country."

It is difficult to interpret these moves, but there is evidence of them in the surviving wi-gi-e that were recorded in the early twentieth century of such moves. The nineteenth-century Osage were divided into twenty-four clans, but within the wi-gi-e and other ceremonial songs there are references made to fourteen clans. The original fourteen grew to twenty-one, and eventually increased to twenty-four. The timing of these changes is impossible to determine, but there is clear evidence of an increase in the number of Osage clans. It is not certain why the Non-hon-zhin-ga increased the number of clans, perhaps to incorporate new people into the group or to expand the number to accommodate a growing population.

The Osage reveal such an addition in an origin wi-gi-e. The wi-gi-e tells that the original Osage were made up of three groups of people, the Hon-ga, or Earth People; Wa-sha-she, or Water People; and Tsi-zhu, or Sky People. These three groups were wandering about the earth when they came upon a village occupied by a filthy people. The Osage invited the villagers to change their dreadful ways and join them. When the villagers accepted and joined the Osage, they were all placed within a single clan named Hon-ga U-ta-non-dsi, or Isolated Earth People, and were placed within the Hon-ga moiety. The "filthy villagers" may have been members of the Oneota culture that archaeologists claim merged with the Osage when they arrived on the prairies in the early seventeenth century.[3]

Two other clan additions are accounted for in a wi-gi-e. In this wi-gi-e the Non-hon-zhin-ga were sitting in the long lodge choosing clan symbols to represent the important elements of Osage life, when they were startled by the appearance of an angry buffalo bull who charged up to their lodge. This fierce charge, accompanied by a loud crash of thunder, came about because buffalo bull and thunder were angry that they had not been chosen as clan symbols. The Non-hon-zhin-ga, recognizing their great importance to the People, created the Ni-ka-kon-da-gi, or Thunder People, clan, and the Tho-xe, or Buffalo Bull People, clan, and placed them as a separate phratry within the Tsi-zhu moiety. They named their phratry Tsi-Hai-shi, or Those Who Were the Last to Come, a revealing title. These last two clan additions may have been newly created to bring strangers into the Osage tribe, or they may have been created to accommodate the Osage who were enjoying new success on the prairie-plains, where buffalo and thunder are ever present and whose former clan ritual roles did not provide sufficient status. Another possibility is that a growing population may have overwhelmed the old structure, so that the Osage were forced to create new positions for their growing population and to provide them with new roles and responsibilities within the old familiar clan framework. It is not clear what prompted the increased number of clans, but the increase was shaped and directed by the Non-hon-zhin-ga, who made the "move to a new country" to deal with some dangerous Ga-ni-tha.

They also designed Osage polity to those same ends. Osage polity was organized according to the spiritual guidance provided to the Non-hon-zhin-ga by Wa-kon-da. Their clan organization was integral to the polity, and the Osage were led by two moiety leaders from specific clans. These two moiety leaders, called *Ga-hi-ge*, were hereditary positions determined by clan membership. The Ga-hi-ge were responsible for keeping peace within the community and protecting the people from outside threats. Ten soldiers, *A-ki-da*, chosen from specific clans, enforced Ga-hi-ge decisions.

The Non-hon-zhin-ga were also engaged in interpreting and explaining Osage religion to their people. The central element of Osage religion was an all-pervasive holy spirit they called Wa-kon-da. The Osage believed that the spiritual presence, Wa-kon-da, was everywhere. Wa-kon-da was not only everywhere, its presence was manifested in everything. Wa-kon-da provided order to the world, an order not understood by humans. What understanding did exist was provided by the clan elders, who used their religious experience and knowledge to pray for direction and understanding of Wa-kon-da, to make some sense of the world, to appease and seek Wa-kon-da's guidance and approval. The Non-hon-zhin-ga, in an effort to appease Wa-kon-da, created, directed, and performed religious rituals to that end.

Rituals served as sacred reminders of those things the Non-hon-zhin-ga believed vital. The Non-hon-zhin-ga organized the people into the twenty-four clans whose names and responsibilities symbolized essential elements of the universe. The two moieties to which all Osage belonged were the earth and the sky. The earth moiety contained phratries that symbolized the two vital planet elements, earth and water. All combined, the Osage were symbolically the universe. Rituals reinforced this symbolic unity and the importance of all Osage in that symbolic oneness.

The Osage had an abundance of religious ceremonies, for spirituality was an integral and ever-present part of Osage life. They began each day by rubbing dirt on their faces and praying to Wa-kon-da for help.[4] The dirt was to show Wa-kon-da how miserable they were and why Wa-kon-da's help was so needed. The Osage implored Wa-kon-da for help and blessings throughout the year in ceremonies to bring rain, to ensure a good harvest of their crops, to bring bountiful hunts, to provide success against their enemies, and to celebrate their victories. There were rituals to name their children, foresee the future, heal the sick, and bury their dead. In addition to seeking Wa-kon-da's help and sanction, the rituals also included symbolic reminders of the importance of all Osage people. Their very names—earth, sky, and water—were constantly repeated to remind them of their important place in the Osage universe and of the vital necessity for them to remain united to survive as a people.

The ritual reminders of their important role in the Osage world went beyond symbols and songs, for the Non-hon-zhin-ga assigned every clan specific responsibilities in the rich ritual life of the Osage. Every clan had a role to play in the yearly ceremonial life, so all were constantly reminded of their place and importance in Osage culture. These all-important rituals called for the recitation of specific clan wi-gi-e. The great variety and number of essential rituals conducted throughout the year ensured that all clan wi-gi-e were involved. The importance of this involvement was reinforced and often duplicated in ritual. Rituals required sacred objects: pipes, looms, bows, arrows, and wa-xo-be that belonged to specific clans. These sacred objects and their ritual manipulation were important parts of Osage religious ceremonies; their inclusion again reinforced the unity of the Osage and the importance of all clans.

Although all clans' participation was vital for Osage survival and success, all clans did not share the same status. Some clans possessed objects with greater spiritual significance. The Tho-xe clan owned the war wa-xo-be. The Osage were required to perform a lengthy and elaborate ceremony before they could take such an important step as to engage in war, and that very important ceremony required the participation of the Buffalo Bull clan and their war wa-xo-be. Their role in that important ceremony gave them prestige and status greater than those of other clans. Despite the varying degrees of ritual status assigned the clans, all were vital elements in the rich spiritual life of the Osage people. All clans had ceremonial roles in all Osage rituals. All were necessary; all were important. The spirit of union and community was continuously being reinforced by the inclusion of all in their spiritual life.

Out of chaos the Non-hon-zhin-ga sought order. They, at the direction of Wa-kon-da, had created a massive, detailed, and formal cultural framework. This large and complex framework provided strength and unity and a place for all Osage people. The cultural framework was filled with elaborate rituals to direct and sanction behavior, provide some understanding of the wide-ranging events in people's lives, and ensure Wa-kon-da's blessing. The framework was incredibly complex, with a pattern established by Wa-kon-da, yet within this complex pattern the Non-hon-zhin-ga created enough flexibility to meet new realities and new challenges, and to make the adjustments necessary to meet new threats and opportunities.

The Non-hon-zhin-ga, however, were able to construct this complex system through the wisdom gathered by experience and through their knowledge of the past as recorded and revealed in their wi-gi-e that they alone preserved in their minds. Wi-gi-e provided the rationale for behavior and the credibility for behavior, and in an oral culture only those who recited the accounts were sure of their consistency and accuracy. Changes could be more easily made in an oral presentation than in one preserved in writing. That helped the Non-hon-zhin-ga make changes, and a vital element of Non-hon-zhin-ga power was their willingness to accept and direct changes. They were able to make incremental social, political, and economic adjustments. Although they indeed changed to deal with recurring Ga-ni-tha, the Osage, directed by their elders, were able to control the rate of change, so that they could incorporate new elements and graft new features onto their older and more familiar cultural framework.

As the Osage went to the prairie-plains, the new environment created new opportunities and new challenges, but their new life often challenged the old patterns. In the eighteenth century when they invaded the plains to hunt the buffalo, they had to fight the plains people to gain entry to the buffalo plains. These conflicts with the Pawnee and Wichita became a large part of their eighteenth-century life, and the Non-hon-zhin-ga had to create cultural changes to recognize and sanction the increased role of conflict in their lives. Ceremonies were redesigned and new ones created to meet the more combative spirit of the eighteenth century.

The increasing violence provided a serious threat to the Osage. Young men too eager to fight their enemies and launch raids would only provoke retaliatory raids on the Osage villages. At other times enemy raids on the Osage might warrant a revenge attack, or perhaps the threat of an attack might only be noticed by the Non-hon-zhin-ga. These growing threats of violence forced the Non-hon-zhin-ga to make another "move to a new country," the creation of a two-week-long war ritual called the *Wa-sha-be A-thin Wa-tsi,* or Dance to Possess the Dark Object. The Non-hon-zhin-ga insisted that war required the support of Wa-kon-da and that the performance of the Wa-sha-be A-thin Wa-tsi was essential for that support; hence no Osage attacks could be launched without first performing the ceremony. This important ritual required the participation of all twenty-four clans, which served to remind them that war demanded they come together as one to confront the dangerous challenge of war. The clever Non-hon-zhin-ga created the ritual to serve a variety of purposes. This lengthy ritual could be used to incite an attack or delay an attack. Because the war ritual took two weeks, it ensured enough time for the tribal leaders to carefully organize and plan the campaign and to avoid carelessly rushing to war. The same ritual could also create an attack, for if the elders believed that a raid was needed, they could call for the ritual that would lead to an attack.[5] With the increased violence of the eighteenth century, response to the

Pawnee, Wichita, Illinois, and Potawatomi raids often demanded an immediate response that the formal war ceremony prevented, so the Non-hon-zhin-ga authorized, within very specific guidelines, permission for immediate response attacks, which loosened Non-hon-zhin-ga control over the growing violence.[6]

The new bounty provided by buffalo hunting redirected their lives, and although they continued to farm along the rivers, hunting became a larger element of their life. These new elements also had to be accommodated within their cultural lives.

The advent of the horse and gun brought about dramatic changes to Osage life. Mounted on horses and armed with guns, the Osage could hunt in smaller groups farther from the prairie villages. With the quickness and mobility of horses, they no longer needed the entire tribe to surround and drive the herds off cut banks and cliffs. Small groups could travel out to the massive buffalo herds on the shortgrass plains beyond the Arkansas, and their guns protected them from Pawnee and Wichita attacks. The success brought about by the horse and gun created a new prosperity for the Osage, a prosperity that included ample food and safe shelter for their people, which in turn created a growing population.

As a result of the growing population, the increased opportunities for smaller groups, the security provided by their size, and the acquisition of guns, families began to leave the core group to form separate bands. Sometime in the early eighteenth century they divided, and again this "move to a new country" was recounted in wi-gi-e. According to the wi-gi-e account the division did not come about because of population growth and increased opportunity for small group success; instead it came about as the result of a great flood that invaded their river-bottom village. As floodwaters roared into the village the people fled from the advancing waters. One group ran to the nearby hills and climbed into the trees, another group ran up a dry ravine filled with brush, while a third group sought shelter on a nearby bluff. A fourth group ran to the bluff, but, unable to climb it, remained under the bluff. A fifth group found high ground in the village and remained surrounded by water.

The Non-hon-zhin-ga sought the cause of the flood, created divisions, and in time explained that Wa-kon-da created the divisions to protect the people. Their village was becoming too large and too vulnerable. With all the Osage in a single village they could all be destroyed in a single attack, so the Non-hon-zhin-ga instructed the Osage to remain in the groups they had created. These five bands were named according to their location during the flood.

The group that fled up the ravine through the brush was named the Wa-xa-ga-u-gthin, or Thorny Thicket People. The group that fled to the hilltop trees became the Pa-ciu-gthin, or Big Hills People, while those that successfully fled to the bluff were given the name Con-dseu-gthin, or Upland Forest People. The ones under the bluff were named the Iu-dse-ta, or Down Below People, and those who remained in the village were the Non-dse-wa-cpe, or Heart Stays People.[7]

A flood may have occurred to divide the people, or the Non-hon-zhin-ga may have created the wi-gi-e to mask the split caused by the growing population and increased opportunities with the cultural approval provided by the wi-gi-e. The Non-hon-zhin-ga sought to keep the Osage united and to maintain their identity as Osage. Although physically divided, they remained united by the culture as defined by their elders.

Economic success and the increased warfare that accompanied it created stress within their social and political system. The continued growth of the economy and continued violence, however, posed powerful challenges. There were new opportunities for wealth and prestige with the lucrative trade and frequent raiding. More Osage enjoyed this new prestige and wealth because of increased hunting and raiding, yet because of the hereditary nature of Osage leadership positions they had no means of gaining political power. The Osage created new clans, positions, ceremonial prerogatives, and ritual activities to provide status to meet the growing demands for power. These "moves to a new country" provided enough flex in the framework to preserve the frame while successfully dealing with the new threats and challenges of the eighteenth-century prairie-plains. These challenges continued into the nineteenth century, and their ability to "move to a new country" allowed them to make their own moves and to avoid those suggested by New England Protestants.

The changes proposed by the Protestants were thus thwarted by a resilient and flexible culture and by a prospering economy. The Osage had created a successful way of life on the prairie-plains that exploited the three ecosystems they inhabited. The Osage established their large towns on the edge environment, that prairie region along the western edge of the Ozark forests. There they planted and cultivated their family plots and hunted in the nearby forest. The large prairie towns, however, were only occupied for a short time in the fall and spring, when the environment would support the large communities.

As soon as the weather permitted, usually in late March or April, the Osage would gather in their towns; families would clear the ground and plant their gardens of corn, beans, squash, and pumpkins. Once their gardens were established, they left for their spring hunt on the plains. They would travel to the shortgrass plains two or three hundred miles west between the Canadian and Arkansas Rivers to hunt buffalo. They would remain out on the plains until early July when the buffalo began to breed, hunting and, if the opportunity arose, raiding their plains rivals. To avoid dangerous attacks from the aggressive buffalo bulls in rut they would make their way back to their large prairie towns.

The late summer and early fall prairie environment would support the large towns: the men would hunt the white-tailed deer along the forest edges while the women would harvest and store their crops for the winter. After the harvest and forest hunts, they would return again to the plains where they hunted buffalo and raided neighbors until the winter weather drove them back to their prairie homes. Upon returning they would, however, avoid their exposed village sites and break up into smaller family groups to spend the winter along the timbered river bottoms hunting bear and beaver in nearby eastern forests to supplement their cached crops.

When the threat of frost subsided, they would gather in their prairie towns and begin their seasonal cycle again. This cycle allowed them to effectively exploit the three ecosystems of their lands and prosper as a people. The seasonal cycle, which worked so successfully for the Osage, doomed the missionaries' plans to change the Osage economy and civilize them.

That same success had created internal problems for the Osage, which the Non-hon-zhin-ga "moves to a new country" had only tempered. As the Osage expanded they met the new challenges. Osage culture had always placed great value on economic and military success. Osage men acquired status as a result of hunting prowess and courage in battle. Men who protected their people and kept their kin well fed were respected. The increased hunting and raiding fit well within the older social framework. Individuals who enjoyed increased status and economic success, however, often had no access to political power within the traditional political system. As in the eighteenth century, heredity remained often more important than ability; unless individuals possessed the correct family ties they could never become an Osage leader. The Osage, however, in an attempt to limit internal strife, had created new kin groups with new positions that provided additional avenues to political power. Although the Osage were able to adapt and avoid internal conflict by creating social and political compromises that recognized older patterns yet integrated new features, the new realities of the nineteenth century placed limits on their flexibility.

Ambitious Osage, denied power within their traditional political framework, left the tribe and established independent Osage bands where they acquired more political power and status. When the Protestant missionaries first arrived, the Osage were living in three large groups. Two, the Big and Little Osage, were living in the north in large prairie towns near one another along the prairies of the Marais des Cygnes,; a third group, called the Arkansas Osage, lived in the south along the Verdigris River.

The Big Osage communities were made up of the Wa-xa-ga-u-gthin, Pa-ciu-gthin, and Non-dse-wa-cpe, who were led by Pawhuska (by 1821 the name *Pawhuska* had become a title for the leader of the Big Osage, a succession of Big Osage leaders were known as Pawhuska). The Little Osage were entirely the Iu-dse-ta. The Arkansas band (led by Claremore, whose name also became a title of Arkansas band leadership) was composed largely of the Con-dseu-gthin and members who had left the other four bands. These Osage splits would continue, and soon after the missionaries arrived another faction would separate and form a large community just north of Clermont's band.

The northern bands, living closer to St. Louis, the home of the superintendent of the western Indian Territory and linked to the powerful Chouteau family, acted as the spokesmen for the entire Osage tribe. Until the southern bands moved north in the 1840s, the U.S. government would deal primarily with the northern bands. The southern bands never surrendered their separate sovereignty to the northern bands and maintained their separate identity throughout the nineteenth century.

Their strategic location on the Arkansas and Missouri Rivers that had once allowed them to limit access to the West would become in the nineteenth century a pathway for outsiders going west. The rich resources of Osage country would attract thousands of outsiders, Indian and non-Indian alike, in the 1820s and 1830s. The Osage were challenged by thousands of eastern Indians who moved into Osage country. Cherokee, Chickasaw, Creek, Potawatomi, Delaware, Shawnee, and other eastern Indians, forced from their homelands by white settlement and the U.S. Indian policy, invaded Osage country. The southeastern tribes settled along the lower Arkansas and along the White River of the Ozarks. These outsiders posed an immediate threat to the Osage.

At the same time the Osage had to deal with this eastern threat, they had to contend with another growing problem in the west. The Kiowa, Comanche, and Pawnee had become a serious threat to the Osage out on the plains. Wedged between the aggressive plains tribes and the large eastern tribes, the Osage had to have guns and ammunition to resist them. They therefore had to maintain good relations with their only trading partner, the United States. The Osage were forced to choose peace with the Americans in the 1820s to survive the wars with their more immediate and pressing foes, eastern immigrant tribes, and the newly armed western tribes. Anxious to maintain trade, the Osage remained at peace with the United States throughout the nineteenth century.

While the Osage fought all of the eastern tribes, the most serious threat came from the Cherokee. The Cherokee, living in the mountains of Tennessee, Georgia, North Carolina, and South Carolina, began appearing in the forests along the lower Arkansas as early as 1786.[8] Small Cherokee bands hunted in the region, and in 1796, ten families, led by Kon-ora-too, moved to the St. Francis River. As conditions became crowded and inhospitable in the east, those Cherokee who wanted to continue their hunting life moved to the St. Francis and White River area. By 1806 there were about six hundred Cherokee there. These people joined the Choctaw, Shawnee, and Delaware and hunted in the Ozark forests.

The migration of southeastern Indians grew, so that by 1816 about six thousand Cherokee had settled on the lower Arkansas. These Cherokee invaders of Osage country were well-armed and skilled hunters. When Cherokee and Osage met on hunting expeditions, violence ensued as both struggled for control of the territory. The competition over hunting grounds was the essential problem between the two peoples, but the economically motivated violence begat additional violence as individuals sought retaliation for the attacks.[9] Economic competition and cultural differences made any successful diplomacy between the two people difficult.

In January 1817 the Cherokee, angered by Osage violence, began planning an attack on the Osage. In October, knowing that most of the Osage men would be out on the plains for the fall hunt, the Cherokee moved against the Osage prairie village, filled with food stored for the winter and left protected only by old men and women. Five hundred Cherokee, joined by Choctaw, Chickasaw, and "several whites," attacked the Verdigris River village, killing eighty people, taking over one hundred captives, setting fire to their lodges, and destroying all their food in the winter caches.[10]

When the southern Osage returned from their hunt and found their village destroyed, they were enraged, but the necessity of maintaining good relations with the United States prevented any large-scale retaliatory attacks. Troops arrived in December and started construction of Fort Smith on the south bank of the Arkansas River between the Osage and Cherokee villages to keep them apart. Fort Smith itself did little to control the violence; the threat to cut off trade was more effective than the little palisaded fort at the mouth of the Poteau.

The soldiers at Fort Smith tried to maintain a peace between the Osage and Cherokee, and repeatedly called on both tribes to meet and hammer out their differences. It was at one such meeting at Fort Smith between the Cherokee and Osage in July 1819 that Chapman met with the Osage for the first time.

The arrival of the New England missionaries had no impact on the violence in the region; it continued. Soon after their arrival Claremore came to the Union Mission and warned them of possible Cherokee attacks. He warned them that his men would be passing through to attack the Cherokee, and that they should gather up their stock and keep a close on eye on them, for some of the warriors from the northern villages he had no control of, and he feared they might misbehave.[11] Shortly after Claremore's visit Skitok, or Mad Buffalo, and about four hundred Osage warriors appeared across the river from Fort Smith, and with a thinly veiled threat to the fort they told the fort's commander, Captain William Bradford, that they were on their way to attack the Cherokee. After a day of shouting and threatening they moved south of the river, attacked a few Quapaw, and returned to the village with stolen horses, but without fighting the Cherokee. Perhaps hoping that the threatened attack on the Cherokee would dissuade them from launching another raid, they soon departed for the plains for their spring hunt. The threatened attack failed to stop the Cherokee, however, and a small group came upriver and attacked, killing Joseph Revoir, an Osage métis living just north of Union.[12]

The Osage returned from their hunt in August angered by the death of Revoir and threatened to send 1,400 warriors against the Cherokee. The threat remained only a threat, and in September, their crops harvested and stored, the Osage return to the plains for their winter hunt.

In early November a group of Cherokee, Delaware, Choctaw, Creek, and Shawnee warriors came by Fort Smith on their way to attack the Osage. The fort's commander, Captain William Bradford, was unable to stop them, and inexplicably gave them a barrel of gunpowder for the raid.[13] Unlike the 1817 attack when the Cherokee defeated a village of women and children, this time the war party split up; while one group attacked the camp containing women and children, the other party collided with a band of Osage warriors who drove them from the Osage plains.[14]

While northeastern tribes were moving into the former Osage forests, there was occasional violence when Osage hunters encountered eastern tribes in their hunting territory, but the northern bands never came under the concentrated attacks suffered by their southern kin. Most of the removed northeastern tribes were settled north of the Missouri River and were able to bypass the northern Osage villages on their way to the plains. The Kickapoo and Delaware who settled south of the Missouri hunted in the Ozarks south of the northern villages, closer to the territory hunted by the southern bands. There was, however, enough violence and tension in the region to occupy the attention of the Osage, and as they struggled to maintain their control of the region they had little time or interest in becoming civilized Christians.

With the combined goals of Christianity and civilization, the good men and women of Union and Harmony set out to convert the Osage. These people were convinced that their religion, values, and overall way of life were proper for all human beings of the world. One has only to read the issues of the society's periodical, the *Missionary Herald,* to see the missionaries' efforts among the native peoples of the world. For alongside the reports of the Osage, Cherokee, and Choctaws missions, one finds accounts of missions among the native peoples from the Sandwich Islands, Malta, Africa, Haiti, Ceylon, Bombay, and South America.

Their efforts to export Christian civilization was based upon a cultural conceit that is inconceivable to us today. They firmly believed that their religion and accompanying way of life were approaching perfection. They conceived of humanity as on a celestial ladder with the Protestant Christian civilization on the top rungs nearest to God, with the more acculturated tribes below on the middle rungs, and with the poor Osage living a life on the lowest rung of the ladder.

These agents of Christian civilization were intent on changing the Osage. They planned to do this by combining correct representative Christian behavior among themselves to serve as an example of the correct life with preaching the gospel. In addition to serving as examples of proper life and preaching the gospel, the missionaries intended to teach the Osage to live in a proper Christian fashion: a life of industry, individualism, and agricultural capitalism. The mission intended to pave the way to Christian civilization by teaching the Osage new skills and a new economy so they would give up their old indolent ways, adopt the new economy, and become prairie Presbyterians.

An important early barrier to such changes, culture aside, was one of language. Cultural barriers could not be approached until the missionaries could communicate with the Osage and describe what they had to offer. The missionaries first met the challenge of language by seeking out interpreters. Unfortunately they had few choices. None of the Osage spoke or understood English. This was partially the result of their long-time isolation from any sizeable English-speaking population. It was also, however, an element of eighteenth-century Osage hegemony in the region, where the Osage demonstrated their power and their feelings of superiority by making all strangers use their language.[15] For most of the eighteenth century the Osage had dominated the region and never deigned to learn French or Spanish, for the French who came among them sought Osage favors, and they learned Osage. Few Spanish speakers ever came to visit, and accordingly, few Osage learned Spanish.

Therefore, although Union missionaries sought out interpreters, they were unsatisfactory, for they had limited command of English, they were not always available, they seldom lived a life representing Christian values, and they were expensive. Within five days after arriving at Union:

Brother Chapman and brother Wm. C. Requa went to the Osage village to procure an interpreter for the Mission. They returned this evening, and think they have been successful in obtaining one who is sufficiently qualified to serve. It would be greatly for the interest of the Mission, could we obtain a person of learning and religion. But the most that we can expect from the man we have in view, is merely a verbal knowledge of the two languages. He has a wife, an Osage woman, and two children who must come with him. His price is fifteen dollars a month.[16]

Apparently this newly hired interpreter was of little help, for two weeks later they complained, "The only interpreter we could obtain at this time being inadequate, we laboured under many disadvantages in making them understand the full import of the papers. Besides this, their language is very barren of terms suited to explain the nature of a Missionary Society, and the meaning of many things connected with the Mission."[17] Later they will discover that the language was rich and possessed an extensive and appropriate vocabulary. Benton Pixley, perhaps the most ardent student of the language, wrote: "But this I would not hesitate to say, that it [Osage language] is undoubtedly capable of communicating all religious knowledge and instruction, and sometimes I think may be seen in it all the fire of poetic effusion."[18] They found yet another interpreter, but the problems continued:

> The Interpreter tarries with us for the present. This man speaks Osage readily; but he understands the English language so imperfectly, that we dare not preach to the Indians through him. He can neither read nor write; is a Catholic by education; has lived with the Osages seven years; and knows but little more about religion than they do. To communicate religious instruction through such an organ would be unsafe, not to say dangerous.[19]

Those at Harmony temporarily escaped such problems, for Bill Williams, the U.S. factory interpreter, was willing to help the missionaries.[20] He began to translate the Bible into Osage for them, but before he made much progress he left the region.[21] With Williams's departure, the Harmony missionaries had to seek out an interpreter, whereupon they had as little success as their Union brethren. Early on the missionaries selected several men to begin learning the Osage language: Benton Pixley and William Montgomery from Harmony, and Epaphras Chapman and William Requa from Union.[22] These men were surprised at the complexity and difficulty of the language, and, despite a great deal of effort, they never really became adept in the language. Pixley and Chapman lived with the Osage in their towns for weeks at a time, and on several occasions they accompanied the Osage on their hunts to stay close to them and improve their language skills. "In order to learn it advantageously, we are reduced to the disagreeable necessity of living among the Indians, wandering with them, and, in a manner, adopting their habits."[23]

As the missionaries struggled to talk with the Osage about Christ and civilization, it became clear that what they wanted to communicate to the Osage would require more than a shared language. The Osage and the missionaries did not share a common view of the nature of the universe, and this lack of a shared understanding would make effective communication and the ultimate conversion of the Osage into model Christian citizens very difficult.

These New England Protestants believed in a natural order of things that was very different from the natural order of the Osage, and those differences were critical for any mutual understanding between the Osage and the missionaries. The missionaries possessed an incredible cultural conceit, a conceit that denied them any real understanding of the people they were trying to help and that prevented any possible cultural compromises in describing and explaining their system. There was thus a paternalizing confidence pervading their beliefs that prevented them from any meaningful dialogue. It was perhaps that smug confidence that had sent them to the prairies, but it prevented any real conversion.

The Osage possessed similar cultural ethnocentrism; however, they were willing to concede that there were other valid cultural systems in the world for other people, and that each group of people had a satisfactory system for their own people. On several occasions when challenged by the missionaries, they suggested that perhaps the Christian religion had been created for white people and did not apply to the Osage.[24]

The New England missionaries claimed that Christianity was the sole religion for the world, and combined their religious convictions with a belief in a natural progression for humankind. They believed that all humans began at the bottom of an economic, social, and cultural ladder. They believed that Christ had come to them to provide a divine direction for them and for all humankind. Once enlightened, all people would make their way to civilization. Crude and uncivilized people whose lives were engaged in hunting and gathering would abandon hunting and gathering and become subsistence farmers. They would continue their journey by becoming profit-making farmers; continuing their progress, they would eventually engage in the commercial world of capitalism.

> Let, then, Missionary Institutions, established to convey to them the benefits of civilization and the blessings of Christianity, be efficiently supported; and, with cheering hope, you may look forward to the period, when the savage shall be converted into the citizen; when the hunter shall be transformed to the agriculturist or the mechanic; when the farm, the workshop, the school-house, and the church, shall adorn every Indian Village . . .[25]

This path, to their minds, was natural and inevitable, and their complete belief in this natural order blinded them to any other paths. They simply could not conceive of anyone being content with their lives. They were convinced that it was human nature for all men and women to "improve" their material condition.[26] They believed all people were ambitious and wanted to accumulate material possessions, and were engaged in the struggle to make progress as defined by nineteenth-century white Americans. This, they claimed was the natural order of things, and they had come among the Osage to start them on their way to farming and civilization. They preached that Christian enlightenment would smooth the path and ensure successful progress. They did, unlike many of their fellow Americans, believe that Indians were capable of such progress, hence their move to the prairies. They wanted to provide Christian enlightenment for the Osage and get them on their way to progress and success.

The Osage were not interested in such a path, for they had already arrived where they belonged, physically and spiritually. Their lives were already successful, and they had no need for missionary pathfinders, for they had already made their way to the prairie-plains where Wa-kon-da had provided ample resources for their way of life. They only needed to conduct the appropriate rituals and live a correct and proper life as defined by their spiritual guides. In 1820 the Osage were satisfied and content with their way of life. As the words of Big Soldiers reveal:

I see and admire your manner of living, your good warm houses, your extensive fields of corn, your gardens, your cows, oxen, workhorses, wagons, and a thousand machines, that I know not the use of. I see that you are able to clothe yourself, even from weeds and grass. In short you can do almost what you choose. You whites possess the power of subduing almost every animal to your use. You are surrounded by slaves. Every thing about you is in chains, and you are slaves yourself. I hear I should exchange my presents for yours. I too should become a slave. Talk to my sons, perhaps they may be persuaded to adopt your fashions, or at least to recommend them to their sons; but for myself, I was born free, was raised free, and wish to die free. I am perfectly content with my condition. The forest and rivers supply all the calls of nature in plenty . . .[27]

They sought protection from their enemies and enough game to feed their people. By the nineteenth century the Osage had gone beyond mere subsistence, and their growing fur trade had brought about a more comfortable life. These new comforts provided by wool blankets, steel knives, and brass pots and pans, however, were acquired through old and familiar means and put to old and familiar uses.

The Osage rejected the touted path of progress for other reasons too. An unavoidable cultural barrier to such change was the communal nature of Osage society. The missionaries' plan for progress and civilization called for an individualism that was inconceivable to the Osage. Progress required competitive individualism. Individualism was an integral part of America, where every single person had the right to life, liberty, and the pursuit of happiness and property. The U.S. government had been created to bring this individual opportunity for success. The spirit of the Second Great Awakening movement that helped trigger the missionary movement also contained elements of individualism, as individuals were given the opportunity to make up their individual minds to accept Christ.

The New England missionaries carried this message of individualism along with their Christianity. They preached that individuals had to look out for themselves, and that in order for them to "succeed" they had to be hardworking, self-disciplined, thrifty, and competitive men and women, who by working hard would achieve their proper place in the world. They believed that all humans were engaged in the struggle, and that Christian enlightenment would provide a clearer vision and ensure eventual success. Material possessions and the accumulation of wealth were signs of God's grace. These beliefs had inspired their missionary efforts. Living in New England surrounded by material comforts, they had felt the obligation to share the word and wealth provided by God's word with the unfortunate heathen mired at the bottom of the ladder.

The individual nature of American Christian culture was an alien one to the Osage. Their whole identity was wrapped up in their tribal community. They were all integral parts of the group, and their entire social, spiritual, and psychological being existed solely in the context of their community identity. They were Osage; they were Hon-ga, they were Tsi-zhu, they were Wa-sha-she—the Earth, Sky, and Water People. The Osage were unable and unwilling to break away from their community and abandon their tribal identity.

The individual nature of Christian civilization was therefore impossible for the Osage to conceive. Osage thought patterns were created and constantly reinforced by their culture. Their survival on the prairie required group effort and shared responsibilities. The Non-hon-zhin-ga, influenced by the realities of the prairies and inspired by Wa-kon-da, taught their people that individuals were all part of the whole and that their survival and identity as humans rested in the survival of the tribe, moiety, phratry, and clan. The group defined them. The Osage were taught that mindset from birth, and living in their crowded villages reinforced their group identity every day of their lives. Those community values were vital, and their religious ceremonies were filled with songs, dances, and religious symbolism that reinforced the importance of the group. Communal sharing was incorporated into ritual religious ceremonies throughout the year, for clan participation in ceremonies included feeding the community gathered for the ceremony. Involving all twenty-four clans in the yearly rituals ensured that all would share their food with the community.

They rewarded individual behavior that benefited the community. Only individual behavior that would contribute to the success of the whole tribe was defined as worthy and valuable. Individual acts of bravery in war were honored because the individual had protected the community. The Osage had a graded system of *O-don,* or war honors, that they awarded their young men for acts of bravery. The most distinguished O-don was earned for defending the village and the gardens.[28] Individual hunters gained status, not by their prowess as hunters, but by their willingness to share the bounty of their skilled hunting. Their individual skills and abilities were redirected from the individual to the group.

Nineteenth-century Protestant Christianity saw economic success as a sign of God's grace. Individuals who followed God's path, worked hard, and saved their money would accumulate wealth and material possessions and be happy Christians. This accumulation of material goods, an integral part of the Protestant success story, was an anathema to the Osage. As Benton Pixley, who was traveling with them on a bear hunt, noted, "the heaping up of treasures, and in this sense the love of the world, seems not to have taken possession of their minds."[29] Individuals acquired respect and status by giving away property, not by accumulating it. Generosity and hospitality were integral parts of Osage culture. One displayed one's good character by sharing and giving, not by hoarding. A thrifty Christian was a selfish Osage.

The means for acquiring such Christian success were also problematic for the Osage. White Christians attacked nature and harvested as much as they could possibly take. The Osage harvested the rich resources of the forest, prairies, and plains but with reserve and some caution. They believed that they were only one of many spiritual creatures inhabiting the universe. They shared their universe with all things, and their shared place within the universe's space was maintained by acts of reciprocity with the others. Christians did not believe in an equality of existence and a sharing of space with the elements of nature. They insisted on seizing, controlling, and consuming nature. White ideologies of domination and submission were not understood, for the Osage ethos was one in which the social, natural, and supernatural worlds were defined and shaped by reciprocity.

In 1821, when the missionaries arrived on their doorstep intent on converting the Osage to civilized Christians, they confronted a people content with their way of life and able, when circumstance demanded change, to shape those changes along familiar lines and within culturally consistent patterns. Because they were satisfied with their way of life, the missionaries would be unable to bring about the complete reorientation of the Osage worldview necessary to transform them into civilized Christians.

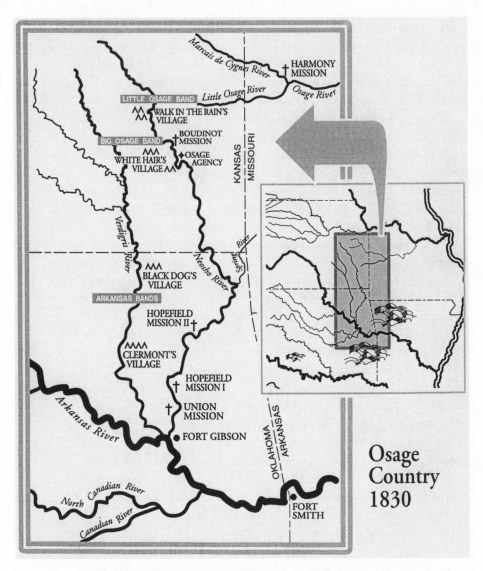

Fig. 5. Osage Country 1830. (Artist, Christine Stergios, 2003.)

5

Peaceful Resistance and the Co-option of the Protestants: 1821–1839

... The reluctance which this people have hitherto manifested in regard to religious instruction, cannot be supposed to arise form any distinct apprehensions of the
nature of the gospel. Perhaps it may, in part, be attributed
to the doubtful state of their minds on the great question,
whether they will adopt the ways of white people, or per-
severe in their wandering life. In their conceptions, the
arts, government, and religion of white people are viewed
as a whole, inseparable from one another. All their traditions and ceremonies lead them to this conclusion. We
have always found that much pains are requisite in order
to prevent them from confounding farming with religion.
While, therefore, their minds are not made up to adopt
our customs, and mode of life entire, they appear to consider it necessary to resist the entrance of light on any subject, and to reject every innovation on the ancient system.
—Reverend William B. Montgomery,
Missionary Herald[1]

The southern Osage did not need Christianity; they
needed tools and weapons. They needed muskets and
gunpowder to fight the Comanche, Wichita, and Pawnee
enemies in the west. They needed those same weapons to resist the
Cherokee, Creek, Kickapoo, and Shawnee invaders in the east. They

needed tools, for knives, awls, axes, hoes, needles, band metal, pots, and pans had all become a necessary part of Osage life, and they could only get the tools and weapons from the American traders. With the establishment of a military outpost in their lands they could not afford to anger or alienate their trading partners, especially when new enemies were arriving every day. They needed allies, and if their would-be allies needed land to farm, the Osage were willing to let them move onto their lands. In 1819 there were few whites in the region, and they were not seen to be as great a threat as were the Natives in the area.

Confronted with powerful Indian rivals, the Osage were not interested in hearing about their sinful and degraded condition. It is not clear what the Osage expected from the missionaries. They may simply have wanted a buffer group between them and the Cherokee. For years the Osage had used their downstream kin, the Quapaw, as buffers from the eastern Indian attacks. With the Quapaw decimated by disease and forced from their homes, the Osage were in search of new buffers, and the mission farms could serve as such barriers between the eastern tribes and the Osage villages. The Osage, recent victims of a Cherokee attack (Claremore Mound Massacre in October 1817), were willing to invite whites to settle between the Cherokee in Arkansas and their home in Oklahoma.[2] Earlier, in the 1816 Osage land cession known as Lovely's Purchase, the Osage claimed that they had ceded the land for white settlement, not for Cherokee villages.[3] In addition to a buffer, the Osage may have expected tangible rewards. They certainly expected more from the missionaries than they received.

When Sans-Nerf complained to McKenney that if the southern bands had a mission the northern bands deserved one too, it is unlikely that he was requesting boarding schools and the Christian gospel. What he wanted was a grist mill for their corn and a blacksmith to repair their metal tools, both promised by the federal government in 1808.[4] It seems obvious from their later treatment that Sans-Nerf did not invite the missionaries to come to his land to denigrate his culture and make his people give up their way of life.

It seems that the Osage, both in the southern and northern band towns, initially expected tangible rewards from the missions. Big Soldier, a prominent member of the northern towns, was an early visitor to Harmony. When he first visited the missionaries in the fall of 1822 he told them "he was glad we had come, because we would teach them to make corn soft; he also inquired whether any of us knew how to make powder, and expressed a strong desire to have one of his sons taught that business."[5]

The Osage came to the missions and brought food to share with their visitors, and initially the missionaries fed them. Later, when they convinced a few mixed-blood Osage to send their children to the mission schools, they fed and clothed them. Although a pattern of friendship and alliance based on reciprocity seemed to be understood by both sides at first, of course it was not understood by the missionaries, and in time this misunderstanding became very clear. The missionaries at Harmony complained that when the children left the schools they took their clothing with them. After one such complaint Sans-Nerf reminded them they had given the mission all of the land for the school and farms, and it was unseemly to complain about the missing clothing. Sans-Nerf further "replied that they had given us a great piece of land, and had not asked anything for it; and, if we wanted more land he would give us another piece for the clothes which he had not brought back."[6] All this explanation was lost on the missionaries, who simply believed the Osage were not properly grateful for the clothing they had provided.

After the Osage discovered that there was little tangible forthcoming from the missionaries in return for listening to sermons and sending their children to live with the strangers, they stopped participating in the missionary enterprise. The Arkansas Osage visited Union Mission but paid little attention to the gospel of the missionaries. Claremore kept the missionaries at arm's length and his village a day's ride away. In 1822, with the closure of the U.S. trading factory, the Harmony missionaries were surprised and dismayed that Pawhuska and Nez-ah-mo-nee moved their villages seventy miles away from the mission to the vicinity of the Chouteaus' new trading post on the lower Neosho.[7] They, along with the southern band, saw no meaningful return on their investment in hospitality. Claremore visited the mission and complained, "You do nothing . . . but talk about books; you have never given me a plough, an axe, or a bake-oven; these are things which I value."[8] It is obvious that the initial acceptance of the missionaries and their "invitation" was based on a great deal of misunderstanding on what was being offered and what was expected by both sides.

Despite the reputation of the northern towns as being more cooperative and more progressive, they too were unwilling to adopt the white ways. The cooperative reputation of the northern towns had come about because the earlier changes urged by the French and Spanish traders had been conducted within a familiar context. The Osage adopted the horse and gun and became active participants in the fur trade because the horse, gun, and fur trade could be incorporated into a familiar pattern. The Osage had hunted for centuries, and with the horse and gun they simply continued to hunt; the hunts in time would change, but the changes were initially subtle. The fur trade was conducted along familiar gift exchange patterns, so when the northern towns welcomed the European traders and became active fur traders, the newcomers came to believe that they were always cooperative with the whites. The northern towns, however, had welcomed the French, Spanish, and early Anglo-American traders into their towns and families largely because the newcomers were willing to become Osage and because they did not demand the Osage become French, Spanish, or American.

The northern Osage who cooperated with the U.S. Indian agents did so, therefore, because the agents did not make any demands for drastic change. When the Harmony missionaries came among the same friendly, cooperative progressives in the northern bands, they met the same lack of success their Union colleagues confronted in the southern towns. Neither the conservative band led by Clermont nor the progressive bands led by Pawhuska wanted to become Christian farmers.

It is clear that the missionaries never fully realized what they were asking the Osage to do. On one occasion a missionary complained that the Osage continued to confuse farming with Christianity. "We have always found that much pains are requisite in order to prevent them from confounding farming with religion."[9] It seems as if the Osage had a better understanding than the good New England missionary about what was really going on out on the Osage prairies.

The missionaries wanted the Osage first to give up their successful and familiar economy of hunting and farming. Convinced that if they remained nomadic hunters and farmers they would never become Christians, the missionaries attempted to convince the Osage to give up their seasonal hunts and to adopt a single-farming economy. Something that seemed eminently reasonable to the missionaries was inconceivable to the Osage. The Osage did not object to farming; they had farmed for years, but in a fashion that was acceptable to them, not to the New Englanders. Not only did the New Englanders ask the Osage to live apart from their people and only farm, they demanded that men do the farming.

This demand was not acceptable to the Osage, for farming was the women's responsibility. A proper Osage man did not plant or cultivate crops. He would help his wife and her mother prepare the garden plot before planting and assist them with the harvesting, but the remainder of the work was women's work. When the missionaries attempted to get the men into the fields to plow, they were met with great resistance. In the first days of the Harmony Mission, Pawhuska, the northern town leader, ever willing to get along and cooperate with the Anglo-Americans, went into the fields and spent an entire day plowing. Even this most obliging of the Osage, a man who repeatedly violated other cultural restrictions, finally could take no more and left the field, never to return. The missionaries never understood what the old man had done, nor why he finally had to leave. Such cultural restrictions were never understood by the missionaries, who thought Pawhuska's and other men's resistance to farming was merely laziness.[10]

The missionaries were asking the Osage to become anti-Osage, and people do not readily behave that way.[11] Given a choice, and the Osage, despite the increasing outside pressures in the east and west, still had a choice, they did not choose to become Presbyterian farmers. They did have to give up more land in 1825, and the political realities of the 1820s and 1830s did compel them to allow the missions on their lands, but in the 1820s and 1830s they did not have to become Christians. They retained their political and economic autonomy. They remained Osage. They remained hunters and farmers living on their prairie lands, living on smaller and smaller territories, but still living their lives shaped by their cultural values.

While Chapman, Requa, Pixley, and Dodge worked with Bill Williams to learn the language of the Osage, the other missionaries launched their crusade to civilize the Osage and transform them into New England farming families. Aware of the hold of the "savage" ways on the adults, they immediately began recruiting children for their schools, convinced that if they took the children before they became set in their Osage ways they could be transformed into Christian citizens. They wanted to convert them and then employ them to convert their fellow Osage. The Osage, however, especially those in the southern band, were not keen on sending their children to school.

In August, as soon as the Osage had returned from their summer hunt, Abraham Redfield went to Claremore's town to recruit children for the Union Mission school. There was little interest in sending their children to the mission schools, for in 1822 the missionaries were simply a group of white strangers who had just moved into the area making promises to help. The nature of that help was not yet clear, and this uncertainty is revealed in an exchange with an early Osage visitor. Big Soldier, an A-ki-da from one of the northern bands, came to Harmony shortly after they arrived and posed a variety of questions about their mission. After a brief exchange, Big Soldier concluded that they were probably good men, but he wanted to wait, for "in about three years he could judge better whether we were good men."[12]

The Osage were naturally reluctant to leave their children with these strangers. In addition, that summer Cherokee raiders had come upriver and, unable to find any Osage in the region, had attacked and killed Joseph Revoir, a métis trapper living just north of Union. With Cherokee raiders in the area and the character of the missionaries unknown, the Osage were unwilling to leave their children at the undefended mission schools.

Despite these reasonable concerns, the New England missionaries continued their recruiting visits to the villages. The missionaries particularly wanted to attract the children of the leaders; Claremore insisted that it was too dangerous for his children, but he promised that after the war with the Cherokee was over he would send his children.[13] Claremore would use that excuse well after the Cherokee threat had ended, and would never send his children to the mission school.

Claremore was not the only Osage who resisted sending his children to the mission school, for in the town of three thousand, Redfield was only able to recruit four mixed-blood children.[14] This number shrank quickly when the eldest, a twelve-year-old girl, fled back to the village bearing tales of beatings, leaving only the French interpreter's three children at the school.[15]

Soon after Redfield's visit, Claremore's village left for their winter hunt on the plains. Another Cherokee raiding party that included Delaware, Choctaw, Creek, and a few whites followed the Osage out onto the plains, and, finding the Osage camp empty of hunters, they fell upon the old men, women, and children, killing and capturing over one hundred.[16] Although the Osage hunters returned to drive the raiders off the plains, this repeat of the earlier 1817 Cherokee attack would make the Osage extremely leery of leaving their children at the mission.[17]

The missionaries at Harmony, settled near the Big and Little Osage villages a safe distance away from the Cherokee threat, had only a bit more success than their Union colleagues when they opened their school in early January. Sans-Nerf, the Osage leader who had met with the UFMS leader in Washington, brought two of his grandchildren to Harmony. They were soon joined by fifteen others, ranging from small children to young adults. Before the school began, however, several mothers came to the mission school claiming they missed their children too much to leave them, and took six of their children back to the village.[18] San-Nerf's daughter came and took her seven-year-old son back to the village, and within a few days her other son had had enough of the school and returned to the village. That first year the two mission schools had little success attracting students, for out of the four thousand Osage they were only able to enroll fourteen students, ten of whom were mixed-blood.[19] As Reverend Nathaniel Dodge wrote, "We find much difficulty in persuading the natives to give up their children and in keeping them after they have been given up."[20]

When students were brought to the missionaries, they were bathed, given American clothing, and given a new name. Contributions were solicited from eastern congregations, and in exchange for donations the missionaries would give the Osage children the names requested by the donors. "Have washed and clad our new pupil, and named him Zechariah Lewis."[21] If the newly named student ran away, which frequently occurred, they would give the name to the next student who arrived at the mission station.

Mission teachers hoped to transform the Osage children into proper, civilized New England citizens. They wanted them to abandon their culture and become industrious, disciplined, punctual, rational young Christians. The mission schools tried to teach basic educational skills combined with Christian morality and vocational training. Students were taught according to a popular new education program developed in the East, known as the Lancaster system, which focused on a curriculum of basic spelling, writing, and arithmetic using printed cards instead of expensive textbooks. Teachers would group the students according to their level and use more advanced students to teach the younger ones. This system was not designed for students who did not speak English, and it made learning difficult for the Osage children.[22] The Lancaster system included a reward system, intended to encourage the students to make progress in their lessons by rewarding them with coupons redeemable for small prizes, such as pictures or booklets.[23] The missionaries, failing to understand that such prizes might not be considered rewards to Osage children, continued to hand out the coupons.

The mission school curriculum combined teaching basic skills with vocational training. The mission farmers and mechanics taught the boys how to farm and tend to livestock. Some of the boys were put to work in the blacksmith shop while others learned carpentry. The mission women taught the Osage girls domestic industries: cooking, cleaning, washing, ironing, sewing, carding, and spinning.

Nineteenth-century Christians considered idleness dangerous to body and soul, so students were kept busy. This attitude toward work was an integral part of New England Protestantism as revealed in a note concerning the acceptance of a young student. "She is a pleasant child, and as her general health is sufficient, we shall do all in our power to teach her to work, and to read."[24] The sequence of the stated goals is revealing.

Convinced that idleness created Satan's playground, the children were placed on a demanding schedule; they were awakened at dawn and put to work for an hour, the boys tending to the livestock and the girls cooking and cleaning or sewing. After working for an hour they were given time to eat, then returned to work at 8:00 a.m. They would work until called to school, where they would remain until 1:00 p.m., when they would work for an hour. They would again return to the classroom for afternoon lessons followed by another work session. After dinner they would work on their lessons, memorizing hymns and portions of scripture.[25]

This type of education was not desired by the Osage. Those who did enroll were almost all the mixed-blood children whose parents, coming from the Euro-American culture, saw value in the vocational training. The few full-blood Osage children were likely sent as gestures of friendship or symbols of alliance by a few of the Osage leaders. They may also have hoped that their children would learn to speak and write English so they could establish more direct communication with the American government and help foster better relations with Americans at Fort Smith and St. Louis. Their stays, however, were brief. Tally, the Tzi-shu Ga-hi-ge, or peace chief, of Claremore's village did bring his fifteen-year-old son, Who-sis-ter, to the Union Mission School in May, where he was quickly renamed Philip Milledoler in honor of the foreign secretary for the UFMS.[26] Tally, however, returned in October to reclaim his son for the winter hunt.[27]

Some children, intrigued by the appearance of strangers, came to the mission out of curiosity or seeking a bit of adventure. Those students seeking adventure soon became disenchanted with the schools. They became bored with the tedium of memorizing biblical verses and copying English sentences and with the strict discipline enforced by the missionaries, so that they usually left after only a few days. Spankings were a part of New England culture, and there were occasional complaints of the missionaries beating the children. The Osage, who never disciplined their children by force, were reluctant to send their children away to such a harsh and threatening place. Mission records are filled with such accounts of children being brought to the school, only to have their parents return within a matter of days to reclaim their children and take them home.[28]

Equally disturbing was the fact that the missionaries were forcing their boys to do women's work. Within Osage culture, a man was to hunt and fight to feed and defend his people, not to work in the fields. Women were placed on the earth to plant the seeds and care for the gardens. Farming was thus women's work, yet the missionaries, operating within their cultural constructs, put the boys to work plowing the fields, planting corn and cotton, and cultivating the fields. This culturally abhorrent work, combined with the strict schedule, ensured that few Osage boys would begin, or continue attending, the mission schools.

The female students were more willing to learn "domestic industries," for the chores the missionaries assigned them were more consistent with their cultural framework. Osage women cooked and made clothing for their families, so the cooking and sewing were culturally appropriate chores. Washing, ironing, carding, and spinning were strange new chores, but were still within an acceptable and familiar cultural framework.

Mission reports are replete with complaints about absences and runaways. With several Osage towns only a few miles away, filled with several thousand Osage, the schools never had more than fifty students at one time, and almost all were mixed-blood children of families who thought that such education and training might be useful.[29] The mission schools were never successful, therefore, because what they were teaching had no application or relevance to Osage life. Mission lessons called for memory of strange stories and odd lessons from an alien culture. Osage children raised in a society that stressed group, and the importance of group sharing and responsibility, were baffled by lessons stressing individuality, modesty, and thrift. Christian thrift was Osage miserliness. Nineteenth-century New England Protestant values were too bizarre a concept for the unwilling Osage students.

The mission schools were thus never attractive to the Osage, and the semi-nomadic pattern of Osage life doomed mission schools already weakened by lack of interest. The distance from the Osage towns forced the Osage to leave their children at the missions year round, which made parents very uneasy. They were uneasy when they were nearby in the prairie villages, but when they left for their spring and winter plains hunts parents simply refused to leave their children so far behind and unprotected, and they would come to the missions to reclaim their children.

While efforts to convert and transform the children had little success, the missionaries' efforts to convert the adult Osage had even less success. The Osage lived communally in villages and towns with their extended kin. Osage towns might have two hundred *Tsi-sté tse,* or longhouses, with each containing several generations of extended kin, all grouped around the wife's family. The missionaries wanted the Osage to leave the security and comfort of their longhouse communities to establish separate single-family farms away from the communal villages, to become hard-working, self-disciplined, self-reliant individuals intent on accumulating property and wealth: to adopt the features of rural New England white culture.

The individualism that the missionaries promoted was unthinkable to nineteenth-century Osage. Communities provided protection and security vital for Osage survival. The Non-hon-zhin-ga, understanding the danger of living apart on the prairies, filled Osage lives with rituals and symbols emphasizing the necessity of community. Their culture, reinforced by their religion, extolled the virtue of group unity.

Individual Osage farms were not only culturally abhorrent, but in the 1820s and 1830s they were dangerous, as Joseph Revoir's family discovered in 1822. The 1817 and 1822 Cherokee attacks on the unguarded hunting camps were ample proof of the necessity of community defense. With the constantly growing invasion of Cherokee, Choctaw, Creek, Delaware, and other eastern tribes, the Osage had to remain united in their large communities, not isolated on separate, individual farms.

The plan to relocate Osage families on individual farms also called for Osage men to become sedentary farmers, which was simply too extreme a transformation for them. As mentioned earlier, Osage culture divided labor according to gender, and an Osage's sexual identity was defined and confirmed by their work.[30] Men were unwilling to abandon hunting, for their hunting skills defined them. Good men were good hunters who provided game for their kin. Cultural definitions aside, hunting was essential for their survival.

The Osage economy was composed of two elements, hunting and farming, and these two components were essential for Osage survival in the nineteenth century. Men had to augment the farm food crops with buffalo and deer meat, for the village gardens could simply not provide enough food to feed their communities. Further, insects, droughts, floods, and bad weather could destroy the crops, and if the Osage relied solely on agriculture, such attacks by nature would kill the crops and decimate the Osage. The hunting and farming economy of the prairie-plains had enabled them to expand and prosper, and they were unwilling to abandon their successful economy for an untried one based solely on agricultural.

Ironically, the missionaries, while constantly urging the Osage to abandon hunting and to adopt farming, were never, despite their sophisticated agricultural skills and the latest in farm equipment, able to survive solely on their farm products. They remained dependent on food shipments from their eastern sponsors.[31] Yet although the mission farms were never self-sufficient, the missionaries never seemed to apply their problems to those of the Osage. Indeed, on several occasions the Osage brought welcomed venison and buffalo meat to the mission.[32]

In addition to feeding their people with game, hunting also was a lucrative and necessary enterprise in the early nineteenth century. Traders flocked to the Osage prairies to trade manufactured goods for furs and hides. Guns and ammunition were always in short supply, and the Osage needed these weapons to defend their homes and families from the growing threats in the east and the west. Hunting was culturally blessed, as good hunters who shared their game with their village were given status and prestige in the Osage community, and was necessary in the increasingly dangerous prairie environment. Osage hunters could ill afford to become New England farmers, so they refused to abandon the hunt and continued their familiar and successful economic roles.

In September 1822, Moi-neh-per-sha, an Osage from Claremore's band who had lost family in the Cherokee attacks, approached the

Union Mission asking for help. He claimed that he wanted "to change his habits" and become a farmer.[33] The missionaries, suspicious of his intentions and sincerity, refused to help him start his farm, but hired him to work for wages, fifty cents a day, on their farm. Several other Osage joined Moi-neh-per-sha and settled near the mission to work for wages. They remained at the mission despite the ridicule given to them by their people, as described by one of the laborers, "My people told me that if I should work I should become a woman; but look, I am a man still, and can now clothe my children handsomely, while those who are lazy are poor and vicious."[34]

After a four-month trial, however, the Osage who had gathered around the mission had satisfied the missionaries they were willing to change. The missionaries then agreed to sponsor an Osage farming community when the southern bands returned from the spring hunt. When Moi-neh-per-sha and his kin failed to return to the mission settlement after the hunt in August, William Requa and Reverend Epaphras Chapman still hoped to establish the farming community. Leaving Union, they traveled a few miles upriver to find a site. They found a location on the east side of the Neosho where they began construction of the cabins for their new community. In February, they were joined there by three Osage families led by Pah-hunk-sha.[35]

Chapman and Requa optimistically named the new community Hopefield, and soon after Pah-hunk-sha's arrival Moi-neh-per-sha and five other families, made up of Osage and French métis, joined the new community. That first spring they planted twenty-four acres of corn, cotton, beans, squash, and watermelons. Although they successfully planted their crops with Requa's help, they were unwilling to depend solely on their farm crops and abandon their proper roles as Osage men, so after planting their fields they left for their spring hunt. Upon completion of an abbreviated hunt they returned to Hopefield to cultivate their fields and build cabins for their families.[36] Their first gardens produced enough for them to take several loads downriver to Fort Smith to sell for cash. This conversion to a cash economy thrilled the missionaries. As they described in their journal, "To see the Osage, for the first time, count his money, the fruits of his industry, affords no small satisfaction."[37]

It is unclear why Pah-hunk-sha and Moi-neh-per-sha left Claremore's village to establish Hopefield, but their separation from the large village may have been simply a part of an already existing pattern of separation and division developing among the Osage. The prairie-plains environment had brought new prosperity to the Osage. Their villages became large towns of three to four thousand people. Hunting and raiding on the plains, prairies, and forests combined with the growing trade in the east had created new opportunities for wealth and status for individuals who were not provided such position and status within the older cultural system. Although the Non-hon-zhin-ga made changes to provide status for the newly created group, their changes did not keep pace with the growing opportunities, and some began to leave the core group on the Marais des Cygnes to form their own communities. The Little Osage had broken away in the early eighteenth century to move closer to the trading frontier along the Missouri, and the Arkansas band had formed in the 1770s when ambitious Osage left the Marais des Cygnes villages for greater opportunity to hunt and raid in the west. The pattern would continue in the nineteenth century, for soon after the missionaries arrived on the Neosho, Shungeh Moineh established a village just north of Claremore's. This separation and creation of faction villages would continue throughout the nineteenth century with the five core groups dividing into as many as ten smaller groups or bands.[38]

Moi-neh-per-sha's approach to the missionaries may have been such an attempt to seek status and autonomy. Moi-neh-per-sha was not seeking Christ and civilization. He was seeking opportunities and status denied him in the larger community, and he was clever enough to secure the mission's support for his faction's community. He did achieve status for himself; in the spring of 1823, when he was a member of Claremore's village, he was referred to as "a young Chief of small influence in the nation," yet by 1825 he is frequently referred to as the Hopefield chief.[39] The mission's support of Moi-neh-per-sha and his faction annoyed Claremore, for he, in one of the few instances of opposition to the mission, openly criticized the mission's support of the Hopefield faction at a meeting at Fort Gibson in 1825.[40]

The single Hopefield community took on a dual identity. Hopefield was a budding Christian farming community in the eyes of the optimistic Union missionaries, while the Osage saw it as another southern Osage band village that had broken away from Claremore's village. Hopefield never grew to more than one hundred people, and while they broke away from the larger village, they never embraced Christianity, despite the presence of the missionaries living among them and conducting weekly religious services. When asked if they wanted to be Christians, "they say they cannot come to a decision on these important subjects immediately, but in the course of a little time they will be able to determine whether *their* religion or *ours* is the best. . . . But they observed, that, 'as they had just begun to hear of Christ, and knew very little of the true way of worship, they could not immediately renounce their ancient customs.'"[41]

The Hopefield band did, however, face problems in their attempt to establish a "civilized farming community." Their small settlement did not contain enough armed men to provide adequate defense against raids, and any rumors of enemy raiders would send them fleeing to the mission or the shelter of Claremore's village, along with other small separated bands. Warned of a possible Delaware attack in April 1826, "[t]hey therefore concluded to leave Hopefield immediately, and join Claremore's town."[42] Borrowing missionary tools and expertise, they expanded their gardens, but their newfound wealth was limited, for their ties to the larger community survived. These newly crafted Osage farmers remained culturally Osage, and their culture required them to share with their people. In the winter their nearby kin would move to Hopefield and consume any and all surplus food produced by Hopefield farmers. Other Osage passing through would help themselves to any crops left in the fields.[43]

The Hopefield band did, however, survive, as did other breakaway bands. The "success" of Hopefield convinced the Harmony missionaries to establish a separate Osage farming community among the northern bands, and in September 1824, Benton Pixley and his family left the Harmony Mission community and moved to the upper Neosho to establish the Neosho Mission for the northern divisions.[44]

Mission communities were not the only sites of missionary activity. The missionaries preached to the adults at all times and at every opportunity. These were not always formal presentations. A simple request to borrow a tool would merit a Bible lesson about thrift and independence. The missionaries visited every Osage town and preached to any group they could gather.

Without an adequate command of the Osage language, however, the missionaries could never convey their belief system, and those Osage who were polite enough or interested enough in listening to the Christians got only clumsy metaphors and simplistic moral tales that rarely fit within the Osage cultural context. Language also prevented the Christians from understanding the complex spiritual life of the Osage. Without a shared language, the missionaries got notions of the Osage religion as simplistic and misunderstood as the Osage had of theirs. Initially, the curious would collect to hear the Anglo-Americans, but the novelty soon wore off, and the missionaries were hard pressed to capture an audience.

The Osage were not interested in attending Christian services, for throughout the 1820s they were confronted with dangerous and growing challenges by Indian invaders. In November 1822 while the missionaries were visiting and preaching about sin and possible redemption, Osage hunters, seeking revenge for the 1821 attack, attacked a group of Cherokee hunting along the North Canadian and killed Red Hawk, the nephew of Thomas Graves, one of the eastern Cherokee leaders. Thereafter the Cherokee sent war parties seeking revenge for Red Hawk's "murder."[45]

In 1824 while stealing horses from the Delaware along the head-waters of the Red River, the Osage killed Kikthawenund, the son of the Delaware leader, who responded with a series of revenge attacks on the Osage. Such attacks fueled still more attacks. Agency records and missionary correspondence from the region in the 1820s are filled with accounts chronicling the ongoing violence between the Osage and emigrant tribes.[46]

While confronting the growing challenge of the eastern invaders, Western Plains tribes began mounting successful challenges to Osage domination of the plains. By the 1820s the Comanche, Kiowa, and Wichita had stopped fighting one another and had joined together to challenge the Osage for the hunting grounds between the Smoky Hill and Red Rivers. By the 1820s the area along the Upper Red, Cimarron, and Canadian Forks, long controlled by the Osage, was being contested by the Comanche, Kiowa, Kiowa-Apache, Wichita, and two newcomers, the Cheyenne and Arapahoe.[47] Attacks like the 1823 Comanche attack killing twenty-five Osage hunters became much more common.[48]

The western tribes had long challenged Osage in the west, but their challenges grew stronger after Mexican independence in 1821 with the opening of the Santa Fe Trail.[49] The Arkansas Valley became a busy thoroughfare for Mexican and American traders whose livestock over-grazed the valley and disturbed the game, particularly the massive herds of buffalo along the river. The new chaos in the west, through some of the prime hunting territory of the Osage, disrupted their summer hunts and threatened their livelihood. The flood of American traders crossing the prairie-plains to Santa Fe and Chihuahua became an even greater threat when they began providing the western tribes with guns and ammunition. The Osage could not stop the nineteenth-century Santa Fe Trail traffic as they had the eighteenth-century French and Spanish, and for the first time the western tribes were able to mount a real challenge to Osage control of the central and southern prairie-plains.

Throughout the 1820s the Osage came under serious attacks in both the east and the west, as more tribes fleeing American expansion invaded the Osage forests and prairies and as better-armed western tribes launched attacks on the Osage plains. The strategic location that had once provided the Osage with power and wealth had become a dangerous position by the late 1820s, as they found themselves caught between two rapidly expanding Indian frontiers.

The Osage of the 1820s, despite the growing dangers, were content with their way of life and worldview (and would keep a firm grasp on both throughout the nineteenth century). What they wanted were friends and allies, and they were willing to tolerate the often annoying presence of the Christians in order to secure their support. The Osage allowed both Protestant and Catholic missionaries into their villages, but not into their hearts and minds.

Nineteenth-century Osage were able to seize and co-opt the Protestant efforts and adapt them to their own ends. The Osage, whose villages had suffered repeated attacks while the men were away hunting on the plains, began leaving their property with the missionaries for safekeeping when they left for their spring and fall hunts.[50] They would also try to borrow guns from the missionaries for their plains hunts. When the Osage were badly injured they would seek the missionaries' help; as one journal notes: "an Indian severely burnt arrives for medical aid."[51] After attacks with other tribes they would bring their wounded to the mission's doctors. The Osages "had a skirmish with the Iaways [Iowas], and killed five men. They lost two men, and had two others dangerously wounded. On their return, they encamped here a few days, that the wounded might be under the care of Doctor Belcher."[52]

While avoiding Sabbath services, the Osage frequently visited Union and Harmony asking for food, blankets, and clothing. Once the missionaries erected their grist mills, Osage women came to Union and Harmony repeatedly to get their corn ground. Osage men came to the mission, not for the word of God, but to get the mission blacksmith to repair their guns and tools.[53] Missionary correspondence is filled with complaints about the unending visits of the Osage, who were eating them out of house and home and not paying any attention to the Christian gospel.[54]

Thus the Osage, in their critical position, needed friends, and they sought those friends among the newly arrived missionaries. The southern Osage bands were in a particularly difficult position for they had no agent to represent them at the all-too-frequent conferences; the single Osage agent lived a hundred miles away with the northern bands. The southern bands never had an agent near them until 1824, when they were assigned a subagent. Tragically, the first subagent assigned to the southern bands died mysteriously shortly after his arrival, and later subagents were seldom present at crucial meetings.[55]

Fearing that the violence between the Osage and emigrant tribes would hinder future immigration of eastern tribes, the federal government tried to stop the Osage attacks on the eastern intruders. Agents and subagents threatened them, and Osage leaders were repeatedly called to come to Fort Smith, and later Fort Gibson, where the commanders would castigate them for their attacks. Osage leaders were also summoned to St. Louis, where Superintendent William Clark would also chastise them for their violence and seize portions of their treaty annuities to pay for damages they caused.[56]

Early on, the Osage visited the missions and asked for assistance at such meetings. They would have the missionaries write letters for them and often had them deliver the messages in person. In January 1823, when the Osage were summoned to Fort Smith to make amends for the murder of a Cherokee, Claremore asked the missionaries to accompany him to the council. "Claremore has renewed his request, to have us attend the council, as he says he desires to have all his white friends present."[57] Any time the Osage were summoned to parley with the government or other tribes they requested the missionaries to accompany them. They would continue to have missionaries alongside them when they held important meetings with the United States in the 1820s.

In 1824 U.S. officials, anxious to quell the violence between the Osage and eastern tribes, closed Fort Smith and sent troops into Osage country. Colonel Matthew Arbuckle took his men to the Three Forks, and near the mouth of the Verdigris River he established Cantonment Gibson in the heart of the southern band homelands, only forty miles from two large southern band villages.[58] The establishment of Cantonment Gibson so close to the Arkansas band convinced them to cooperate with the United States. By 1824 both the northern and southern bands understood their delicate position and the necessity for peace in the east in order to survive in the west. This new awareness was clearly revealed when the southern Osage finally began working with the United States to maintain that peace.

The previous fall a group of Osage had set out on a mourning ritual. The group had sought to kill a Pawnee to accompany their dead, but when they failed to find the Pawnee and stumbled upon a group of Americans and Quapaws hunting illegally along the Blue River, they attacked and killed four of the hunters. When word of the attack reached Fort Smith, Colonel Arbuckle demanded the Osage surrender the warriors accused of the attack, but the southern band leaders only surrendered some of the horses and furs stolen in the raid. The arrival of four hundred soldiers at the Three Forks, however, convinced them to make further concessions to keep the peace. In June the entire southern band, consisting of about four thousand Osage, along with members of other Osage bands, came to Fort Gibson accompanied by Reverends William Vaill and Epaphras Chapman, George Requa, and Vaill's son, Richard.[59]

Although the fort consisted only of a collection of tents and wagons surrounded by a pile of brush and driftwood, the Osage surrendered six of their young men accused of the Blue River attack. The surrender was telling, for the southern band of Osage had always been the most independent and defiant, yet by 1824 they recognized their weakened position and made the necessary sacrifice. It was also remarkable, for the Osage accused of leading the attack was Skitok, a prominent southern band warrior and the son of Claremore, the leader of the Arkansas Osage. To preserve the eastern peace the southern bands surrendered their sons, but they punctuated this concession with a demonstration of strength. Their juxtaposition of great power alongside great capitulation only emphasized their earnest desire for peace with the United States.[60]

That desire grew as more eastern tribes moved into the region. The ever-growing presence of eastern tribes continued to challenge the Osage. The northern bands, hoping to escape the Kickapoo, Delaware, and Potawatomi raids, moved west in the early 1820s, finally settling on the plains along the upper Neosho River in 1824. While the northern bands searched for a safer village site, the Arkansas band remained at the Three Forks and continued to resist the eastern tribes. With the 1824 surrender of Skitok, however, the Arkansas band conceded some sovereignty to the United States. Not all, however, for when their new agent came to their village in January 1825 and told them to move north to join the Little and Big Osage villages, they refused.

Aware that they should not defy the United States, for such defiance might halt trade and curtail their access to the vital guns and ammunition, they used a technique they had been using with the missionaries regarding their children. They agreed to the demands, but failed to carry out their promises; they stalled. After a lengthy conference with the agent at Fort Gibson they reluctantly agreed to move north, but "they begged the indulgence of Government while they planted corn once more on their old spot. This was cheerfully granted."[61]

The agent's January visit was followed by a summons for Claremore to come to St. Louis to negotiate the proposed move. Pawhuska, Nez-ah-mo-nee, and the other northern band chiefs who had already moved north in 1824 joined Claremore in St. Louis and agreed to cede the southern lands. Claremore was coerced into signing the treaty that ceded almost all of their remaining lands, save a narrow fifty-mile strip of land in the north where the northern bands were living. Although southern band leaders "signed" the treaty, once they returned to their villages they ignored the provision calling for their removal. Claremore would continue to delay the move for another fourteen years, and he and his village would remain along the lower stretches of the Verdigris until 1839, when, bribed with large gifts and urged along by Fort Gibson soldiers, they moved fifty miles north.

This 1825 treaty alarmed the missionaries, for the Osage land cession appeared to remove the Osage from the missions' sites. Both Big and Little Osage villages were now seventy miles east of Harmony, and the southern bands had promised to evacuate the region. The missionaries feared their move north would leave Union and Hopefield more than one hundred miles from their villages. The treaty cessions also concerned the UFMS, for they had incurred an enormous debt establishing their Osage missions that were about to be abandoned by the Osage, and by 1825 they were not sure they would be able to meet the ongoing financial demands of the missions.[62]

After much prayer and deliberation, they decided to dissolve the UFMS and transfer their missions to the larger, more financially stable ABCFM. Claiming that they shared common goals and a common theology, the UFMS formally transferred their Osage missions to the ABCFM in May 1826, and thereafter the Union, Harmony, Hopefield, and Neosho missions were under the direction of ABCFM in Boston. Once they assumed control of the Osage missions, the ABCFM immediately begin urging caution and extreme frugality. "This state of uncertainty has rendered the Committee unwilling to extend large sums of money on either of the stations among the Osage."[63]

Although the times were uncertain for the ABCFM, the times were far more uncertain for the Osage. A conversation with Claremore provided a vivid description of the Osage situation: "I have many foes. I am like a man who is attacked by twenty angry dogs at one time, he knows not which to strike first."[64] The Osage were indeed being attacked both by those who wanted to "save" them and those who wanted to drive them from their prairie lands.

In 1828, to provide room for white settlers, six thousand Cherokee living between the White and Arkansas Rivers were forced from their Arkansas homes and removed to the Three Forks region.[65] In May 1830, President Jackson pushed the Indian Removal Act through Congress, which formalized and broadened the earlier piecemeal policy and accelerated the process of removing the eastern Indians to the western prairies. With the passage of the act thousand of Indians would be bribed, threatened, and coerced to exchange their eastern homelands for lands in the West. The act brought about the removal of over fifty thousand eastern tribal peoples to the western prairie-plains. The Osage had seized this land from the Wichita in the eighteenth century, and it had been their home for over one hundred years.[66] From 1830 on, the flood of emigrants grew as Choctaw, Chickasaw, Seminole, Creek, Cherokee, Seneca, Miama, Wea, Piankasha, Peoria, Kaskaskia, Ottawa, Kickapoo, Mesquakie, Sauk, Potawatomi, Delaware, Wyandot, and Shawnee would be forced into the western prairies.[67]

The good missionaries continued their efforts to civilize and Christianize. The Hopefield community, despite the ridicule of their kinsmen and the threat of Indian attacks, survived. Moi-neh-per-sha and his small band of Osage and métis part-time farmers took advantage of the new market created by Fort Gibson and managed to survive. Those who abandoned the plains hunts and stayed home that first year paid a very high price, for the summer and fall hunts were important for Osage survival in the winter. Without the meat and the buffalo robes from the plains hunts, winter found a Hopefield poorly prepared. The Hopefield people went hungry that first winter.

A single economy was a dangerous undertaking, and after the first miserable winter the Hopefield settlers left their farms for part of the summer and continued their summer hunts. When the floods of 1826 completely washed away their cabins and wiped out their fields, the Hopefield farmers starved. They suffered from hunger that winter, and many died, but they were determined to remain separate from Claremore's village, and the Hopefield band survived.

While Requa and Chapman ministered to the Hopefield band, the Union missionaries continued to run their mission school with only limited success. The Osage still refused to send their children to Union despite the blandishments of Vaill and Dodge. Gradually the Union school began accepting students from the newly migrated tribes, and soon their school was filled with Creek and Cherokee students.[68]

Although the northern bands accepted the missionaries into their villages, they too continued to ignore or merely tolerate the visits. Benton Pixley at Neosho, perhaps the only missionary to ever really become fluent in Osage, began delivering sermons and singing Christian hymns in Osage. Unfortunately, Pixley's knowledge allowed him to understand the ridicule and rough insults that some of the Osage hurled at him. He became angered by ribald Osage humor and responded to the Osage ridicule with his fists.

In 1828 Pixley also became engaged in a controversy with the agent and agency farmers. What began as criticism quickly became accusations of fraud. Pixley accused the agent, the agent farmers, and the agency blacksmith of appropriating Osage livestock, destroying village gardens with their cattle, and refusing to do any blacksmith work for the tribe. The agent, John F. Hamtramck, and A. P. Chouteau, the sub-agent, used their influence with the Big Osage leaders, and together they had Pixley removed from the Neosho Mission.[69] Reverend Nathaniel Dodge moved from Harmony to replace Pixley; he relocated the mission downstream and renamed it Boudinot, in the name of Elias Boudinot, who had made generous contributions to the ABCFM. With the help of farmer William Bright from Harmony, Dodge continued Pixley's efforts to transform the Osage into New England farmers, with little success.

While ignoring their Christian message, the Osage continued to take any help available from the missionaries—who accompanied them to meetings, wrote letters for them, tended to their sick and wounded, and fed and housed them when they passed through the mission stations. Union and Harmony mission workers spent more of their time accompanying Osage leaders to meetings, writing letters to St. Louis and Washington for them, grinding their corn, repairing their tools, and feeding their families than they did preaching the gospel and converting the heathen. The Protestants persisted, however, and they continued to work among the Osage in hopes of converting them into Protestant Christian farmers. The Osage also persisted and resisted.

While they often listened politely to the proffered words of Christ, they continued their morning prayers of supplication to Wa-kon-da, not Jehovah. They cordially accepted the help of the Christians, but resisted their message of conversion. The Protestants, mistaking the cultural tenacity of the Osage for ignorance and savagery, labored on in the "heathen wilderness." The ABCFM, however, was reluctant to invest great sums of money, for after the 1825 treaty cessions the future of the Osage missions became uncertain. Harmony Mission was no longer on Osage land, for after the 1825 treaty cessions the Osage found themselves in the state of Missouri, where they were soon be surrounded by white settlers hostile to any Indian community in their neighborhood.[70] "Considering the present perplexing state of the mission [Harmony], the mission families & property being off the Indian lands, & it being uncertain how long they will be permitted to remain where they are; of what course of policy the agent of the government will pursue or what influence he will exert in respect to the mission, the Committee hardly know what course to adopt."[71] The land cessions of 1825 would, in time, also affect Union and Hopefield.

Union and Hopefield lands were not transferred to any other tribes until May 1828, when western Cherokee took title to the land. The Cherokee demanded that the Hopefield settlers move, but the settlers were able to stall and delay their evacuation until the spring of 1830, when they were finally forced to leave Cherokee lands. They crossed to the west side of the Neosho and moved twenty-five miles north, where they began erecting cabins in their new community, which the missionaries christened New Hopefield.

As the Osage entered the 1830s and their prairie homelands filled with eastern emigrants, they maintained their earlier patterns, trading prairie-plains products of deerskins, buffalo hides, horses, and mules with the Three Forks merchants. They also continued struggling with the Pawnee, Kiowa, Comanche, and Wichita. The earlier struggles of the 1820s, however, worsened in the 1830s, for the Osage confronted new and powerful enemies they could not defeat: influenza, cholera, and smallpox.

Smallpox attacked the Osage in the late 1820s, and smallpox epidemics in 1827 and 1828 sent them fleeing to the plains. Because of these smallpox outbreaks, the federal government authorized Osage vaccinations in 1832, but not all of the Osage were inoculated. The doctor went to their prairie towns during the summer when most were out hunting on the plains, and some of his vaccine was damaged by improper sealing and summer heat; only one-third of the Osage were vaccinated.[72]

Vaccination saved some of the Osage from the scourge of smallpox, but nothing saved them from the terrible outbreak of cholera of the 1830s. By the 1830s, the Osage were hemmed in by expanding and often hostile tribes, who pushed the Osage closer together where these epidemic diseases could spread more easily. Removal had surrounded them with thousands of eastern Native Americans who, along with the hundreds of soldiers, hunters, and traders in the region, brought diseases to the Osage.

Throughout the 1830s, the Osage confronted successive and sometimes simultaneous attacks by diseases.[73] From 1829 to 1831 the Osage suffered from influenza and were thus in a weakened condition when repeated attacks of cholera struck in 1832, 1833, and 1834.[74] ABCFM missionaries reported, "Sickness prevailed extensively and was unusually mortal. It is estimated that as many as 300 or 400 Osages died of the cholera."[75] When the Kiowa and Wichita came to Fort Gibson in 1834 to meet with the Osage, they asked the soldiers where the Osage were, and the soldiers told them the Osage were dying of cholera.[76] Missionaries reported that the Osage fled out onto the plains to escape "the prevalence of cholera among the Osage, causing them to forsake their towns."[77] Despite their flight to the plains, over four hundred Osage died in the summer of 1834.[78] Cholera returned in 1835, and the Osage lost still more.[79]

Living in the sedentary community, Hopefield settlers became the victims of disease that some of their semi-nomadic kin avoided. When the cholera epidemics came to New Hopefield, the Osage fled their farming community and escaped to the plains.[80] After 1834 New Hopefield was abandoned by most of the Osage, with only a few remaining at the settlement.[81]

Despite the onslaught of deadly diseases, the Osage remained determined to preserve their way of life, so they compromised where necessary and maintained their power whenever possible. Claremore and Black Dog still reluctantly received the missionaries' visits. They let them stay in their lodges and allowed them, if convenient, to preach in the village. Their village gatherings were always being ignored or interrupted by Osage village life, as evidenced in their journals: "Toward evening, we arrived at the little Osage town, where we were saluted with a war party, preparing for a war expedition, and with whom we were annoyed all the time we spent at the town, for they were extremely tumultuous and noisy."[82]

The missionaries never seemed to understand their insignificance to the Osage, as revealed in Vaill's account. "Visited White Hair's village, and collected a few of the people; but they appeared reluctant so to do, as they had come in from their buffalo hunt on purpose to dance over the scalps of the slain; and their minds are all taken up with their victory."[83] The missionaries also never seemed to truly understand what they were asking of the Osage. On a visit to Claremore's village they expressed disappointment when the people of the village failed to stop working and respect the Christian Sabbath. When they protested to a respected elder he explained "that there would be a heap of corn lost if the women should quit planting for the *Umpah Who-kun-dah,* the day of God."[84] Visiting a Little Osage village they complained, "Saturday, visited Belle Oiseau's town and spent the Sabbath; failed, however, to preach, on account of their great religious ceremony which took place on that day."[85] They also sometimes arrived at the villages when the Osage were celebrating a victory over their enemies, or conducting a necessary ritual on their yearly spiritual calendar. In May 1833 the Osage surprised and attacked a Kiowa village in the Wichita Mountains.[86] Vaill, at the Osage village when the warriors returned from their victory, complained:

> On reaching town, at evening, we found all in commotion.
> For five days the Osage warriors have been coming in from an
> excursion against the Pawnees [Kiowa]. . . . [T]here was great

rejoicing over the multitude of scalps brought in—drumming, dancing, and yelling. . . .

One heart and one soul animates the whole town.[87]

Their letters are filled with outrage and self-righteousness as they describe the Osage living their lives according to their culture. "And truly, the more we see of the Osage religious customs, the more we learn, that we have to contend, not merely with ignorance, but with deep-rooted and long-confirmed idolatry."[88] The Osage, with more pressing concerns and the growing need for spiritual help from their faith, sometimes discouraged the missionaries from visiting and preaching.

> Though in the habit of spending much of their time in large companies, when a missionary proposes to preach, a tedious negotiation has to be entered into, when all their ingenuity is put in requisition, either to prevent the meeting by getting up a council or a dance, or to render it almost nugatory by calling on none but a few old men, or in some way preventing the people from attending.[89]

Another missionary noted: "Thursday we did what we could to collect the people, and gained some small audiences; but we found them much indisposed, especially the chief, young Clermont, who evidently strove to keep us from preaching to his people."[90] Still again, "The opposition of Belle Oiseau, (who is both a Chief and a *Who-kun-duk-ka*) to our holding forth the word of God in his town, was very great . . ."[91] Their correspondence is filled with such complaints.

By 1834, Montgomery and Requa had gained enough knowledge of the language to create *Wabashe Wageressa Pahogreh Tse,* or *The Osage First Book,* a book written in Osage. Believing that if the Osage could learn to read and write in Osage they could more easily acquire those skills in English. *Wabashe Wageressa Pahogreh Tse* contained an Osage alphabet and sample sentences in Osage to read and copy.[92] Unfortunately the practice sentences the book used extolled the virtue of Anglo-American cultural values, such as Anglo-American gender roles and the virtues of log cabins and stone fireplaces for individual families. Sentences praised the virtue of farming, advantages of private property, and benefits of Christian civilization.

The Osage First Book, therefore, was for naught, for the meager gains made with language were lost in culture. The struggle of culture was never fully understood by the missionaries. They could understand the problems of language—which they never really overcame—but they never understood what they were really asking the Osage to do, which was to stop being Osage.

Events in the early 1830s began to reshape the mission efforts. Jackson's forced removal policies flooded the region with eastern tribes. As more Creek and Cherokee arrived in the area, the ABCFM decided to close the Union school in 1833. The deadly cholera and smallpox epidemics also attacked the mission families, and after ten years of little success among the Osage, several of the missionaries decided to abandon their missionary efforts and leave the field. In 1834 Reverend William Vaill and his wife, visiting their families in New England, decided to remain in the East and not return to the Osage missions.

In 1835 the ABCFM transferred most of the Union buildings to their Cherokee missionaries, where Samuel Worcester and Elias Boudinot set up the Cherokee printing press.[93] That same year the ABCFM released their missionaries at Harmony from their duties and put the mission settlement on the market. Later, Boudinot missionaries Nathaniel Dodge and his wife decided to retire from their missionary efforts, and they abandoned the Boudinot Mission. With the closing of Union, Harmony, and Boudinot, only New Hopefield, ministered by William Requa and his wife, survived.

The New Hopefield Mission's survival would be short-lived. Because New Hopefield was located on Cherokee lands, the ABCFM in early 1836 asked Requa to move north and reopen the Boudinot Mission. "We hope to obtain a missionary for the place [Boudinot] next fall. It is exceedingly mortifying and distressing to reflect how the Osage mission has dwindled, after all the expense, labor, suffering and life which have been devoted to it."[94] Requa gathered the few remaining families at New Hopefield and made his way to the upper Neosho mission, where he arrived in early 1837. Requa confronted Osage opposition, and he struggled to maintain the mission.

Osage life, despite all of the changes they had made since the first European strangers came among them in the seventeenth century, remained Osage. Despite the destructive disease, despite the political factionalism and social divisions, and despite the economic and political changes forced upon the Osage, they remained strong enough and flexible enough to shape those forced changes forced into a familiar and acceptable pattern. The missionaries, however, demanded changes that could not be molded into familiar patterns. The missionaries asked too much and gave little in return, and as a result they failed. The Osage enjoyed their way of life, and the changes demanded by the Christians were simply too drastic and unnecessary. Unable to drive the meddling newcomers away because of their need for peace and trade with the federal government, the Osage were forced to endure the sermons, visits, and insulting demands made by the missionaries. The Osage moved away from the missionaries when they could.[95] When moving away failed, the Osage simply ignored the missionaries. They refused to send their children to the mission schools, and only allowed the preacher to come among them because they had no way, short of violence, from preventing it. The Osage had more pressing concerns in the 1820s and 1830s. Busy defending their land and resources of the prairie-plains, they merely tolerated the missionaries. The missionaries finally conceded defeat in 1837 and with the permission of the ABCFM closed the last Osage mission.[96] The few Osage living at Boudinot and New Hopefield rejoined their kin in the nearby Osage towns, and William Requa, the last Osage missionary, moved to nearby Missouri, where he became a preacher and carpenter for white settlers living there.

Good men and women and children toiled and died on the Osage prairie, working for what was in the 1830s an impossible goal, for as long as the Osage remained able to hunt and farm and live their way of life, New England Christian civilization had no charm for them. The Osage had "scarcely a motive to be any thing after all their improvements, but Osages."[97] Indeed, in 1832, as Dodge noted, the Osage did go to their graves unaffected by the Christian gospel, but filled with the gospel of the Osage.

The missions at Union, Harmony, Hopefield, Neosho, and Boudinot failed because the missionaries never understood their challenge. They were asking a people to give up a successful and satisfying way of life, to adopt an alien, and frankly ill-adapted, way of life for the prairies. They asked them to adopt a life of loneliness, miserliness, and effete behavior, to ignore their kin, and to challenge the fates by giving up the hunt. As they could only ask, not force, the Osage to change, the Osage could, and did, resist.

6

Spiritual Victories, Secular Compromises: 1838–1859

A retrospect of the history of this mission cannot be taken without awakening many painful emotions. Very few, if any, of the adults of the tribe have been induced to exchange their savage and migratory habits for a civilized and industrious life; or to substitute the Christian doctrines and practices for the ridiculous and absurd superstitions; or have been in any other manner benefitted as to the condition of their character. . . . The amount of funds expended on the mission has been great; and so also has been the number of laborers who have engaged in promoting it. Not a few of these, after going through a course of arduous service, have gone down to the grave, the victims of disease and hardship; others, worn down by toil and disheartened by opposing difficulties, have retired from the field with broken constitutions; while the remnant, after having labored with much fidelity and patience nearly fifteen years, have felt themselves compelled to abandon the work, leaving the Osages, with scarcely an exception, more miserable and hopeless, both as to condition and character, than they were when the missions was commenced among them.
—Report of the American Board for 1836[1]

Although there is no evidence the Osage celebrated when William Requa closed the Boudinot Mission and retreated to the Missouri frontier, his departure in 1838 signaled the Osage victory over Protestant colonialism.

Subjects of sixteen years of zealous proselytizing, the Osage had successfully and nonviolently resisted the concerted and diligent efforts of the New England Protestants to transform them into Protestant New England farming people. Evidence of this spiritual victory is shown in the above ABCFM account of their Osage missions. Nineteenth-century ethnocentrism and cultural arrogance aside, it is clear from this account that the Protestant Osage missions were a grand and expensive failure.

In 1838, the Osage were not miserable and hopeless; instead they were a people who had successfully made the necessary compromises and had retained control of their spiritual and secular lives. The Osage had perhaps made some changes in their spirituality, but those changes were directed by the Non-hon-zhin-ga, not by Presbyterian pastors. Osage social structure and Osage spirituality were so intertwined it is impossible to separate them. Osage society underwent changes in the early nineteenth century, and those changes were accompanied by spiritual adaptations.

Spiritual changes were merely an expansion of the familiar and were consistent with the Osage worldview. These were not compromises, for the core beliefs remained unchanged. Wa-kon-da continued to inhabit all elements of the universe, and the Osage continued to seek, through prayer, songs, and ritual, the blessings of Wa-kon-da. What appears to have occurred is the democratization of Osage spirituality. The pre-eighteenth century Osage culture had been organized around a small elite whose positions were defined and sanctioned by Osage spirituality. The increased economic opportunities of the eighteenth century had created a new and growing body of Osage whose hunting skills and fighting abilities had to be recognized and incorporated into Osage society. The Non-hon-zhin-ga made the changes necessary to accommodate the growing demands of the increasing number of successful Osage; they made the necessary "moves to a new country." They created new clans and gave them important ritual responsibilities that provided their members with elevated status. The newly created clans were given important roles in Wa-sha-be A-thin Wa-tsi, the ritual required before going to war (see chapter 4).[2] This ritual sought Wa-kon-da's blessings, and with the increased violence in the late eighteenth and early nineteenth century this frequently performed ceremony provided the necessary status for the growing Osage elite.

A vital element of Wa-sha-be A-thin Wa-tsi was the Hawk wa-xo-be.[3] That wa-xo-be contained the sacred hawk skin, scalps, and other sacred objects wrapped in deerskin and buffalo wool and was used to provide necessary blessings and sanctions in Osage ritual. Most Osage ceremonies required the unwrapping of specific clan wa-xo-be accompanied by the recitation of the appropriate clan wi-gi-e. Reverend William Vaill wrote about the unwrapping of a wa-xo-be during a ceremony at Belle Oiseau's town: "It is now more fully ascertained, that the Osages are gross idolaters. It was with great solemnity that they exhibited their god, the painted skin of a bird, with a scalp affixed. They prayed to this god, worshipped it, and called upon it to witness their sincerity."[4] The Osage were not worshiping the hawk as a god, but Vaill was partially correct in noting that it was used as a witness to their sincerity.

It is not clear what specific ritual Vaill was observing, for the unwrapping of a wa-xo-be and the display of the sacred hawk skin was a feature of many Osage religious ceremonies. Its presence sanctified the ritual, and indeed was testimony to their sincere commitment to the ritual's true function. Wa-xo-be were accorded great respect, and initially only clans possessed them. By the nineteenth century, "moves to a new country" enabled individuals to purchase wa-xo-be and their accompanying ritual roles and responsibilities.[5] This increased access to these valuable ceremonial items provided the ambitious Osage another avenue for status within the familiar spiritual context. The spiritual context of Osage religion remained consistent and the contents remained intact, despite the Protestants' sincere efforts to destroy it and replace it with Protestant Christianity.

In the summer of 1840, just three years after the closing of the last Osage mission, a French doctor, Victor Tixier, visited the Osage. Tixier and three companions from France came to the Osage prairies and were welcomed into the northern band community. Tixier kept a detailed account of his visit with the Osage, and his vivid descriptions provide an excellent view of Osage life in 1840.[6] He spent several months with the Osage and accompanied several bands of Big Osage out onto the plains on their summer buffalo hunt. After crossing the Arkansas they came upon massive herds of buffalo and conducted a successful hunt. With the conclusion of the hunt, the young men prepared to launch a raid against the Pawnee. Because such an attack was dangerous, they had to conduct the Wa-sha-be A-thin Wa-tsi in order to sanction the attack and secure Wa-kon-da's blessing. The *Wa-sha-be,* or dark object, is a ceremonially prepared charcoal that is used to paint the faces of the warriors so they will be as fierce as fire in their attack on their enemies.[7] Tixier witnessed the four-day ritual, which he called the *danse du charbon*. He described how the young warriors unwrapped their wa-xo-be and placed the sacred hawk skin around their necks, so they would be as swift and ruthless as the hawk in their attack. Tixier provides a wonderful description of the four days of fasting, dancing, and singing of the Wa-sha-be A-thin Wa-tsi as the Osage prepared for war.[8] Nowhere within the lengthy ritual was there a hint of Christianity, for the missionaries had made no impact on the spiritual life of these strong and resilient people. The sixteen years of proselytizing were for naught, for the Osage had ignored the Protestants' message and resisted the changes they demanded. The Osage in 1840 continued to leave their prairie villages to go out onto the plains to hunt the buffalo, and when they left to pursue the Pawnee they directed their prayers and songs to Wa-kon-da, not to Jesus.

While they retained control of their spiritual lives, they were confronted with serious challenges to their secular lives. Perhaps the most serious challenge was the Removal Act (see chapter 4). The early migrations of the Cherokee and Choctaw continued to grow, followed by seven thousand Chickasaw, who began arriving in 1837, along with the last of the fifteen thousand Creek forced from their Alabama homes. The southern bands became surrounded by the eastern emigrants, and despite their land cessions in 1825 they remained along the lower Verdigris. Finally, in early 1839, just before another wave of five thousand Cherokee arrived, Major Arbuckle of Fort Gibson called them to the fort, and with the promise of twenty years of annuities, thousands of heads of livestock, and the threat of military action, Claremore and Black Dog agreed to move to their lands in the north. Despite the threats and promises, they did not go far, however, for they established their villages only about fifty miles upriver, well south of their 1825 reservation. They would remain in that area until 1870, when they would regain title to that land.

The Osage, the "great nation of the south," while no longer the dominant power in the south, remained strong. They would retain power and continue to exert influence in the region, but their domination collapsed in the 1830s as thousands of invaders, both native and white, poured through the Osage prairie-plains on their way west. Weakened by deadly disease and warfare with their expanding eastern

Fig. 6. *The Charcoal Dance (Médecine du charbon)*. This is an 1839 drawing by Victor Tixier, who visited and hunted with the Osage. It portrays the Osage conducting a Wa-sha-be A-thin Wa-tsi (Dance to Possess the Dark Object). This ritual had to be performed before the Osage could go to war. (Victor Tixier is the author of *Tixier's Travels on the Osage Prairies,* edited by John Francis McDermott. Copyright © 1940, 1968 by the University of Oklahoma Press. All rights reserved. Reprinted by permission of the publisher.)

and western tribal foes (see chapter 5), the Osage were also confronted by the United States, whose monopoly of trade and power forced them to accept the new conditions in the eastern prairies.

Despite the onslaught of deadly diseases, the Osage remained determined to preserve their way of life, so they compromised where necessary and maintained their power whenever possible. Throughout the 1830s they maintained their forced peace in the east and continued their struggles in the west. They still fought for control of the western hunting territory. Their weakened circumstance in the 1830s, however, brought about some changes in their western campaigns. Although in 1833 they destroyed an entire Kiowa village camped just west of the Wichita Mountains, they began to accept compromises to avoid some of the western violence.[9] Sometime in the mid-1830s, realizing they could no longer defeat the Comanche, they made peace with them and began sharing the buffalo herds with these former enemies.[10] That peace would, in time, include the Wichita and the Kiowa.

The Osage's violent campaigns against the Pawnee in the western plains, however, would continue, because these longtime enemies were being pushed south by the Lakota invasion of the northern plains. Violence also broke out with Southern Plains newcomers, the Cheyenne and the Arapahoe, so that for much of the 1840s the Osage would compete violently with the Pawnee, Cheyenne, and Arapahoe.

Much of the ongoing violence with the eastern emigrant tribes, however, came to an end in the mid-1830s, for the Osage, caught between the expanding Indian frontiers, created new alliances with the newly expanding powers, thus retaining their autonomy and some of their former power. As they gradually made peace with their new eastern Indian neighbors, this peace help create closer ties with the United States. In 1834 Osage scouts joined Cherokee, Delaware, and Seneca hunters and scouts to lead the Dragoons out onto their former battlegrounds along the Red River, where instead of attacking the Comanche, Kiowa, and Wichita they talked of peace.[11] The 1834 summer peace expedition had limited success, for after meeting at the Taovayas town only a few Kiowa and Comanche were willing to return to Fort Gibson to meet with the removed southeastern tribes.

In August the next year, however, another effort for peace was launched, and the Osage journeyed with the Cherokee, Creek, Choctaw, Seneca, and Quapaw out onto the plains to a site on the Canadian River named Camp Holmes, where they met with the Comanche, Kiowa, and Wichita bands. After days of negotiations, they all agreed to sign a treaty of peace, which promised peace and perpetual friendship among all participants. All agreed to share the hunting territory west of the Cross Timbers, and the Comanche and Wichita agreed to treat all Indians from the east with "kindness and friendship."[12] After distributing presents, all around the council broke up. This promised peace of 1835 was short-lived, for with the exception of a peace established between the Osage and the Comanche and Wichita, the violence continued between the Western Plains tribes and the removed southeastern tribes. Eastern tribes would frequently cross the Red River and hunt in Comanche lands not included in the Camp Holmes agreement, and plains tribes would attack eastern people found hunting on "their lands." The violence continued, despite the federal government's attempt to bring peace to the region.[13]

In the 1840s the Osage found themselves in a unique position, for they had established peace and were able to maintain peace with both the eastern emigrant tribes and their former western enemies—the Comanche, Wichita, and Kiowa. They took advantage of that unique position, for the eastern tribes, led by the Creeks and Cherokee, continually sought peace with their Western Plains neighbors, and the Osage became unofficial intermediaries between the two groups.

The eastern tribes, though large and powerful, throughout the 1840s were threatened by the Western Plains tribes. The Osage confined their depredations to occasionally stealing horses or, when driven by hunger, to taking the eastern tribes' cows and pigs. These thefts seldom caused violence, for compensation was provided by payments from the Osage agency; thus the Osage were able to maintain their peace in the east. The Comanche, Wichita, and Pawnee, however, were seen as dire threats to the eastern tribes, for eastern tribes venturing out onto the plains were often attacked by the plains tribes.[14] In the 1840s the southern removed tribes convened several large gatherings of local tribes to bring about peace and order among themselves and with the Western Plains tribes. Led by the Creek and Cherokee, the newly removed southeastern tribes sought peace with the Pawnee, Comanche, Kiowa, Wichita, and Caddo. In 1842, the Creek called all the tribes together to meet and establish peace, but no western tribes appeared. The Creek meeting was followed by a meeting arranged by the Cherokee at Tahlequah in June 1843. The Osage were active participants in both meetings; they agreed to peace with their eastern neighbors and promised to take words of peace to the plains tribes. The Osage may have taken words of peace to the Comanche, but they continued their campaigns against the Pawnee. At the close of the Creek peace conference in 1842, Black Dog and his warriors left and attacked a group of Skidi Pawnee on the Canadian River.[15]

The Creek, victims of Pawnee raids, tried to convince the Osage to stop their western attacks and organized another peace gathering in June 1845, which they urged the Osage to attend. Black Dog and other Osage attended, and as the meeting closed Black Dog agreed to meet with the "wild Indians" at the Great Salt Plains and to take the Creek message of peace to the Comanche.[16] Black Dog met with the Comanche that summer, but it is unknown what message, if any, he relayed to them. The Osage in the 1840s were involved in a reorganization of their economic base, and while they met, ate, and talked with the eastern tribes, their energies were focused on their own survival. The Removal migrations of thousands of eastern Indians had forced a peace upon the Osage, and that forced peace denied them access to their former eastern forest resources. The Cherokee, Creek, Choctaw, Chickasaw, Delaware, Shawnee, Seneca, and Kickapoo people now occupied Osage forest hunting territory. Their large presence limited Osage entry, and their hunts soon depleted the forest resources. The growing white community in western Missouri and Arkansas also denied the Osage access to any other eastern resources, so the Osage were forced to surrender their eastern economic base, reorganize their tribal economy, and make compromises in the west.

The newly created peace with the Comanche was one of these compromises. The Osage had fought the Comanche for control of the plains until 1835, and perhaps as a result of the Dragoon peace expeditions in 1834 and 1835, they met and made peace with the Comanche. The Osage were clever enough to maintain the peace of 1835, for it was to their advantage to share the western plains in exchange for new economic opportunities.

The Osage became the middlemen in a lucrative Comanche trade. The Osage would acquire guns, powder, lead shot, blankets, stroud, and other manufactured goods from the Neosho traders, and take those goods with them when they left for their summer buffalo hunt. Upon completion of the hunt, they would go to the Great Salt Plains, where they would meet with the Comanche and exchange the manufactured goods for Mexican mules and horses. "Both parties [Comanche and Osage] place a high estimate on this trade, which is itself calculated to cement them in friendship. The Comanches in consequence of the Mexican tariff can sell their guns for thrice their value & the Osages can get three times first cost for the mules."[17]

This trade would continue until 1854, when the United States made a peace with the Comanche that would provide them with manufactured goods but that almost eliminated the Comanche trade with the Osage.[18] The Osage would meet the challenge of the declining Comanche trade by harassing traders crossing along the Santa Fe Trail, stealing horses and mules. In the summer of 1854 the commissioner of Indian Affairs complained that the acts of the Osage were "intolerable: emigrants and freighter will scarcely be permitted to pass the road next season, unless something is done."[19]

While the Osage established peace and trade with their old plains enemy, they continued their attacks on the Pawnee. Attacks similar to Black Dog's attack on the Skidi in 1842 would continue. The Osage also began to fight two new western rivals, the Cheyenne and the Arapahoe. Southern Cheyenne and Arapahoe bands began venturing out onto the Osage's plains hunting territory in the 1840s, and the Osage would attack any they came upon.[20] The violence with the Cheyenne and Arapahoe would be short-lived, however, for the Osage discovered that peace and trade with the Cheyenne were more advantageous than warfare, so they made peace with the Southern Cheyenne and Southern Arapahoe and began trading with them.[21] This new peace went beyond trade, for they all understood their reliance on the massive herds of buffalo along the Arkansas and, when some of the removed northeastern tribes began intruding on their shared plains hunting territory, the Cheyenne and Osage joined together to attack the eastern intruders. In 1854 they attacked a group of Potawatomi hunters at Pawnee Fork. That same year they joined with the Comanche and Kiowa to fight a group of Sauk and Mesquakie hunters. In both instances, the better-armed eastern tribes defeated them.[22] Despite such defeats, the Osage were able to retain power and influence in the region. Their skillful if forced compromises in the east and west allowed them to remain "the notorious Osage."[23] While they no longer dominated the region as they had in the eighteenth and early nineteenth centuries, they had made the necessary compromises to remain a significant presence on the southern prairie-plains.

Engaged in ongoing cultural transformation, the Osage were becoming Plains Indians. While they retained their traditional band identities, they continued to break into smaller groups that established separate villages. Tixier had noted in 1840 that a group of young warriors who called themselves *Bande-des-Chiens*, or Dog Band, had broken away and formed their own village that was similar to the soldier societies of the Cheyenne and Crow.[24]

By the mid-1840s the three major bands of the Osage were loosely divided into seventeen villages. Although they often traveled separately onto the plains, they shared the same general hunting region and they all returned to their village sites along the Verdigris and Neosho valleys, where they spent the winters and planted their spring gardens. The Big and Little Osage bands lived in a string of villages along the Upper Neosho, and their villages attracted traders. This Neosho trading community, made up of métis traders and their families, was dominated by the American Fur Company trading post operated by Paul Papin and owned by the powerful Chouteau family of St. Louis. Also scattered along the Upper Neosho were mixed-blood Osage who were trying to farm and to continue the economic changes they had begun at Hopefield and Harmony. The southern bands of Claremore and Black Dog, forced north by the arrival of the removed tribes and the 1839 treaty, lived in a group of villages along the Verdigris about sixty miles southwest of the northern bands.

Compressing all the bands together created internal conflicts. Since the eighteenth-century split between the northern and southern bands, there had been tension between the leaders. Thomas McKenney described the situation in 1820 when the ABCFM was preparing to establish the Harmony Mission: "The Arkansas Osages, and the Osages of the Missouri, are not on friendly terms. Out of the schism which sundered them, originated much bad blood."[25] Pawhuska had seized leadership of the northern Big Osage with the help and support of the Chouteau family, and the seizure had prompted Claremore's move to the southern bands. Claremore and Tally in the south had maintained their autonomy and a distinct separation from the Big and Little Osage bands in the north. Pawhuska and his heirs maintained close ties with the Chouteaus and their fur trading company and were ever responsive to the Chouteaus' requests and needs.

The Chouteaus used their connections with Pawhuska's northern band and their power as traders to maintain influence and power with the U.S. government. As agents for Superintendent of Western Indians William Clark, the Chouteaus secured the necessary signatures for all of the early treaties. When controversy arose about the first 1808 treaty negotiated by Clark, August Chouteau returned to the northern villages, redrew the treaty, and secured the signatures for Clark. Pawhuska and the Chouteaus, without the knowledge and consent of Claremore and the other southern band leaders, made treaties and other important agreements. The tension and animosity created by Pawhuska's usurping of Claremore's position was only exacerbated by Pawhuska's repeated acquiescence to the Chouteaus' demands.

Sans-Nerf's complaints to McKenney and Milledoler on his visit to Washington in 1820 revealed such tensions. After Sans-Nerf spoke with McKenney the latter wrote: "I find that these Osages are jealous of their Arkansas Brethren."[26] After the two missions were established, Sans-Nerf appeared at Harmony complaining about the missions' catering to the southern bands. The death of the first Pawhuska and later the first Claremore did little to ease the tension between the northern and southern leaders. The tension, however, was somewhat mitigated by the distance between the northern and southern villages, and by the power and autonomy of Claremore that allowed him to ignore any direct control by Pawhuska or the Chouteaus.

With all of the Osage bands living closer together, factional disputes that likely would have been ignored were no longer ignored. By the 1840s there were more divisions within the Osage, for the Osage were in the process of becoming nomadic plains people, and their bands continued to split into smaller living groups. This decentralization of the Osage led to increased political competition for power and influence, and created more factional disputes. The creation of more divisions within the tribe, combined with their being pressed closer together, created new tensions, exacerbated older divisions, and combined to created a chaotic and tense situation. Agents interfered to bring order, and in the process exacerbated the situation.

Agents would also come to the Osage reservation with preconceived ideas about what was best for the Osage without discussing those ideas with the Osage. Factions and power were constantly shifting, and it required great knowledge and insight into Osage society and culture to understand what was really occurring in the various disputes and controversies; agents seldom, if ever, had such knowledge and insight. At times, the agent would think he had the approval of the Osage for some proposed change when he had only the approval of a small clique. When he began the changes he would be confronted by opposing factions, and his power and position would be challenged. Support might slip away with little warning, and several agents were dismissed when they failed to remain aloof from the conflicts.

One such agent was the well-intentioned Robert Calloway, who came to the Osage in 1841. Calloway would eventually move to the Neosho and set up his agency near the American Fur Company trading post.[27] This 1843 move was the first instance of an Osage agent actually living among the Osage. Prior to Calloway's move, agents and subagents, with the possible exception of the Chouteaus, who, when they visited, stayed at their families' nearby trading posts, had lived miles from the Osage and only visited them a few times a year. Calloway became involved in a series of controversies that would eventually lead to his dismissal in 1844.

In the summer of 1842 a group of Osage, primarily from Claremore's band, sought to remove George White Hair [Pawhuska], the federally recognized chief of the Osage. The dissidents maintained that Shin-gah-wah-sah was the choice of the whole tribe, and Calloway, perhaps naïvely, supported the removal of White Hair. His support of Shin-gah-wah-sah angered White Hair, who, with the support of the Chouteaus' traders Paul Papin, M. Girand, and Edward Chouteau, sought to have Calloway removed. The confrontations grew, with Calloway removing White Hair from his house and cutting down his peach orchard. Calloway complained in repeated letters to St. Louis and Washington whether "the Osage and their affairs be continued to be managed by a little French trader—assisted by a chief or chiefs of his own creation and for their own . . . interest—who has long lived and ruled amongst them—or shall they be managed by an agent of the government, assisted by the chiefs who are the choice of the Osage people."[28] Calloway received his answer when he was removed in 1844. Calloway's removal revealed that the connection between Pawhuska and the Chouteaus, which had begun with their grandfathers in the eighteenth century, remained strong in the 1840s. This political strife continued on the Osage reservation for the remainder of the nineteenth century and became more heated and complex when more outsiders invaded the region. The Neosho settlements began to attract bootleggers, and the Osage, for the first time, began to drink alcohol.

Prior to the 1840s the Osage were noted for their sobriety. James Miller, the territorial governor of Arkansas, who spent two months among the southern bands and the Cherokee, wrote in September 1820 that "they [the Osage] know of the use of money, nor do they use any ardent spirits."[29] Reverend William Vaill reported in 1821, "As they [the Osage] have not been corrupted by ardent spirits, they are comparatively pure."[30] In 1826 he reported to the ABCFM: "Nor are they intemperate. In six years, I have not seen one of them drunk. They are afraid of whiskey, and call it *fire-water*. They like the water, but not the *fire*. Their manners are simple, and their morals untainted by intercourse with the whites."[31] Liquor had always been an important element of Indian trade, but the Osage, while active participants in the fur trade for over one hundred years, had never before been involved in the liquor trade. In the 1840s, however, they did become involved in the liquor trade.

It is unclear why they began to drink. One theory is that before the 1840s their political leadership, seeing the danger of liquor, had been able to control the traders coming into their villages and thus kept liquor from the Osage towns. When the Osage lived in a few concentrated towns, the Osage Ga-hi-ge, using their A-ki-da, could have prevented the traders from introducing liquor. By the 1840s the Osage, fast becoming Plains Indians, were living in seventeen separate villages along two river valleys. The separation into smaller distinct villages had weakened the power and influence of the traditional band Ga-hi-ge and their A-ki-da enforcers. While cultural compromises had weakened the Ga-hi-ge's power, the very separation of the villages prevented them from controlling traders. With the Ga-hi-ge living miles from their band villages, liquor traders could easily slip into the small villages without the knowledge and control of the Ga-hi-ge.

Another possible explanation for the use of alcohol by the Osage might be found in the dramatic changes in Osage life and culture brought about by the invasion of the eastern tribes and the growing power of the plains peoples. The Osage, although still powerful and influential, did not any longer have hegemonic control of the region. This loss of power was accompanied by a drastic decline in game in the region, which deprived them of their eastern economic base. The plains hunts were now constantly threatened by the western invaders, and these changes, together with the repeated deadly attacks of cholera, smallpox, and measles, might have combined to create such trauma that the Osage would seek solace and escape in liquor.

It perhaps was a combination of factors. By the 1840s there were simply more opportunities and more exposure to liquor. The white invasion of Arkansas, Missouri, and Kansas in the 1830s and 1840s had brought more Anglo farmers into the region. The prairie-plains tribes were no longer isolated from the white frontier. Instead they were now in close contact with hundreds of white farmers who planted large fields of corn. White frontiersmen were very familiar with the simple process that transformed bulky corn into more easily transportable liquor. The arrival of fifty thousand eastern Indians, who were forced into the region by Removal, also provided white bootleggers a new and growing market.

All of these elements may have combined to bring about Osage drinking, but whatever the cause, liquor had become a part of Osage life. In 1837 the ABCFM reported:

> In the mean time the number of white travellers and traders
> who had been passing through or residing among the Osages

has been increasing. New temptations have been presented to them. Intoxicating liquors have been introduced in great quantities, and the Osages, though slow to imitate either the whites or their red brethren of other tribes, have at last contracted a fondness for them, which their ignorance and a feeling of their humbled and melancholy condition well fitted them to indulge.[32]

Robert Calloway, the agent who moved to the Osage reservation, was concerned about the liquor in the Osage villages, and his correspondence is filled with complaints about the liquor trade. Calloway noted that the livestock and farm equipment provided in the 1839 treaty were being taken to Missouri and traded for whiskey. He complained that the Missouri border was filled with grog shops, and while he could keep the whites out, he could not prevent the Osage from crossing into Missouri and getting whiskey. He claimed, "The tribe as a whole has drunk more whisky [sic] (an ounce of which would kill the most poisonous snake) in the last three months than they have in the previous ten years."[33] Calloway later organized a group of Osage and sent them into Missouri to destroy whiskey stored at two Missouri farmhouses.[34] Calloway was soon removed, in part for encouraging attacks on whites, and the liquor trade continued.

The Neosho community surrounding the agency and the American Fur Company trading post was later described by Osage agent John Richardson as an area "infested, overrun with vendors of whiskey, horse thieves, and other low base characters."[35] It was into this wild and "infested" community that another group of Christian missionaries would launch another attack on Osage spirituality. In April 1847 five Jesuit priests arrived at the Osage agency, just two miles from the Neosho, and began their campaign to convert the Osage to Roman Catholicism.

7

The Catholics Return: 1820–1870

It is impossible, the Bishop [Du Bourg] said, to describe the attention that these poor savages paid to him, and the emotion which they experienced when the interpreter repeated to them the words of the Bishop. They raised their eyes and their hands to heaven and then to the crucifix. All the spectators were moved by the scene. Before taking leave of the Bishop, Sans-Nerf said to him, through the interpreter, that if he wished to come and visit them in their homes he would be well received, that he could do a great deal of good, and that he could pour water on many heads. The bishop promised to do so, and presented each one with a little crucifix and also a medal which he hung around their necks with a ribbon, admonishing them to guard them carefully. They promised to do so, and have kept their word.

Father Eugene Michaud,
Annales de la Propagation de la Foi[1]

In April 1847 Fathers Schoenmakers and John Bax, along with Brothers John De Bruyn, Thomas Coghlan, and John Sheehan, arrived at the Osage agency on Flatrock Creek to begin their work of converting the Osage to Roman Catholicism and civilization. This spring 1847 arrival was not the first contact the Osage had had with Roman Catholic missionaries, for Jesuits had been visiting the Osage since the seventeenth century. Early French explorers were accompanied by Roman Catholic priests, and French Jesuit Jacques Marquette, traveling with Louis Jolliet, was the first European to record Osage existence.

In 1699, priests from the Seminary of Quebec established the Cahokia Mission on the east bank of the Mississippi, just across from the future site of St. Louis. A Jesuit priest, Father Gabriel Marest, in 1700 followed a group of Kaskaskia Indians from Illinois, who established a village across the river from Cahokia on the west bank of the Mississippi. Father Marest established a mission among those Kaskaskia near the mouth of a river that would be known as the Des Peres. French traders collected around the Cahokia and Kaskaskia missions, and Osage families who visited the trading posts at the mission sites to acquire hatchets, knives, awls, and other metal goods probably met with Father Marest.[2] The Des Peres Mission was abandoned in 1703, and the Kaskaskia, along with their Jesuit priest, moved seventy-five miles south and crossed to the east bank of the Mississippi, where they reestablished Kaskaskia.

In 1723, the French Company of the Indies sent Etienne de Véniard, sieur de Bourgmont, west to establish peace and trade with the plains tribes. Bourgmont brought one of the Cahokia priests, Father Jean Mercier, up the Missouri River on his way west. Before setting out for the plains, Bourgmont established a base named Fort d'Orléans just across from several Little Osage villages.[3] From this river outpost, Father Mercier and Bourgmont exchanged visits with the Osage. It is not clear what impact and impression Mercier made on the Osage; however, when Boganienhin, the Osage chief who traveled to France with Bourgmont, was introduced to Louis XV, he asked him to send additional priests to them.[4] "Our lands have been yours for a long time; do not abandon them. Move Frenchmen there; protect us as your true soldiers and give us White Collars [Foreign Missionary priests], Chiefs of Prayer, to instruct us. Have pity on us here and everywhere."[5] While it is unclear what Boganienhin was asking for with this request, it sounds very similar to the later requests of Sans-Nerf, who was clearly not asking for spiritual guidance. It is more likely that the eighteenth-century Osage chef was asking for French trade and assistance. Whatever he was asking for, he would not receive it, for The Company of the Indies that had helped fund Bourgmont's expedition was unwilling to fund missionaries among the Osage and had already reneged on its promise to pay Father Mercier. When Fort d'Orléans was abandoned by the French in 1728, Father Mercier left his Osage charges and returned to Cahokia.[6]

In 1686, Henry Tonty established a French trading post near the mouth of the Arkansas River. Although he promised the Jesuits he would establish and support a mission there, he never provided the funds nor support, and the outpost was abandoned in 1699.[7] In 1721, John Law's Compagnie d'Occident established a colony near Tonty's site, and a Jesuit priest, Father Paul Du Poisson, was sent to minister to the Quapaw people of the region. This small outpost on the Arkansas became an important trading center, and Osage hunters who visited the post throughout the eighteenth century would have come into some limited contact with the Jesuit fathers there. Other French settlements, Ste. Geneviève and Cape Girardeau, were established along the west bank of the Mississippi, and these trading post communities were ministered by Jesuit priests who met with any Osage who visited the French traders. These occasional meetings with Jesuit and Seminary priests, however, were so brief and cursory that they were of little spiritual consequence. Thus the expulsion of the Jesuits from Louisiana in 1763 had no impact on the Osage.[8]

The cession of Louisiana to Spain in 1763 did have an impact on the Osage, but it was an economic impact, not a spiritual one. While the Spanish supported Franciscan missionaries in the West, Franciscans were never sent to the central prairie-plains and they never visited the Osage. The Osage might have encountered Roman Catholic priests when visiting St. Louis, but again any contacts would have been very brief and inconsequential. The contact between the Roman Catholic Church and the western Indians, however, would increase dramatically after 1820.

In 1812, Sulpician Father Louis Valentine Du Bourg was sent to New Orleans to administer the diocese of Louisiana and the Floridas. Du Bourg, a former president of Georgetown College and the founder of St. Mary's College, was very committed to educational projects for the Church. In 1815, Du Bourg traveled to Rome, where he was named bishop of Louisiana and the Floridas. While in Rome he contacted Father Brzozowski, general of the Jesuits, and asked for Jesuit missionaries for his huge diocese. Father Brzozowski replied that since the Jesuits had only been restored to the world for a year, he did not have any priests to spare, so Du Bourg returned to New Orleans without any Jesuit missionaries. Encountering opposition in New Orleans, Du Bourg established his headquarters in the more friendly environs of St. Louis, where he continued his efforts to enlist the Jesuits.

So far I have scarcely been able to turn my attention to the conversion of the savages, who are in great numbers in the upper part of my diocese. But even if I had been able to do so, there are no laborers. For some time past I have been thinking, for this paramount work of charity, of the Fathers of the Society of Jesus and have left no stone unturned in order to secure some of them.[9]

While Bishop Du Bourg was trying to secure priests for the Indians of Louisiana he was visited in 1820 by a group of Osage led by Sans-Nerf. Sans-Nerf and *"plusieurs des chefs"* spoke with Du Bourg and invited him to their village, "where he could do a great deal of good, and that he could pour water on many heads."[10] Sans-Nerf also met with Philip Milledoler of the UFMS that year and "asked" for missionaries to come to his villages. We cannot be certain whether Sans-Nerf met Du Bourg before he met with Milledoler, as the account of the Du Bourg meeting is only dated "En 1820."[11] The sequence is not important, for the intent of Sans-Nerf's visits to Du Bourg and Milledoler was the same. He was seeking support and assistance for the northern bands and was willing to ask both Protestants and Catholics for their help, for he was more interested in their practical help than their spiritual messages. Sans-Nerf did not seek Catholic Christianity any more than he sought Protestantism; he only wanted assistance from the white community and took these opportunities to ask for it.

Du Bourg, like the Protestants, promised to visit; however, unlike the Protestant Milledoler, he gave Sans-Nerf gifts. He gave the Osage small crucifixes and hung religious medals around their necks. It is not clear what Sans-Nerf and companions thought of the figure of a man nailed to a cross; however, when they saw a crucifix on Du Bourg's wall they were struck with astonishment. Michaud [the author of this account] claims that they looked upon it with avid and gentle eyes, and that Bishop Du Bourg took the opportunity to explain that Jesus had come from the heavens and suffered and bled for them and that he had sent him [Du Bourg] to make his will known to them.[12] This brief visit reveals the marked difference between the Protestants' approach and that of the Catholics.

The crucifix, while gruesome, was familiar. Although the cross meant little to the Osage, the figure was real and concrete, not an abstract cultural construct. It was a figure of a suffering man who, the strangers told them, had been tortured for them. It had substance in a familiar form. The Osage, although they did not torture their captives, were certainly aware of the practice. The Catholic meaning of the crucifix was lost on the Osage, for symbols are given meaning by the culture that produces them. Sans-Nerf was not a member of the Roman Catholic culture, and he knew nothing of Catholic Christianity. However, he had before him a recognizable symbol of bravery and sacrifice that he could understand and appreciate, and could carry with him for good luck.

The medals Du Bourg hung around their neck were welcome gifts, not for their sacred quality but instead for their metallic quality, for Osage men liked jewelry. Sans-Nerf and his companions had come to visit in formal dress that Michaud described in a letter:

> Their hair was arranged in tufts. Bracelets, ear-rings, rings in their noses and lips completed their head-dress. Their shoes are made of buckskin which they ornament with difference designs in feathers of various colors; hanging from their robes are little pieces of tin, shaped like small pipes. These are to them the most beautiful ornaments. Their great object is to make a noise when they walk or dance.[13]

The bishop had simply, to their minds, given them attractive metal jewelry to add to their dress. These gifts fit a familiar pattern, for the Osage established friendships with gift exchanges, and despite the fact that their Catholic meaning was lost, the gifts were welcome, and the people who gave them gained goodwill by providing them.

Those New England Protestants who were about to descend on Sans-Nerf and his people had no such objects as parts of their faith and culture. The Protestants had crosses, but their crosses were completely abstract symbols, unlike the Catholic cross that had a recognizable human figure, not a symbol to the Osage but a man, nailed to it, who they were told had sent the bishop to help them. This visit of Sans-Nerf with Bishop Du Bourg provides clues as to why the Osage would, in time, prefer Catholic visits to those of the Protestant missionaries. That preference had little to do with theology. It had everything to do with behavior, for the Osage shared enough form with the Catholic culture to make them welcome, but not enough substance to make them Roman Catholics.

After this meeting Sans-Nerf either made his way to Washington to seek the goods promised in the 1808 treaty and to ask for Protestant missionaries, or returned to his village where he made ready to welcome both groups of invited white strangers. Sans-Nerf would wait a year before the Protestants arrived in his homeland, and Bishop Du Bourg never made a visit to the Osage, for he departed St. Louis that November to reestablish his diocesan headquarters in New Orleans. He did, however, send one of his parish priests, Father Charles de La Croix, who two years later made a visit to the Osage. La Croix made his way to the northern band villages in May 1822, but his visit was ill-timed, for most of the Osage had already left for their summer hunt, so he only visited one Big Osage village, accompanied by Paul Liguest Chouteau, the Osage subagent. There he was welcomed by Sans-Nerf and Pawhuska, the son of the recently deceased Pawhuska. La Croix described his entry into the village:

> After conveying our thanks we invited them to come the next day to Mr. Chouteau's place, where I had prepared a pretty altar, so that they might assist at the Divine Sacrifice and at the baptism of a number of persons. I began by explaining in French for the benefit of the many persons present who understood that language, the ceremonies of the Mass and afterwards those of Baptism. I told the chiefs through an interpreter that I was going to speak to the Master of Life and that I would speak to Him for them. (1:180–81)[14]

The following day La Croix conducted Mass, baptized twenty métis, and presented medals and ivory crucifixes to the village leaders, promising to return in the fall (1:180–81). With this brief visit, the nineteenth-century Roman Catholic missionary work began among the Osage.

Father La Croix returned to the Osage in August, accompanied by Osage agent Richard Graham. After celebrating Mass and baptizing thirteen métis, he observed negotiations between Graham and Osage leaders regarding the closing of their Marais des Cygnes trading factory. He later served as a witness to the agreement and signed the treaty authorizing the closure.[15] Despite La Croix's visits, the Catholic missionary work among the Osage was limited, for there were no missionaries available in the region. La Croix was an obliging parish priest from Florissant who would make occasional visits to the northern band villages, but his parish responsibilities limited his visits to the Osage.

Bishop Du Bourg, working from New Orleans, continued his efforts to recruit Jesuit missionaries for his diocese's Indians. His efforts would succeed through a curious chain of circumstances. Father Charles Nerinckx, a Flemish priest from Belgium, had gone to Kentucky in 1805 to serve the Catholics there. An ardent religious leader, he traveled across the state ministering to the needs of the Catholic community. He founded a congregation of nuns, the Sisters of Loretto, to teach in Kentucky, and he made several trips home to Belgium to recruit priests, nuns, and financial support for his Kentucky missions.

Preparing for his first trip, he visited Georgetown College, where the Maryland Jesuit superior asked him to find recruits for the newly established Jesuit novitiate. Nerinckx recruited eight young men who returned with him in 1817. When he returned to Belgium in 1820 he again agreed to recruit Jesuit seminarians. These recruiting trip were done with the utmost secrecy, because William I, Calvinist king of the Netherlands, was hostile to Catholicism, and Nerinckx feared arrest if Belgian officials caught him recruiting priests. Despite the threat of arrest, Nerinckx gathered a small group of young seminary students who wanted to serve as Jesuit missionaries to America and smuggled them out of the country in July 1820 (1:19).

Upon arrival in Baltimore, Father Nerinckx and his nine young men met with Archbishop Maréchal, who invited them to stay in Baltimore. Two remained with the archbishop while the other seven, hoping to become Jesuit priests, continued to the Jesuit novitiate at White Marsh, Maryland, to begin their education and preparation for the Jesuit priesthood. Curiously, their arrival was not particularly welcome, for the Maryland Jesuit Mission was in poor financial shape. The added burden of seven new students severely threatened the survival of the novitiate. These financial hardships were exacerbated by an attack from Archbishop Maréchal of Baltimore, who, in 1821, claimed that the White Marsh property belonged to the Catholic Church of Maryland, not to the Society of Jesus. The Jesuits and Archbishop Maréchal bickered, and the novices went hungry. The Maryland Jesuits were so desperate they directed the novices to seek financial support from their families in Belgium. When the families failed to send funds and the pope granted the property to the Baltimore archbishop, the superior of the Maryland Mission ordered Father Charles Felix Van Quickenborne, the master of the novices at White Marsh, to close the Jesuit novitiate and to release the seven young men from their vows.

Before they were dismissed, however, Bishop Du Bourg arrived and provided a solution to the Jesuit crisis (1:32–34).

Bishop Du Bourg had gone to Washington to settle some affairs concerning title to church property in New Orleans. While in Washington he stayed at Georgetown College where he heard of the distress of the Maryland Jesuits. Du Bourg, who had been seeking Jesuits for his Indian missions, quickly made arrangements with the Jesuit Superior of the Maryland Mission to take three of the Jesuits back to Missouri. Having secured a promise of Jesuit missionaries, Du Bourg then met John C. Calhoun, secretary of war, and asked for financial support for his proposed western Indian missions. In a letter to Calhoun, Du Bourg made this interesting offer:

> I should then, with due deference, think that for those distant missions at least, the work of civilization should commence with harmonizing them by the kind doctrine of Christianity, instilled into their minds not by the doubtful and tedious process of books, but by familiar conversation, striking representations and by the pious lives of their spiritual leaders. Men, disenthralled from all family cares, abstracted from every earthly enjoyment, inured to fatigue and self-denial, living in the flesh as if strangers to all sensual inclination, are well calculated to strike the man of nature as a supernatural species of beings, entitled to his almost implicit belief. Thus become masters of his understanding, their unremitting charity will easily subdue the ferocity of their hearts and by degrees assimilate their inclinations to those of the fellow-Christians. (1:48)

Although Calhoun had already approved a very different missionary proposal by the UFMS in which Protestant families, unlike Du Bourg's supernatural Jesuits, would use the "doubtful and tedious process of books," he agreed to this proposal. With the approval of President Monroe he agreed to provide two hundred dollars per year for each missionary to go among the western tribes and work to civilize them. Calhoun also offered some financial assistance to construct buildings for the missionaries.

With this promise of support Du Bourg began arranging to take four Jesuits (he had persuaded Calhoun to provide for the additional missionary) to St. Louis, where he planned to establish a boarding school for western Indians. Upon his contacting the White Marsh Jesuits, they, however, insisted that he transfer the entire novitiate to St. Louis (1:58). Despite the opposition of the Baltimore archbishop, who wanted to retain some of the novices for his diocese, Du Bourg secured Jesuit approval and directed Father Charles Felix Van Quickenborne to prepare the novices for their transfer to Missouri.

Du Bourg had secured funding for the missionary efforts in Missouri, but he had not secured funds necessary to pay for their move to St. Louis, so he sent Van Quickenborne on a fund-raising trip to cities along the East Coast with these instructions: "But for yourself, keep on begging as long as anything comes of it. You will have great need of money in the beginning" (1:71). Van Quickenborne collected $963 and a promissory note for $432.50, and with that he and his party left for St. Louis (1:49).

The party was composed of Van Quickenborne, master of the novices; his assistant, Father Peter Joseph Timmermans; and seven Belgian novices: John Anthony Elet, Francis de Maillet, Peter John De Smet, John Baptist Smedts, Judocus Van Assche, Peter John Verhaegen, and Felix Levinus Verreydt. They were accompanied by three coadjutor-brothers, Peter De Meyer, Henry Reiselman, and Charles Strahan, along with six African American slaves from the White Marsh plantation: Tom and his wife, Polly, Moses and his wife, Nancy, and Isaac and his wife, Succy.[16]

The group loaded their belongings in three wagons, but their shortage of funds forced them to walk to Wheeling, Virginia. They followed the Cumberland Road and spent their nights at Jesuit residences or with sympathetic Catholic families. In Conewago, Pennsylvania, mission supporters gave them $128 for their mission. Upon arriving at the Ohio River, they discovered that steamboat tickets were too expensive, so they purchased two flatboats. Their limited finances prevented them from hiring an experienced pilot to take them down the Ohio; instead, Van Quickenborne bought a copy of the *Riverman's Guide* and directed Brother Strahan to take them downriver (1:85). Fortuitously they made their way safely down the Ohio to Shawneetown, Illinois, where they unloaded their flatboats, arranged for much of their baggage to be shipped to St. Louis, and began walking the 150 miles to St. Louis, where they arrived on May 31, 1823.

Bishop Du Bourg owned a farm at nearby Florissant where the Sisters of the Society of the Sacred Heart had established a convent.

After meeting with the Indian superintendent, William Clark, the Jesuits made their way to the bishop's farm at Florissant, where the sisters welcomed them. They immediately began construction of several buildings to house themselves, and began working to make the farm productive and profitable. While the novices worked on the mission farm, Van Quickenborne ministered to the local Catholic parishes and instructed the novices.

The first year was difficult for Van Quickenborne and the novices. With limited resources the novices worked to construct the buildings for their novitiate, while operating the farm to provide food for themselves and the nuns, in addition to seeking the education and training to become Jesuit priests. Two members of the Maryland group left, and Father Timmermans, Van Quickenborne's assistant, died. While building the seminary, running the farm, and ministering to the parishes, Van Quickenborne was expected to instruct the novices so they could be ordained as Jesuit priests and be sent out to the missions in the West as Bishop Du Bourg had promised Secretary of War Calhoun. That year was incredibly demanding, but somehow Van Quickenborne and the novices were able to successfully reestablish the Jesuits in the region.

Another element of Du Bourg's plan called for Van Quickenborne to collect a number of Indian children for the mission. He was to bring children to the mission school where they would be converted to Catholicism, and then sent out with the Jesuit missionaries to convert more of their people. "I propose to receive into the Seminary a half dozen Indian children from different tribes, so as to begin to familiarize my young missionaries with their manners and languages and in turn to prepare the children to become guides, interpreters and helpers to the missionaries when the time comes to send the latter forth to the scattered tribes" (1:147). Although Du Bourg claimed the children were being brought to the school to be converted, often they were also used as laborers on the mission farm.

Van Quickenborne was a bit more ambitious than Bishop Du Bourg; he proposed creating a boarding school that would both produce future Indian assistants for the missionaries and make a big step toward converting the western Indians to Catholicism and civilization. He believed that to bring about change among the western tribes, the missionaries had to take Indian boys from their native environment when they were young and "pliant," and to instruct them in "the practice of the true religion and in the ways of civilized life."[17] Isolated from their families, Van Quickenborne believed, Jesuit teachers could instruct them in basic English language skills, and in the course of this instruction the missionaries would acquire the children's native languages which they could use to convert Indians in the field. Along with these language skills, the missionaries would convert the boys to Catholicism and teach them mechanical skills. Having converted and educated the Indian children, they would send them back to their people where their exemplary lives would convince their families to abandon their native cultures and become Catholic farmers. With such hopes, the St. Regis Seminary for Indian boys was opened in May 1824 when two Sauk boys were admitted, followed in June by three Iowa boys. Father Van Quickenborne believed that unless the boys were provided with educated Catholic Indian wives, their education and conversion would be for naught when they returned to their people, so he convinced the Sisters of the Sacred Heart to establish an Indian girls school nearby. The girls school opened a year later, in April 1825 (1:158).

Van Quickenborne solicited the help of William Clark and sought children from any Indians visiting St. Louis. This practice severely limited the number of Indian students, so Clark urged him to visit Indian villages and seek out children for his school. He made his first visit to the northern band Osage villages in August 1827—five years since La Croix's last visit. Accompanying Osage agent Hamtramck, he journeyed to Harmony, where he stayed with Reverend Nathaniel Dodge, whom Father La Croix had entrusted with his church vestments. The first night's dinner was followed by a spirited religious discussion. Van Quickenborne also asked Dodge if he would excuse the Catholic students in the Harmony school so they could attend Mass the next day, which Dodge graciously agreed to do.

The next day Van Quickenborne heard confessions and baptized eighteen whom he had "prepared." His celebration of Mass was attended by Reverend Nathaniel Dodge and his wife, who, upon completion of the service, asked to speak to the group. Van Quickenborne did not think such a talk was proper, so he refused to allow Dodge to address his congregation. After the service, Van Quickenborne gave each of those baptized a medal and a crucifix. He also took them aside and told them to avoid any Protestant instruction and to never join Dodge in any religious services, "and that if they should preach to them, they should not listen to their preaching" (1:190).

After the services at Harmony, Van Quickenborne traveled to the Osage villages on the Neosho, where he stayed at the Chouteaus' trading post and celebrated a jubilee "for the Creoles living among the Osage" (1:190). He stayed in the area for two weeks visiting the northern band villages along the Neosho, where he met with unnamed "principal chiefs" who promised to send their children to his school. His description of his visit is revealing:

> When I walked through the village, my religious garb easily marked me off from the others, and a troop of youngsters followed me. Nothing could have given me greater pleasure; but as soon as I turned around to say something to them, off they would scamper and hide behind the first house on the way. However, two little fellows, sons of the chief, having each received a medal from me ran off at once to show themselves (with their new decorations suspended around their neck by a pretty ribbon) to their companions, who thereupon were ready enough to approach me. How gladly I should have taught them some catechism! But not knowing their language, I could only give them the little presents I carried with me, while praying their guardian angels to obtain for them soon the favor of becoming members of the Church of Jesus Christ. . . . Sixteen square miles of land have been given to the metifs at a distance of fifty miles from the great village, besides twenty-three square miles at a distance of seventy miles. They are anxious to settle on these lands provided they can have a priest to instruct them and their children. Let us pray the Lord of the harvest to send good workers. (1:190–91)

Van Quickenborne, pleased with this first trip, returned in 1828, visiting Harmony and the Neosho villages, where he baptized seventeen people, preached the gospel, and administered the sacraments. He returned to Florissant with two boys identified only as Osage "princes," apparently the sons of the bands' leaders. Van Quickenborne made his third and last visit to the Osage in June 1830 when he baptized nine and married three métis couples.

His recruiting trips to the Neosho villages gathered only a few Osage students, however, and their stays at the mission school were brief ones, for the mission school was not a pleasant place for the métis and Indian children. Van Quickenborne and his Jesuits were demanding. They woke the boys up at dawn and after meditation, prayer, and breakfast they sent them out into the farm fields to work, where they remained until 11:45 a.m., when they returned for lunch. After lunch they studied in the classrooms until 2:00 p.m., when they were sent back into the fields to work until 4:45 p.m. They were fed dinner and then taught until it was time for bed (1:162).

This demanding schedule was too extreme for these young boys who had spent their lives playing around the villages, and the demands to work in the farm fields were demeaning and improper, for within their worldview only women worked in the gardens. Van Quickenborne writes, "They [the students] all wept when the hoe was put into their hands for the first time" (1:162). Their tears did them no good, and if they misbehaved, Van Quickenborne was quick to whip them. On one occasion novice Peter De Smet was dismayed at the whipping Van Quickenborne delivered to an Osage student. The beating was so severe De Smet feared it would damage their relations with the tribe for generations (1:165).

The schools were never able to attract many students, and the most they ever had was thirty, twenty of whom were métis and the other ten from five different tribes. The school eventually failed, for the parents objected to their children being so far away from them, and this combined with "the disinclination of the young Indians to bend under the yoke of discipline" doomed the school.[18] Parents thought the Jesuits too harsh in their discipline and too demanding in the fields. The school finally closed in 1830. Father Verhaegen wrote the Maryland Superior, Father Francis Dzierozynski, in August of that year: "I suppose your Rev. knows that our Indian college has definitely ceased to be. I am surprised, not that it ended, but that it continued as long as it did" (1:167).

The school had been expensive and had taken time away from the novices' studies to become ordained Jesuit priests, and there were hints of tensions created by the demands of the school in some of the novices' letters (1:162). The Belgian novices, however, were admitted to their first vows in October 1823; the first two received their orders in early 1826, and the remaining four received theirs in September 1827. Their third-year probation was completed in July 1828, and the six Belgian novices became Jesuit priests ready to serve the western Catholic communities, be they white or Native American.

The closure of the school disappointed Van Quickenborne, but he remained committed to a Jesuit Indian mission. Other Jesuits were not convinced of the need, nor the possibility of success. Some were disappointed by their work with the Indians and questioned whether the efforts for the Indians should be attempted when they still had so much work to do with the white communities. Van Quickenborne, still intent on converting and civilizing the Indians, would lobby for five years for the creation of a Jesuit Indian mission. In 1830, however, he stepped down as the Superior of the Missouri Mission and was replaced by Father Theodore De Theux, who did not share his enthusiasm for Indian missions. Having surrendered his administrative position, Van Quickenborne offered to go himself to the Osage and establish a mission along the Neosho, but Father De Theux, arguing that such a mission was beyond their means in terms of both priests and finances, would not allow it.

Van Quickenborne continued his lobbying efforts and in 1832 wrote an impassioned letter to the father general in Rome asking for the establishment of such a mission. The father general agreed that an Indian mission should be begun by the Missouri Jesuits; however, he insisted that Van Quickenborne not be sent to that mission. Van Quickenborne had gained an unpleasant reputation among the Catholic community in Missouri. Local clergymen complained of his bad temperament. They described him as gloomy, secretive, and not easy to work with. He was described as being "hard on himself, hard on others" (1:304). With such a temperament the father general decided that he should continue his work as a rural missionary to the white settlers of Missouri and Illinois rather than be sent to the Indian community of the prairie-plains, where diplomacy and cultural sensitivity was required for any real success.

With De Theux's lack of enthusiasm for a mission among the western tribes, the preliminary efforts to form one proceeded slowly. Despite the father general's admonitions to remain a parish priest, Van Quickenborne continued to urge the father general and Father De Theux to establish an Indian mission and to send him to minister to the Indians. Pressured by the father general, De Theux finally began to make preparations to establish a Jesuit Indian mission. He, however, thought that the Jesuits should focus on those tribes already missionized by the earlier Jesuits, people with some experience with the Jesuits and somewhat familiar with the Catholic faith. The Osage had

had only brief contact with the earlier Jesuits, so they were eliminated as candidates for the proposed mission.

Another candidate for the mission appeared when Father Roux, the Catholic priest at Kawsmouth (also known as "Chouteau's"), a métis trading community located at the mouth of the Kansas River, reported that there was a large and growing community of Kickapoo settling there. The Kickapoo were familiar with the Catholic faith because of earlier Jesuit efforts among them and seemed good subjects for the proposed mission. Father Van Quickenborne made a trip to the settlement and met with the spiritual leader of the band, Kenekuk. Kenekuk, the Kickapoo Prophet, had recently been forced from Illinois for preaching his message of spiritual revival.[19] Van Quickenborne almost immediately got into an heated argument with Kenekuk.[20] Despite the incident with Kenekuk, Van Quickenborne returned to Florissant and reported that it would be an ideal place for an Indian mission, and with De Theux's approval set about to create it.

Father Van Quickenborne and three fellow Jesuits arrived at Chouteau's in June 1836 and quickly moved into a cabin provided by one of the French traders. There they set up a chapel and conducted Mass "in the presence of the wondering Kickapoo" (1:397). Van Quickenborne had finally, after thirteen years, established his Indian mission in the West, ironically among eastern Indians forced from their forest homes. While he had intended to establish a mission among the Osage, he eagerly began his Kickapoo work.

Curiously, Native Americans had taken on a generic identity for Van Quickenborne and his colleagues. His earlier letters were filled with emotion as he called for establishing a mission among the Osage, yet he was quick to discard his Osage ambitions when offered an "Indian mission." One Indian was as worthy, or perhaps unworthy, as another, and all needed salvation, so he quickly moved on to "save" the Kickapoo.

Despite their earlier years with the Jesuits, the Kickapoo Mission met with little success, and the letters and reports coming from the mission are reminiscent of those sent from Union, Hopefield, Boudinot, and Harmony. "Father Van Quickenborne has made but little progress in the Kickapoo language. . . . Of the 1000 souls that constitute both villages, hardly thirty regularly attend church on Sundays. . . . They [Kickapoo] are a set of independent beings; they will have their own way in everything to show that they do no act from compulsion"

(1:405). The Kickapoo explained that "We want no prayer [their term for religion]; our forefathers got along very well without it and we are not going to feel its loss" (1:406).

Van Quickenborne's personality and temperament caused problems among the Kickapoo, and his Jesuit colleagues complained that his "despotic manner of government" was causing great problems at the mission (1:408). He was recalled from the mission in July 1837. Upon returning to St. Louis he was stricken with a bilious fever and died soon after, on August 17, 1837. Van Quickenborne's death saddened his Kickapoo Mission colleagues, but they continued their efforts to convert the Kickapoo. Their efforts were unsuccessful, and as their mission school averaged only eight Kickapoo a year, the federal government stopped its financial support of the mission. With the end of the federal appropriation and the general lack of success among the Kickapoo, the Jesuits were convinced to close their Kickapoo Mission in 1840 (1:418).

The failure of the Kickapoo Mission did little to dim the ambitions of the Jesuits, for in May 1838 they began work on a new mission among the Potawatomi at Council Bluffs. Father Peter De Smet had been sent to them, and he worked diligently among them until he departed for the Northwest, where he was to spend much of his life. Fathers Van Assche and Verreydt, who remained with the Potawatomi at Council Bluffs, became discouraged. "Our people here [Potawatomi] like us very much; but they do not want to listen to our good counsel. Getting drunk is the only fault they have; otherwise, we would live here in Paradise. But now, in the condition they are, it is indeed very disagreeable to live among them" (1:445).

Several other groups of Potawatomi from Indiana had moved west and settled on two tributaries of the Marais des Cygnes, miles from the corrupting influence of Missouri River trade. One group settled along Sugar Creek and were visited by Jesuits from the Kickapoo Mission. Welcomed by the Indiana Potawatomi, the Jesuits began ministering to them in 1838 when Father Christian Hoecken moved into the community. With little chance for success among the Council Bluffs Potawatomi, Father Verreydt sought permission to abandon them and join the small mission among those Potawatomi living on Sugar Creek. Father Verreydt joined with other Jesuits already among these Potawatomi and opened a school in July 1840.

By 1840 all of the Osage bands had moved north, and the northern band villages of the Big and Little Osage were only about fifty miles

southwest of the Sugar Creek Potawatomi Mission. In June 1843
Pawhuska, along with three other Osage, wrote a letter to President
John Tyler asking for schools and missionaries.

> We prefer Catholic missionaries & would not wish to have any
> other—and until we have them to educate our young men
> and teach them how to use the implements of husbandry, it
> is not worth while to provide us with ploughs & such articles,
> not knowing how to use them, they are of no value to us. . . .
> As game is becoming scarce & the living dependent upon it
> more and more precarious every year, we see the necessity of
> turning our attention to agriculture, and for this purpose the
> missionaries are much needed & from the little acquaintance
> we have with the missionaries heretofore sent among us as
> well as among other indians [sic], we think the Catholics
> would send us the best.[21]

This is a curious letter, for the Osage had not shown any interest in
farming in the past and would continue to hunt plains buffalo until
the 1870s. Also unusual is the juxtaposition of the missionaries with
agricultural skills; there is no apparent religious connection, for religion is never mentioned in the letter. They only link the Catholic missionaries with teaching them agricultural skills. Nothing came from
this appeal, but in May 1844 Father Verreydt visited the Osage community gathered about the American Fur Company trading post.[22]

Shortly after this first visit a letter signed by George White Hair,
Clermont, Tally, and six other Osage band leaders was sent to the commissioner of Indian Affairs, T. Hartley Crawford, asking for a school:
"we are disposed to better our condition by the introduction among us
of education and the domestic arts. That a school being felt by us necessary for the instruction of our children we wish to see one established
among us with as little delay as possible" (2:495). They also specifically
requested that Catholics be sent to operate the requested school.

The contents of this letter must be viewed with some suspicion, for
just two years earlier, in August 1842, Pawhuska, Claremore, and
thirty-one other Osage leaders claimed that they were not interested in
missionary schools. Perhaps this 1844 request for a school should be
seen in the same light as Sans-Nerf's repeated requests for Protestant
and Catholic missionaries.[23]

Despite the Osage request for a Catholic school, their petition was largely ignored by the Indian Bureau. Nothing came of the Osage request until the summer of 1846, when the Missouri vice-provincial, Father Van de Velde, was in Washington and met with William Medill, the new commissioner of Indian Affairs. Van de Velde reminded Medill of the Osage request and offered to send missionaries to the proposed Osage school. After some discussion, Medill made an offer to provide some support for the proposed school. The Jesuits rejected the initial offer, feeling it did not provide adequate financial support. When Medill, however, agreed to give the Jesuits one-half of the year's interest on the Osage education fund as provided for in the 1839 treaty (which amounted to about one thousand dollars per year), they quickly agreed and promised to create a school among the Osage. They agreed to teach them the skills to cultivate the soil and learn the arts of civilization.

With the agreement finalized in August 1846, the Missouri Jesuits set about to organize the Osage Mission. They chose Father John Schoenmakers, a forty-year-old Jesuit from Holland, and Father John Bax, a Belgian Jesuit, to set up and direct the missionary efforts among the Osage. Father Schoenmakers went to Osage country, met with the Osage agent, and arranged for the construction of the buildings for the mission school. Together they selected a site near the agency and the American Fur Company trading post on Flat Rock Creek, only a few miles from the Neosho River. The following spring Father Schoenmakers and Father Bax, along with Brothers John De Bruyn, Thomas Coghlan, and John Sheehan, left for the Neosho. They arrived on April 23, 1847, to begin their work of converting and civilizing the Osage.

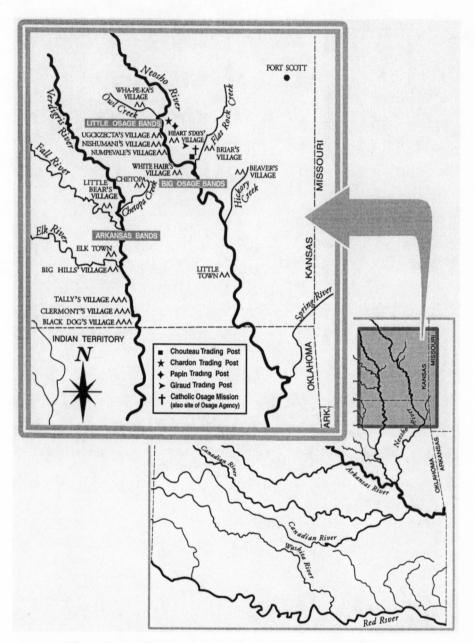

Fig. 7. Osage villages and the Jesuit mission in the late 1860s.
(Artist, Christine Stergios, 2003.)

8

Resisting the Catholics

Whether the labors and expenses undertaken by the
Mission for the civilization of the Osages, have been of
real utility to the Indian, I do not now intend to discuss.
We know this much from the perusal of history; that to
bring aborigines from their barbarism to a state of civilization, and then to make of them good Christians, has
always been the work of centuries, not of a few years.

—Father Paul Mary Ponziglione,
"Origin of the Osage Mission" [1]

The object of the establishment of this Mission of St.
Francis of Jerome being the instruction of the Osage
Indians in all that concerns religion and civilization. So
from the very first day we came here we tried all the
means in our power to succeed in this work, and though
we must acknowledge that we did not do much, yet
thank God we have not been idle.

—Father Paul Mary Ponziglione,
Western Missions Journals No. 2 [2]

So these two Indian Missions [St. Mary's and St. Francis]
have proved after all that they were not useless. And
though the good done in the conversion of Indians, especially the Osages has not been much, yet this is also certain that if his State of Kansas to day [*sic*] numbers over
30,000 Catholics it is in great part due to the work of
these two Missions.

—Father Paul Mary Ponziglione,
Western Missions Journals No. 2 [3]

Theuits established themselves in the small métis trading community along Flat Rock Creek, just two miles from where it joined the Neosho. The mission was set amid métis traders' homes, and alongside the Osage agency and the trading post of the American Fur Company. The métis community was made up of French-Osage families who shared a language and a common culture with the European Jesuits, so that the French-speaking Jesuits were able to go into the homes of the métis trading families and speak directly to the people. All of the early Flemish Jesuits spoke French and thus could communicate without the problems encountered by the Protestants, who were only able to speak English.

The métis traders, while not fervent Roman Catholics, did seek some spiritual blessings from the Jesuits. They sought religious sanction for their unions with Osage women and baptism for their mixed-blood children. Father Ponziglione wrote that the members of the community "belong to that class of French who though can treat the Priest very nicely, and profess to be nothing else but Catholics, yet they do not care of practicing their religion."[4]

In addition to the métis trading families congregated about the trading posts, there were other mixed-blood Osage families living nearby. Some were remnants of the Hopefield and Boudinot farming communities who had managed to remain distinct from the band villages, and they were joined by the mixed-bloods from the old Harmony Mission site who had been driven from Missouri by white settlers in the late 1830s. Together they settled in small family groups along the Neosho River. Father Ponziglione, who arrived at the mission in 1851, described the region: "When the mission began none but the Osage Indians lived in this Country they numbered a little over 7000 all pagan with the exception of Some 500 Halfbreeds most all baptized in the Cath. Church but knowing nothing of our holy Religion."[5]

The Big and Little Osage towns were not far from the mission. About twenty-five miles north of the mission on the west bank of the Neosho were four villages of the Little Osage. Just south of the Little Osage towns were the first of five Big Osage villages extending along the Neosho north and south of the mission. Pawhuska's town was just a few miles due west of Flat Rock Creek. There was another Osage town thirty miles south of the mission just outside the Osage reservation, located on Cherokee lands. The former southern Osage bands of Claremore and Black Dog, who had reluctantly left the lower Verdigris in 1839, were living in seven separate towns along the Verdigris just inside the Osage reservation, about forty miles southeast of the mission.

When the Jesuits arrived, their buildings, although under construction for over a year, were still not complete, so they were forced to stay with the traders while they completed the school. While Father Schoenmakers and the three brothers worked on the buildings, Father Bax visited the Osage towns to recruit male students for their Manual Labor School for Indian Boys. Father Bax enjoyed as little success as the earlier Protestants had had in recruiting students from the Osage villages, for the Osage, despite their concentration in the north, were still unwilling to surrender their boys to the Catholic strangers. They had no desire to send their boys away from their communities to learn unneeded foreign skills. The Osage were not interested in having their boys trained as Christian farmers, and it made no difference to them whether the teachers were Catholic priests or Protestant pastors.

Father Bax had some success in the nearby mixed-blood communities where the families were trying to continue earlier efforts to become livestock growers and small-scale farmers. Despite the general lack of interest, the Jesuits opened their Osage Manual Labor School and welcomed thirteen mixed-blood boys to the school within two weeks of their arrival. With the boys' school begun, Father Schoenmakers traveled east to Louisville, Kentucky, where he recruited four Sisters of Loretto to come to the Osage Mission to establish a convent and boarding school for Osage girls. Mother Concordia, along with Sisters Bridget, Mary, and Vincentia, left Louisville and arrived at the mission in October, and within five days the four nuns had opened their school for Osage girls.[6]

In both the boys' and the girls' school the Catholic brothers and nuns taught religion, literature, and labor. The children began their days with morning prayers followed by daily Mass. After breakfast they attended classes and worked about the mission throughout the day. Soon additional priests were sent to teach and work at the mission. Within the year the school had sixty-five students, and it remained small until the 1850s, when other Indians' children were admitted. In 1853 Quapaw children were enrolled, and by 1860 there were 236 Native students.

The actual racial makeup of the school is unclear. The fathers acknowledged that most of the students were mixed-bloods, but they also claimed that some full-blood Osage students were enrolled. Isaac Gibson, an Osage agent, who became embroiled in a controversy with the Jesuits over tuition fees for Osage boarding students, claimed

> that five years ago [1870] when I assumed charge of the Osages, Sixty Osage pupils were in this Catholic School, nearly all were mixed bloods most of the full bloods were homeless orphans no chief, or leading man (full blood) patronized the School which shows the little interest in education and civilization the Catholics had been able to excite in the leading men of the tribe at the end of twenty years constant effort through a great number of Teachers Missionaries and Priests.[7]

Surviving mission records substantiate Gibson's remarks, for almost all the students at the Catholic Mission school were from the métis communities along the Neosho. Father Bax continued to visit the mixed-blood communities and the Osage towns, trying to secure more students for the mission with very limited success, for they never had more than seventy-six Osage students, almost all of whom were mixed-blood, and this from a community of approximately three thousand Osage.[8]

It appears that the Catholic boarding school at Osage Mission experienced much the same Osage behavior as the Protestant boarding schools at Union and Harmony. The Osage were cordial and polite to the missionaries, but refused to participate in any meaningful way in the conversion efforts of the good Jesuit Fathers. The Osage, despite the drastic changes and reduced circumstances, were still able to live their familiar hunting and raiding lives. They continued until the late 1870s to hunt the buffalo on the western plains and return to their river villages to harvest their crops and visit the nearby traders to exchange buffalo hides, horses, and mules for necessary trade goods.

Their lives, despite the invasions of the eastern tribes and increased competition in the west, remained intact and successful enough to resist unnecessary changes urged by the Jesuits. Students might be lured to the school for a short time, but they quickly became bored with the schoolwork and manual labor, and would either run away or leave when their families arrived to visit the agency or trading posts. Father Ponziglione described this situation: "For since the Osage youth do not understand how important it is to furnish the mind with learning and doctrine, they think that they are here as some state of punishment, and they desire nothing so much as to shed the clothing of the white men in which they now are dressed, and return to the ancient customs of the Osage."[9] One such account was reported by Father Ponziglione about an Osage named Man-sha-kita, who brought his nephew to the school one fall day, telling the priests "to make a smart man of him and a good Christian."[10] The Jesuits eagerly took him in; they baptized him, named him Peter, and soon gave him his First Communion. With the beginning of spring, however, Man-sha-kita came to the school to reclaim his nephew, claiming he needed him for some important ceremonies. He promised Father Schoenmakers he would return him promptly after the ceremonies were completed.[11] Father Schoenmakers protested that he had been working to teach Peter what is right, and that Man-sha-kita wanted to destroy all the good he had done and give him up to the "evil spirit." Man-sha-kita protested that he had no such intentions. He explained, "If I wish him to come with me to the medicine worship, it is not that he may do homage to the evil spirit. No, I wish him to get some meat and buffalo robes. . . . I am a poor man, Father, and must try to make a living somehow; so I wish Peter to come with me, not on account of the worship, but on the account of the meat."[12]

It was more than meat, but the true nature of Man-sha-kita's spirituality was lost on the Fathers Schoenmakers and Ponziglione, for neither spoke Osage and any spiritual subtlety was lost in the translation. Man-sha-kita was not praying to an evil spirit, and he was seeking more than meat, but to the good Fathers, the basis for Man-sha-kita's and other Osage's worship was simply greed. "They [Osage] attend the worship through a motive of gain."[13] Man-sha-kita and the Osage participated in worship to ensure success, as did most Christians. They sought the help of Wa-kon-da as Christians sought the help of Jehovah. One of the major differences was that the Osage religious beliefs were inclusive, and they were willing to pray to both Jehovah and Wa-kon-da for success; Peter was needed to solicit the help of Wa-kon-da for his family. The Jesuits were exclusively Christians and branded any other spirituality as evil, and they could only bemoan the departure of Man-sha-kita and Peter. Such misunderstandings colored Jesuit relations with the Osage and their métis kin. There were enough superficial similarities between Roman Catholicism and Osage spirituality to attract the Osage, and perhaps unintentionally to mislead the Catholic priests into believing that the Osage were sincere converts.

The Protestant missionaries preached a version of Christianity that precluded any such misunderstanding. The New England Presbyterians preached the doctrine of original sin and predestined salvation. There was little dramatic ritual in their religious services and little to attract the Osage. Their Sunday services involved hours-long services conducted by preachers dressed in plain clothing, delivering lengthy sermons about sin and salvation in English. The services contained only limited music and little visual or dramatic ritual. Protestant religious services focused on words and ideas, and their ritual was expressed in language and sequence. Such ceremony was lost to those who did not share the language and the culture. Opening prayers and closing benedictions were vital elements of Protestant services, but any drama present was contained solely in the language, not in the activity or behavior of the spiritual leaders or worshipers.

The Osage did sometimes attend the Protestant Sabbath services, and while they enjoyed the music portions of the services, the Sabbath services held little attraction for them. The few dramatic rituals of the Protestants, such as baptism and communion, were only conducted a few times a year. The rituals of baptism and communion were also very restrictive. Only those who had had been taught Protestant Christian doctrine, understood and accepted it, and were then visited by the holy spirit (a visit verified by a congregational examination) could then be baptized and take communion.[14] Protestant services were therefore intellectual exercises requiring common language, mutual understandings, and shared beliefs to have real meaning and any attraction for the Osage.

The lengthy Protestant ceremonies that demanded a common language and mutual cultural understanding were in striking contrast to the Roman Catholic ceremonies, which did not require real understanding to attract attendance. One could attend a Roman Catholic service and be engaged by the activity of the priests. Roman Catholicism was filled with vivid ceremony, dramatic expressions, and ritual, unlike the Protestant services that contained little entertaining activity. Individuals did not have to share a common language to engage in Catholic ceremonies, for they were all conducted in Latin, a language their own parishioners seldom understood. For the services to have any real spiritual meaning they of course required shared beliefs and cultural understandings. A shared culture and a shared language, however, were not essential for a dramatic and entertaining experience.

Jesuits also went among the Natives as unattached single men who had the support of a highly organized and disciplined organization and were relieved of the responsibilities of family. Almost all of the Protestant missionaries, however, were married, with the added responsibility of families that detracted from their task of converting the Natives. Although Pixley and Chapman occasionally went on hunting trips with the Osage, they could never stay long, for they had to return to care and feed their families back at the mission station. The freedom provided by celibacy allowed the Jesuits to travel among the villages and to attempt to convert the Osage.

The activity and behavior of the priests and their services were certainly more attractive than the Protestant services and attracted more Osage attention, but that increased attention should not be interpreted as Osage conversion to Catholicism. If one carefully examines the Osage Mission records it becomes clear that while there were some sincere spiritual conversions, very few Osage people became converts to Roman Catholic Christianity. Records contain hundreds of names of baptized individuals living on the Osage lands in Kansas. These names are only lists of individuals baptized, married, and buried by the Catholics, individuals who, the priests concede, seldom practiced the Catholic faith. The names are of individuals almost solely from the métis Osage community; the lists contain very few names from the Osage communities. Further, the names were taken by the priest, not given by the Osage—the Jesuits created the records, not the Osage.

The Jesuits seemingly had more success among the Osage, however, for a variety of reasons. The Osage sought good fortune and spiritual blessings, and were willing to incorporate additional spiritual help. The Osage would have likely incorporated elements of Protestantism into their spiritual lives if there had been any familiar or spiritually recognizable ingredients to adopt. Nineteenth-century New England Protestantism, however, as entirely an intellectual exercise defined completely by Euro-American Protestant intellectual culture, had simply nothing to offer nineteenth-century Osage.

Roman Catholic theology had little more to offer the Osage, but their religious culture and dramatic services contained elements that attracted some Osage attention. These elements were, however, almost entirely external, for they were merely shared behavior, not shared beliefs. The Osage practiced a complex religion filled with lengthy and elaborate rituals, conducted by a spiritual elite attired in specific and elaborate dress. Rituals were sanctified by the smoke of the calumet and were accompanied by chanting and the recitals of lengthy sacred stories [wi-gi-e]. The meaning and intent of the Roman Catholic Mass, conducted by priests wearing sacred vestments and accompanied by the burning of incense and the songs and chants, were surely misunderstood by the Osage. The rituals, however, contained enough familiar activity to be recognized as sacred and to be given some Osage regard, respect, and interest.

Both the Osage and the Roman Catholics shared a visual religious culture. They shaped their religious thoughts and beliefs visually, and expressed their spiritual beliefs with elaborate ceremony.[15] Those conducting religious ceremonies among both the Osage and the Catholics wore special ceremonial clothing. The Catholic priests, unlike the Protestant clergy, wore elaborate ceremonial vestments when they conducted their religious ceremonies. Priests wore elaborate stoles, cinctures, and the chasubles in red, green, violet, black, or white, each according to the appropriate liturgy. Osage participants also wore sacred clothing appropriate to the specific ceremony.

At the beginning of the Wa-sha-be A-thin Wa-tsi participants would place a red deer tail with an eagle feather on their heads. They would paint their bodies with black splotches and wear specially embroidered breechcloths along with specially ornamented leggings and moccasins.[16] The style and color of the ceremonial clothing had symbolic meaning and was necessary for the proper conduct of the ritual for both the Osage and the Catholics. While Osage and Catholic religious clothing had nothing in common save a shared belief that religious ceremonies required ceremonial clothing, the fact that both used special sacred clothing for religious ritual was significant. It was familiar and expected by both. The Osage celebrated most of their religious ceremonies clad in sacred dress, and the absence of any such special clothing in the Protestant services may have lessened Osage spiritual regard for their ceremonies.

Osage religious ceremonies required the recitation of the lengthy clan songs called wi-gi-e. As described in chapter 4, the wi-gi-e were inspired by Wa-kon-da and given to the clan's Non-hon-zhin-ga. They were the possessions of individual clan members who had met specific ceremonial requirements, purchased the songs, and committed them to memory. They could only be performed by those who owned them.

Every Osage ritual called for a variety of different wi-gi-e, and all were integral portions of the ceremonies. The lengthy wi-gi-e were chanted throughout the various Osage rituals, providing a rhythmic backdrop.

The rich Catholic ceremonial cycle, with its diverse and elaborate songs and chants, would be a customary ceremonial form for the Osage. The repetition of the Hail Marys of the rosary prayers would be a familiar and recognizable lyrical pattern to the Osage. Again, they would not understand the substance of the prayers, but the sound and pattern would be easily recognizable as familiar and sacred. Roman Catholics conducted other sacred acts familiar to the Osage. Priests began their religious services with the burning of incense. The fragrant and smoky incense was to symbolically purify the church and altar before the priests began the sacred service. Smoke was also an element of Osage religious ritual. The Osage used ceremonial pipes and tobacco smoke in all of their rituals.[17] The smoke was a symbolic offering to Wa-kon-da, and although the pipes involved took on much more symbolic and spiritual significance than the smoke offering, the element of smoke in Catholic religious ceremonies would be an accustomed and recognizable sacred pattern to the Osage.

There were other seemingly common features. The Osage believed that objects could possess a spiritual presence, and that objects and their ritual manipulation could bring about good fortune. The Osage had a variety of objects that possessed spiritual power: sacred rattles; pipe bowls and stems; *Tse-ha-wa-gthe Zhu-dse,* or shields; *zhon-xa wa-zhu,* or rods; and a collection of sacred items wrapped in the wa-xo-be. Roman Catholics agreed with the Osage that objects administered by priests could possess spiritual power. They also believed that specific religious objects could provide grace, forgiveness of sins, and protection from evil spirits.[18]

When Sans-Nerf visited Bishop Du Bourg, the bishop gave him and his men crucifixes and medals of the saints. When Fathers La Croix and Van Quickenborne visited the Osage villages, they too handed out medals and crucifixes. Visitors to the mission were also given similar items. These objects were popular among both the Osage and the Catholics, but for somewhat different reasons. Neither group shared an understanding of what the objects meant to the other. The crucifixes and saints' medals had very specific spiritual meaning for the Catholics, while the Osage thought they were attractive as jewelry and that they could perhaps provide good luck. While there was no real shared understanding of their meaning, there was enough shared appreciation to value the objects as sacred items that could bring good fortune.

Father Ponziglione wrote of sacred objects and revealed some of the misunderstandings: "The Osages as well as all these western Indians have a great respect not only for the priest, but for anything concerning our holy religion, though but simple crosses, holy pictures, medals, and above all prayer-beads, nay the wearing of these is equivalent, I would say, to a profession of our faith."[19] Having stated that the beads were a profession of their faith, he then provided several examples where they were clearly not evidence of Catholic faith. The father wrote about a group of Osage who came upon a band of Comanche out on the plains; the Osage decided to attack the Comanche, and as they prepared for the battle the war chief noticed that one of his young men was carrying a rosary given to him by Father Schoenmakers. The war chief demanded the young man give him the "prayer-beads" since he was the leader and would need more protection. When the young man refused to surrender the beads, he was told to lead the attack, since he was better shielded than the rest. The young man agreed, and the next morning, protected by the rosary, he led a successful attack on the Comanche.[20] On another occasion Father Ponziglione spent the night at the house of a Delaware chief who had a rosary hanging by his bed. "I asked him whether he was a Roman Catholic? He answered he was not. Then, said I, why do you keep those beads hanging there; what do you mean by it? Oh, he replied, those beads are the great prayers of the Osages; they made a present of them to my wife, and as long as we keep them in the house no evil spirit will trouble us."[21] Here were two examples of spiritual misunderstandings. In the words of Father Ponziglione, "they forget the reasons why the prayer-beads are to be respected, so that many look upon them merely as a talisman, we must not wonder; the best garden's soil, if left uncultivated for but a few years, will reproduce briers and thorns instead of flowers and fruits."[22] The Osage and Delaware recognized that the rosaries had spiritual value, but mistakenly believed that they provided spiritual protection. Rosaries are strings of beads used to count prayers and guide meditations, not good-luck charms. They are very similar to Osage zhon-xa wa-zhu, flat wooden sticks that have lines carved across them to act as mnemonic devices to help the Osage remember their sacred songs. There is no evidence that the Osage or Catholics ever saw the connection between the rosary and zhon-xa wa-zhu, for their shared meaning was hidden by their different external appearance.[23] Such misunderstandings reveal the real nature of their "shared spirituality." The similarities were only superficially shared forms, and these shared externals never contained any true shared religious beliefs.

These misunderstood objects, however, provided some attraction to Catholic worship, attractions that the Protestants never had. Nineteenth-century Protestantism was devoid of sacred objects possessing any spiritual powers. The New England missionaries never handed out crosses nor erected them at their missions. Their chapels were plain and simple, with little decoration to distract worshipers from listening, hearing, and understanding the word of God and the messages of their pastors. Instead of elaborate churches and mighty crosses, they constructed sawmills and grist mills, and while the grist mills were attractive to the Osage women, the mills and modest churches never provided any shared or understood spiritual message for the Osage.

Ironically, while there was clearly little real shared spirituality between the Osage and the Catholics, they did at least share an intensity and spiritual immediacy in their services that was totally absent from the Protestant services. The irony stems from the fact that while neither the Catholics nor the Protestants shared ritual forms, they were both Christians and shared many common spiritual beliefs. They both believed that Christ, the Son of God, came to earth, was crucified, died, and was buried, yet rose from the dead to save humankind, and that shared belief was central to the existence of both faiths. Christ's sacrifice was commemorated by both groups in the ritual and ceremony of Communion.

Communion among the Protestants, however, was a symbolic act, a reminder of Christ's sacrifice, and the wine and bread consumed in the service remained wine and bread, merely acting as symbols of Christ's body and blood. For the Roman Catholics, however, the wine and bread of Communion was more than a symbol of Christ's sacrifice and presence in their lives; sanctified by the ceremony of Mass, the bread and wine were transformed into the actual body and blood of Christ. The act of transubstantiation, wherein the bread and wine become the body and blood of Christ, could have been accepted more readily by the Osage than the New England Protestants, for the Osage believed that religious ceremonies were more than symbolic reminders of their faith. They believed that ritual performances could evoke real spiritual presence among them. While it is unlikely that the priests were able to clearly and completely communicate the significance of the sacrifice of Mass, the concept of consuming the body and blood of a human to acquire his power and presence was believable to the Osage.

The Osage were not cannibals, although tribes in the region had in the past eaten the hearts of their enemies to acquire their power.[24] Transubstantiation could have been accepted and believed by the Osage. They believed in the ability of their ceremonies to transcend symbolism and create real spiritual presence, as did the Roman Catholics. Such spiritual reality was absent from Protestant services. Furthermore, Mass was a daily Catholic ritual, conducted frequently, and while only the converted and confessed could take the Eucharist, the dramatic ritual was open for all to observe. Catholics also moved quickly to convert the Osage and administer to them their First Communion. Ironically, the Catholics moved quickly to prepare the communicant for a real spiritual act, while the Protestants moved slowly and deliberately for a merely symbolic act.

Another instance of shared ritual may be seen in Osage and Catholic use of ashes in a religious ceremony. The Osage Wa-sha-be A-thin Wa-tsi called for the ritual creation of charcoal. Specially empowered individuals sing specific sacred songs, or wi-gi-e, as they prepare the charcoal, which they later smear on the faces and bodies of the ritual participants. The Roman Catholics also prepare charcoal for a sacred ceremony: the palms from Palm Sunday are burned, and the resulting ashes smeared on the foreheads of participants in Ash Wednesday services. Protestants do not observe such rituals and never use ashes in any of their religious ceremonies.

Again, there is no spiritual connection between the ashes of Osage Wa-sha-be A-thin Wa-tsi and the Catholic ashes of Ash Wednesday. The Osage ashes are to symbolize the heat and power of fire, and the Osage warriors are to attack their enemies with equally fiery intensity. Catholic ashes represent the frailty and mortality of humankind and are taken as a sign of penance as worshipers begin Lent. There is no shared understanding, only the shared use of ashes. Although the meaning is not shared, the activity is similar and familiar enough to evoke some interest in the Catholic faith or at least attendance at some of their services. There were never any such similarities in the Protestant services, hence the slight preference for Catholicism. That preference was, however, extremely slight.

The Jesuit priests made regular visits to the métis homes along the Neosho, where they baptized the children, administered extreme unction to the dying, and celebrated Mass for those they could convince to participate.

> And so going about from camp to camp, I visit them trying to give them good advises—. I convalidated [sic] some marriages among the Half-breeds, baptized some children, and gave Extreem [sic] Unction to a dieing [sic] girl. I came next to what is called Papin Settlement at the Junction of the two Cany, and here I had the happiness of reading Mass, a thing I could not do at the Agency for want of proper room.
> ... I read mass in different places to give all an opportunity of approaching to the Sacraments. Some I am happy to say did comply with their Christian duties, but the majority did not.[25]

The majority, indeed, did not, for few if any Osage were Catholics in the 1850s and all had more pressing concerns than attending Mass. The Osage were facing growing internal and external threats.

Black Dog died in 1848, followed by White Hair in 1852. The death of such prominent leaders only exacerbated political strife among the Osage, and competing factions vied for control of the tribe. The Verdigris bands, who had largely ignored the political strife of the Big and Little Osage of the Neosho, began to challenge their leaders for position and access to the federal agents.

The internal struggles were overshadowed by external threats. The eastern removed tribes who had long competed with the Osage for the resources of the prairies began traveling further out onto the plains and aggressively challenging the Osage and other central and Southern Plains tribes for the buffalo. On several occasions, the Osage joined with Western Plains tribes and fought the eastern tribes. In 1854 the Osage joined with the Southern Cheyenne and challenged a group of Potawatomi hunters at Pawnee Fork; later that year, along with the Comanche, Kiowa, and Southern Cheyenne, they attacked a group of Sauk and Fox hunting on the plains. In both battles the better-armed eastern tribes defeated the Osage and their plains allies and drove them from the field.[26] Such defeats posed serious challenges to the Osage.

They confronted additional challenges in the 1850s. In 1853 Thomas Fitzpatrick negotiated a treaty of peace with the Comanche, Kiowa, and Kiowa-Apache that provided for eighteen thousand dollars in yearly annuities for them.[27] These annuities provided the Comanche with needed trade goods, so they no longer needed Osage trade. The Osage had been acting as middlemen for the Comanche trade since the mid-1830s, and the trade in Comanche horses and mules had been very lucrative for the Osage. The loss of this trade severely damaged the Osage economy. Some of the bands tried to compensate for the loss of the Comanche trade by stealing horses, mules, and cattle from the Santa Fe Trail traders.[28] The increased thefts brought unwanted attention and visits from Fort Scott soldiers.

Fort Scott soldiers would offer protection both for the Santa Fe Trail traffic and for another growing eastern invasion. White settlers began flocking to Kansas in the 1850s, and Kansas was made a territory in 1854. Attracted by the rich soils and the political struggle being waged by the pro- and anti-slavery factions, white settlers began squatting on Osage lands and soon demanded the removal of the Osage from Kansas. These sentiments would grow with the ever-increasing white population of Kansas, and once Kansas became a state in 1861, pressures to remove the Osage would grow dramatically.

Accompanying and adding to the growing challenges of the 1850s were deadly outbreaks of disease. In 1852 the Osage were attacked by the Black Measles; Asiatic cholera returned in 1853 to kill hundreds of Osage, and the cholera outbreak was followed by an attack of smallpox in 1854 that killed three hundred Osage.[29] With such immediate and dangerous threats, the Osage were not interested in attending Mass and praying the rosary. Nor were they willing to surrender their children to boarding schools and leave them miles away from their villages. The challenges of the 1850s were twofold. They were crucial enough to concern the Osage and occupy their attention, but they were not so threatening as to persuade them to surrender their culture. Their core patterns, although modified, remained unchanged.

The Osage might have divided into smaller communities, but they still planted their gardens along the river bottoms in the early spring. They might plant them along new stretches of the Neosho and Verdigris, but they continued to greet the spring by clearing the fields and planting their corn, beans, and squash. They continued to travel out to the shortgrass plains to hunt the buffalo in the spring with their band kin. After a successful hunt, they would still go on to attack their plains rivals to drive them from the region and to capture horses and mules. While their rivals changed from the Wichita and Comanche to the Potawatomi and Sauk and Fox, the Osage still fought for control of the plains. They still returned to their river villages to harvest their crops, visit the traders, and enjoy the bounty of the plains hunt and the prairie harvest. They would then leave for their winter hunt in late fall and remain out until the weather drove them back to the sheltered river bottoms, where they would spend the winter resting and preparing for the new year. The pattern survived, and despite the geographic limits imposed by the new invaders, the Osage could successfully continue their old and familiar way of life.

Thus able to live their lives in familiar successful patterns, the Osage still saw no need to become Roman Catholics. Although the Catholics performed ceremonies that seemed familiar, they only appeared familiar, for they were Christian ceremonies and not Osage ceremonies, and the Osage were willing only to add Catholic elements to their faith, not to substitute them for their own. They might observe the ritual of Mass; they might allow their infants to be baptized; they might hang crucifixes in their lodges and wear rosaries into battle; but they would never abandon either their Wa-sha-be A-thin Wa-tsi or their Mourning Rite for a Catholic funeral Mass or replace their wa-xo-be with Catholic prayer-beads. Some were willing to add, but few, if any, were willing to replace.

It was relatively easy to resist the Catholic efforts to Christianize. The Jesuits had no means to force their conversion; their invitations to services could be ignored, their visits to the villages tolerated, and any attempts to take their children away to boarding school could be prevented. Events of the 1860s would further challenge the Osage and attempt to change their lives, but those challenges would do little to convince them to become Roman Catholics and to surrender their children to Jesuit schools.

The 1860s began with a dramatic change. The federal government had been paying the Osage $20,000 every year, with part, $12,000, in the form of currency distributed to the band leaders or the traders who held Osage debts, and part in the form of cattle and swine that were typically consumed rather than raised. The payments were in exchange for Osage lands they had ceded in the south in 1839. The 1839 treaty that had forced the Osage north had provided for only twenty years of payments, and they came to an end in 1859.

The Osage had grown accustomed to the annuities, so that the halt of the payments, combined with the end of the Comanche trade and increased competition for plains buffalo, caused real concern among the Osage leadership. Some immediately began clamoring for another treaty to secure continued payments. Their cries for annuities were accompanied by increased demands by white Kansans to remove the Osage from Kansas. In 1861, when Kansas became a state, and throughout the 1860s, despite the violence of the Civil War, Kansas settlers, joined by Kansas politicians, demanded the removal of the Osage. The Osage were engaged in a series of treaty conferences throughout the 1860s and ceded much of their Kansas lands in an 1865 treaty, followed by another final cession in 1870.

The Civil War also brought about dramatic changes to the Osage. Although they had no interest in the status of slaves or the federal structure of the United States, they participated in some of the Kansas Civil War violence. Kansas was the scene of sporadic raids by regular troops and local volunteer units from both sides. Initially the Osage ignored the conflict, but in time some would be drawn into the violence. In September 1861 John Mathews, a trader living at White Hair's village, led a group of southern sympathizers on a raid of Humboldt, Kansas. Several Osage from White Hair's village, along with some métis living near the mission, joined Mathews on the Humboldt raid. The raid was soon followed by a revenge attack by a group of Kansas home guards that killed Mathews and burned White Hair's town.[30] Most of the Osage had been out on the plains hunting buffalo and had avoided the early violence. That first winter hundreds of Quapaw, Tonkawa, Wichita, Creek, and other Native refugees fled the violence of Indian Territory and established communities on Osage lands and amid their villages.[31] The Osage allowed the southern refugees to settle along the Neosho and Verdigris in and among their villages, and with the exception of some horse thefts committed by a few of the young men from all the tribes, they remained at peace with one another.

In the spring of 1862, two hundred full-blood and mixed-blood Osage were recruited into the Kansas Volunteers. A group of "able-bodied half-breeds" and Catholic Mission schoolboys joined the Ninth Regiment of the Kansas Volunteer Cavalry. Few of the Osage would submit to military discipline, however, and soon almost all deserted to go on their summer buffalo hunt. A few remained with the Kansas Volunteers to serve as scouts.

In the spring of 1863 a group of Osage on their way to hunt buffalo came upon a group of Confederates. The Osage confronted the soldiers and demanded they surrender. Instead of surrendering, the Confederate soldiers shot and killed one of the Osage, which triggered an Osage attack. The battle was brief, and the Osage killed all save one of the Confederates. This successful attack garnered great praise for the Osage; the Union commander at Fort Scott came to the Osage and presented them with lavish gifts for their victory over the Confederates.[32] For the remainder of the war most of the Osage avoided the war and continued their summer and winter buffalo hunts on the plains. A few from Claremore's and Black Dog's bands would join with the Cherokee and continue the small-scale violence until the war ended in 1865.

While the war continued, federal agents approached the Osage several times to try to persuade them to cede their Kansas lands. The Osage were still being pressed by white squatters, and they desperately needed the resumption of annuity payments, so they agreed to meet with the Indian commissioner and negotiate a new agreement. They met with federal agents in August 1863 and agreed to sell a twenty-mile-wide strip of land along their northern border to the U.S. government for at least $1.25 an acre. Since the government insisted that the funds from the sale of the northern strip should remain in trust for the Osage, the Osage offered to sell a thirty-mile strip along the eastern border for $300,000, so they could resume the needed annuity payments. The treaty was sent off to Washington, and the Osage moved onto their diminished reservation in hopes of soon receiving compensation for their ceded lands.

The payments did not arrive, however, and although thousands of white settlers had moved onto the strips of Osage land they had left, the treaty was not ratified. The Osage had included a gift of one section of land to the Osage Mission School, which some in Washington found objectionable. Washington officials also decided to limit payments to the Osage to $300,000 for all their land cessions and to place any additional revenue in the Indian Civilization Fund that was a common fund for all tribes in the United States. The changes required renegotiations with the Osage, and in the midst of the discussions, white settlers, not content with occupying only the northern portion of the Osage lands, lands not yet legally ceded, began moving onto the diminished reserve of the Osage.[33]

When the Osage met with federal agents in September 1865, they finally agreed to a new version of the treaty. They were able to reserve a section of land for Father Schoenmakers, but they conceded all the other changes to the treaty. They surrendered all funds from land sales over $300,000 to the Civilization Fund, and they agreed that they might in the future sell their remaining Kansas lands and remove to Indian Territory. The treaty was not ratified until June 1866, and almost immediately Kansas politicians began again to demand that the Osage leave the state.

Kansas Senator Edmund G. Ross began aggressively lobbying the secretary of the Interior, Orville Browning, and the commissioner of Indian Affairs, Nathaniel Taylor, to remove the Osage. Ross was able to convince them, and in May 1868 Taylor traveled to Kansas and met with the Osage at Drum Creek Springs. Taylor had first met the Osage at early treaty negotiations at Medicine Creek, where Taylor had brought the U.S. Peace Commission. Because the Osage were not at war with the United States, the Peace Commission ignored their presence at the meeting.[34] Taylor, however, returned to the Osage in 1868, presented them with a treaty, and demanded that they sign it. He threatened to cut off their provisions and open their Kansas lands to white settlement if they did not sign the treaty. Taylor's threats convinced the Osage to sign, for they had just returned from a disastrous winter hunt where they had been attacked several times by the Arapahoe. These attacks had forced them to leave the plains before they had taken any buffalo, and they had spent the winter with little food.[35] The government had provided provisions for them in March and April, but Taylor threatened to end the provisions unless they signed the treaty. These threats were enough to force the Osage to sign the treaty, which Taylor took back to Washington.

Taylor's treaty, however, contained direct transfer of Osage lands to the Leavenworth, Lawrence, and Galveston Railroad. These land cessions, excluding all preemption and homesteading of ceded Osage lands, combined with reports of Taylor's threats, convinced the House Committee of Indian Affairs to launch an investigation of the treaty. The investigation took months, and in the course of the investigation a new administration took office in Washington. President Grant and his commissioner of Indian Affairs, Ely Parker, became involved in the investigation, and Grant eventually withdrew the treaty from the Senate in February 1870.[36]

While the 1868 treaty languished in Washington, pressures to drive the Osage from Kansas grew stronger. White settlers invaded their diminished reservation and threatened to attack and drive the Osage from Kansas. When the Osage returned from their fall hunt in 1869 they found white settlers occupying their villages. Their newly appointed agent, Isaac Gibson, sought help from Fort Scott troops to protect the Osage, and when he met with the settlers, several threatened to kill him.[37]

In the summer of 1870 Congress decided to avoid another treaty controversy and simply added provisions to the Indian Appropriation Bill that authorized the purchase of Osage lands in Kansas for $1.25 an acre and called on the president to remove them to Indian Territory.[38] Federal commissioners were sent to meet with the Osage to secure their agreement, and on September 14, 1870, at Drum Creek Springs where the 1868 treaty had been forced upon the Osage, they met with the commissioners, accepted the appropriation act's provisions, and agreed to move to Indian Territory.[39]

The move would be delayed, however, by problems with the Cherokee, government surveyors, and white squatters. The Cherokee had been forced to sell portions of their land to the Osage, but they were demanding a higher price for their lands than the government had offered the Osage. The government offered Cherokee land for fifty cents an acre that the Osage agreed to; however, the Cherokee refused to sell their land for less than $1.25 an acre. Negotiations over land prices would continue for three years, until President Grant stepped in and set a compromise price of seventy cents an acre, which the Osage and Cherokee finally accepted in September 1873.

Although they could not agree on the price of the land, Gibson moved the agency south and began construction of new Osage agency buildings. They had neared completion when he discovered that surveyors had erred, so that the agency buildings had been constructed three miles into Cherokee country. The Cherokee claimed the buildings and forced Gibson to move west and begin construction anew on Osage lands. While he argued with the Cherokee about land prices and rebuilt the agency, he discovered that hundreds of white squatters had settled on the newly acquired Osage lands. The squatters refused to leave and threatened to attack the Osage if they moved onto the land. Gibson was forced to get troops from Fort Scott to expel the illegal settlers. While Gibson was dealing with the growing crisis, most of the Osage remained in Kansas; some, leaving for their winter hunt, sent word to Gibson that they would stay out on the plains until he had settled affairs.

Affairs remained unsettled throughout 1871 while Gibson tried to solve the many problems. The three thousand white squatters occupying Osage lands effectively defied Gibson until he was finally able to secure enough troops from Fort Gibson to remain in the area long enough to keep the whites off the land and complete construction of the agency buildings. Most of the Osage stayed away from their new lands in Indian Territory until the spring of 1872, when instead of returning to Kansas they established their towns on their new reservation in Indian Territory.[40] Ironically, their "new lands" were lands that they had formerly occupied until driven north by the 1839 treaty.

When the Osage left Kansas they left the Jesuits behind. When they agreed to surrender lands in 1865, they had included in the treaty a provision that gave the Jesuits title to the land where the mission was located. When they moved south to Indian Territory they made no provisions to provide land and support for the Catholic mission, and the Catholic Church declined to fund a move to their new reservation.[41]

Few Osage cared about the mission, and those that did believed they had paid any debt incurred to the Jesuits with their 640-acre gift in 1865. The small group of mixed-bloods who had established close ties with the Catholics and sent their children to the school thought, as a result of provisions in the 1865 treaty, that they would retain individual ownership of their Kansas lands and would remain near the mission.[42] Although they were eventually issued patents for their Kansas lands and were supported by Father Schoenmakers, the Osage "half-breeds" would be attacked, their homes burned, and their stock killed until they were forced to flee their Kansas lands and settle among their full-blood kin on the reservation.[43]

The Osage had left the Jesuits behind, but the Jesuits did not relinquish them; they continued to pursue the Osage. The Jesuit Fathers traveled south several times a year to baptize children, bless and sanction marriages, and offer Mass. They also continued to try to recruit children for their boarding school, with limited success. Osage enrollment dropped and, deprived of Osage students, the school was renamed St. Francis Institution for Boys and St. Ann's Academy for Girls and became a Catholic boarding school for the children of white Catholic Kansans.[44]

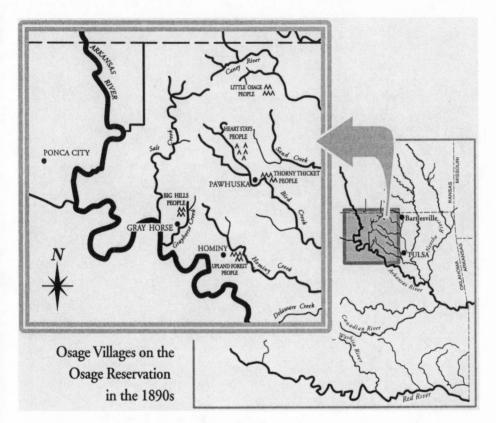

Fig. 8. Osage villages on the Osage Reservation in the 1890s.
(Artist, Christine Stergios, 2003.)

9

Ga-ni-tha—
"Move to a New Country"

The Osage gave but little heed to the story [*Ghost Dance*], perhaps from the fact that, as they are the wealthiest tribe in the country, they feel no such urgent need of a redeemer as their less fortunate brethren.

—James Mooney, *The Ghost-Dance Religion
and the Sioux Outbreak of 1890*[1]

I use the peoti bean in my religious ceremonies. We use it in our meetings same as you white people worship God in your churches. It does not make us crazy or cause us to do any harm and I can see nothing wrong in it. When I eat it I feel happy and good and thank God for his many gifts. As we use peoti in our meetings we realize that we have to die and it aids us to do right. It helps us to live better lives and enjoy happier experiences and we trust you will allow us to retain this channel through which so many gifts flow.

—Testimony of Chief Black Dog before the
Committee of House of Representatives
of the State of Oklahoma, January 21, 1908[2]

By 1872 all the Osage had moved to their new reservation. Most had arrived in 1871 upon completion of the winter hunt. Others, uneasy about the Kansas lands but unsure of the new lands, had remained in the west for another season. Some mixed-bloods had remained in Kansas, because the "treaty" gave them title to their individual farms. They soon joined their kin on the reservation, however, when they were attacked by Kansas settlers who beat them, burned their homes, killed their stock, and drove them from their lands.[3]

The four thousand Osage congregated in five groups on their reservation. The Iu-dse-ta moved to the region between the Caney River and Sand Creek just north of where the Non-dse-wa-cpe, who had merged with the Wa-xa-ga-u-gthin, settled along Bird Creek where Gibson had constructed the agency headquarters. The Pa-ciu-gthin settled in the southwest portion of the reservation along the Arkansas near Salt Creek, not far from the villages established by the Con-dseu-gthin on Hominy Creek. The mixed-bloods established a community of farms in the north near the Kansas border along the Caney River.

The Catholics did not abandon them; Fathers Schoenmakers and Ponziglione continued to care for the Osage despite the move south. Father Schoenmakers continued to lobby for the Osage. He defended the rights of the mixed-bloods in Kansas, to no avail, as they were being driven from their lands, but he later successfully lobbied to have portions of the Osage trust fund distributed to the Osage.[4] While Father Schoenmakers campaigned for Osage rights, Father Ponziglione visited the Osage on their reservation, where he administered baptisms to infants, extreme unction to the dying, and marriage vows to those who were living together. He of course celebrated Mass and preached the gospel of the Roman Catholic Church.

At the Osage agency Father Ponziglione celebrated Mass for those Osage interested and visited the government school to teach the children boarded there. He solicited students for his Kansas school, and generally irritated the Osage agent and the agency teachers. He attacked the agents for not sending all of the students to the Jesuit school and not agreeing to tuition increases for those Osage attending. He also attacked the agency staff's religion, which by the 1870s was Quakerism. President Grant, as a part of his Peace Policy, had begun to send Quakers to Indian reservations to promote peace and to ensure honest dealings with the Indian people. This combination of peace and Quaker Christianity greatly offended Father Ponziglione. He charged the Quaker teachers with teaching heresy, and annoyed them when he told the children that if they listened to Quaker teachings they would burn in hell.[5] "We have listened from time to time to his abusive discourses, describing us as heretic, & etc. When he publicly denounced the system of civilization adopted by the Government for the Osage, he was not molested, because he evidently desires to be made a martyr."[6]

He had little to fear, for the Osage paid little attention to the religious teachings of the Quakers. Agent Gibson had established a boarding school at the agency in 1874 and brought in Quaker teachers to teach the Osage children English literacy and other basic skills. They did not teach religion in the classroom, but forced the students to attend Sunday school and other Sabbath services.[7] There is no evidence that the Quakers had any more influence than their ABCFM predecessors did in converting the Osage children to Protestant Christianity. They would later have better attendance than either the Protestant or Catholic mission schools, for in 1884 Agent Laban Miles made the Osage council institute a compulsory education rule. If students missed class they would lose their annuity payments, and this threat ensured Osage school attendance.[8]

Despite his uncompromising and often annoying religious fervor, the Quaker agents continued to give Father Ponziglione access to agency buildings for his religious ceremonies and the opportunity to teach the children. Father Ponziglione continued to visit once or twice a year until the 1890s. The mixed-bloods welcomed him into their homes and participated in ceremonies when pressed, but paid little attention to the faith when he was gone. "Here I visited the Chief, and Some of the principal men, who treated me very kindly, but I could do nothing with them in the way of Spiritual instruction. . . . I spent one week going around through the different settlements of half-breeds. . . . I tried to give them good advise [sic], but I found them as indifferent as ever in matters of religion."[9]

The Osage in the 1870s were still uninterested in Christianity, whether it was Catholic or Quaker, for in the early 1870s the age-old cultural and economic patterns continued. The Osage continued to make their summer and winter buffalo hunts on the plains followed by occasional raids on plains rivals. They still returned from their plains hunts and raids to spend their winters along the prairie rivers. In 1871, they simply shifted south when they returned from their winter hunt and continued their traditional pattern, ignoring the Catholics and the newly arrived Quakers.

Things were to change dramatically. In the winter of 1873 they conducted a successful hunt, securing ample meat, tallow, and 10,800 buffalo hides.[10] This 1873 hunt would be their last successful one, for soon after they left for their summer hunt in 1874 they were called back by the agent, because the Kiowa, Comanche, Southern Cheyenne, and Arapahoe had left their western reservations and the U.S. Army was trying to drive them back to their reservations. This Red River War continued through the winter and prevented them from going out on their winter hunt. In early 1875, with conditions remaining tense in the West, Agent Gibson forbid them to go to the plains and ordered them to stay on the reservation. A small group defied Gibson and left for the plains, but they had little success hunting buffalo.[11] In the spring of 1876, the Osage conducted their last plains buffalo hunt when a large group ignored Gibson and went out onto the plains.[12] This last hunt was a failure for they found no buffalo, and troops dispatched from Fort Leavenworth forced them back to the reservation. That year was a desperate time for the Osage. Father Schoenmakers visited them in the fall and upon seeing the suffering made a desperate appeal to the commissioner of Indian Affairs to allow the Osage to go hunting, an appeal that was denied.[13]

The canceled and failed hunts were disastrous for the Osage, for those same years were years of drought and grasshopper invasions that destroyed their village gardens. The 1870s were hungry times for the Osage. Their agents, Gibson and Beede, exacerbated the suffering, for they distributed larger shares of the food rations to those Osage who agreed to settle down and become civilized.[14] Those rations soon ran out, and the Osage starved. Three families, desperate for food, slipped away from the reservation and began stopping the Texas cattle drovers on the Chisholm Trail, demanding food as a tax to cross their land. News of the cattle tax brought soldiers to the trail, where they drove the Osage away, killing an old man in the process.[15] Horrifically and ironically, while the Osage were starving, their Kansas land sales revenues had grown to over one million dollars, so although they had one million dollars in the national treasury bank, they starved on the prairie-plains.[16]

These grim times, however, were to mark a critical change for the Osage people. In 1879 a group of Osage went to Washington to talk with the commissioner of Indian Affairs about the dreadful conditions on their reservation and to propose solutions. The Osage asked to replace the food ration system, which made some feel like dogs, with cash payments. The commissioner listened to their complaints and agreed to pay them the interest earned on the revenues from their land sales in Kansas. Equally important, he also agreed to distribute those cash payments individually to each Osage four times a year.[17]

These direct, individual cash payments would make dramatic changes for the Osage people, for these payments would provide more than enough cash to adequately feed, house, and clothe all the Osage. After 1880, the Osage began to enjoy prosperity unique for Native Americans. This prosperity grew in the 1880s, for the Osage tapped another source of revenue in 1882. Texas cattlemen had been driving their cattle north to the Kansas railheads since the late 1860s across the Osage prairies. They often paused on the rich Osage pastures to fatten their herds before they reached the Kansas markets. Kansas farmers had also used Osage pasture without paying for it, so in 1882 their agent, Laban Miles, came up with a plan to lease the pastures to white farmers and ranchers. They soon leased 350,000 acres of pasture for four cents an acre, earning the tribe fourteen thousand dollars per year that was also distributed individually.[18]

The annuity payments and the pasture leases were soon joined by another source of revenue in the 1880s. When they first arrived on the reservation, Agent Gibson had urged each Osage family to claim land they wished to farm. Upon registering the claim, the agent would offer help in fencing, plowing, digging wells, and eventually supplying live-stock for the Osage farmer. Few Osage took advantage of the agent's help, and by 1872 there were only forty-eight full-bloods farming.[19] There were, however, many white farmers in the region who sought land and opportunity, and who were willing to work for the Osage on their land. A tenant farm system developed, and soon thousands of acres of the Osage reservation were being farmed by white sharecrop-pers.[20] This unique combination of annuity payments and pasture lease payments, increased by the farm commodities produced by white sharecroppers, made the Osage of the 1880s a prosperous people.

The passage of the Dawes General Allotment Act in February 1887, however, would soon bring about new challenges to the Osage. The Dawes Act gave the president permission to allot Indian lands pro-tected by treaty. The president would have the reservations surveyed and then allot the land to individual Indians. Each head of the family would be allotted one-quarter section (160 acres) with 80 acres allot-ted to each household member over eighteen years old and 40 acres to those under eighteen.[21] Any land remaining after the distribution to the tribal members would be declared surplus and would be opened to white settlement. The prospect of acquiring land in Indian Territory brought thousands of white settlers into the territory eager to obtain Indian lands. The Osage, because they had directly purchased their land from the Cherokee, believed they had clear title to their land, so they petitioned Congress to exempt them from the Dawes Act, and Congress obliged them. Osage lands were not subject to the Dawes Act, but much of the land around them was allotted, and soon the Osage found themselves surrounded by white settlers. Pressures for Osage allotment began in the early 1890s. Many of the Osage opposed allotment and campaigned against it. They also resisted allotment by pulling up the surveyors' stakes and tearing down their rock cairns. Despite Osage opposition, demands grew to break up their reservation until their lands were finally allotted in 1906.

Into this crowded and confused place came even more Christians to convert the Osage. Episcopal-Methodists built churches on the reservation along with Baptists and Catholics. This new invasion by the Christians was greeted liked the earlier invasions, with courtesy and indifference, and there is little evidence these latecomers had any more success than the earlier missionaries. In 1889 the agent complained:

> In religion the full-bloods nearly all cling to a creed of their own and a large portion of the summer months is taken up by many of them in observation of their form of worship, which is peculiar to the Osage, none of the surrounding tribes joining with them. They are very devout and earnest and will any sacrifice demanded of them to obtain preferment in their "church" and learn new religious forms.[22]

No longer able to hunt the buffalo in the summer, there was little left for the Osage to do except gather together, sing their songs, and try to make some sense of their ever-changing lives. The Osage are an amazing people who have consistently maintained as much control of their own lives and culture as possible. Their spiritual and secular leadership was very conscious of the ongoing struggle and made deliberate moves to shape their perceptions of realities. In times of crisis and in times filled with chaos, those times called Ga-ni-tha, the Non-hon-zhin-ga gathered to find answers to meet the new challenges. The Non-hon-zhin-ga contemplated and pondered the chaos, and then made the "moves to a new country," which meant metaphorically to make the changes necessary to survive.[23] These necessary changes were accompanied by a spiritual rationale and were always placed within a familiar cultural context recognized as Osage and sanctioned by the Non-hon-zhin-ga. In earlier times, the challenges came slowly and the necessary changes were less dramatic. Basic patterns of consciousness and spirituality created in the eighteenth century had served the Osage well into the 1870s.

But the 1870s and 1880s were filled with chaos and crisis. They were times of enormous change and forced adjustments. In 1874, 1875, and 1876 they were denied permission by the federal agent to go out onto the plains to hunt buffalo in the summer. Their 1876 hunt was carried out without permission, and it was a failure; perhaps more important, it was their last plains hunt. The expanding Osage of the eighteenth century, who had extended their hegemonic control over the prairie-plains, were now confined to their reservation.

No longer could they go out onto the plains and hunt the buffalo, for the buffalo were gone and white farmers were farming in their place. No longer could they gain status and wealth by attacking the Pawnee, or any other plains tribes, and stealing their horses. The plains tribes were all defeated, confined on small reservations with little to steal, and they were no longer threats to the Osage villages. No longer could Osage warriors earn O-don by attacking the enemy or defending their villages, the O-don that was necessary for initiation into some of the clans' religious degrees. The recitation of war honors was essential in certain important ceremonies, those ceremonies that required men who possessed all thirteen O-don. Without opportunity to earn the O-don necessary to be initiated or to qualify to participate in the traditional and essential ceremonies, the ceremonies would not survive.

Equally important was the fact that Osage rituals and ceremonies were created when they dwelled on the prairies. Living on the prairies between the rich, game-filled forest and the plains, the Osage were able to live in large communities filled with hundreds of people; the Non-hon-zhin-ga had created a ritual life incorporating these large numbers of people in long, elaborate, and complex rituals. The significant ceremonies required the attendance and participation of all the Non-hon-zhing-ga initiated in all seven degrees of religious knowledge from each of the twenty-four clans. In earlier times, single bands had contained the required twenty-four-clan Non-hon-zhin-ga and were able to conduct their own ceremonies.

In the 1870s, however, there was a shortage of Osage men possessing the requisite O-don. The Osage, weakened by starvation and attacked by measles, smallpox, and influenza, had lost many of their very old and very young. The many deaths on the reservation caused a shortage of Osage men able to become O-don, but this was the least of their ritual problems.[24] Bands could no longer supply ceremonial participants from all twenty-four clans; they had to solicit them from other band villages. By the early 1880s death had devastated the Non-hon-zhin-ga, and there were no longer twenty-four fully ceremonially initiated clan Non-hon-zhin-ga. Their elders were dead, and there were no new initiates to replace them in the ceremonies or to teach them the wi-gi-e. In some cases, uninitiated clan members were simply placed in ceremonial positions as symbols of their clan, and their wi-gi-e were deleted from the ceremonies.[25]

This spiritual crisis was aggravated by other new elements of Osage life. The new prosperity of the Osage in the 1880s would create problems. The revenue from the Kansas land sales amounted to $160 annually for each Osage; more importantly, now each individual Osage received the money, not their band leaders.[26] Before the 1879 distribution, all earlier distributions had been given to Ga-hi-ge and to band leaders who had never distributed gifts or payments equally to all members of their bands.

There had been a nascent class structure among the Osage, with a leader class and a commoner class. In early Osage history certain families had been successful hunters and warriors, and they had enjoyed greater wealth and prestige. They had solidified their status with moves to a new country and had created clans with enough status to ensure their elevated status. Commoners would give gifts to the leaders to show respect and regard, and to gain favorable attention. The leaders receiving gifts from the commoners would accumulate property and in turn distribute them back to the commoners, maintaining status and ensuring loyalty.

Such reciprocity was culturally codified by the Non-hon-zhin-ga within Osage religion and culture. The elite always kept the best for their immediate kin and never gave it all away, always keeping enough for their families before handing out any gifts. Father Ponziglione described the process in a letter: "During the year the big chief receives by way of taxes, an abundant supply of provisions. After helping himself freely, he distributes what is left among the people and thereby gains their good will."[27] In fairness, the differences of wealth were relatively small—distinct, but small. This distribution monopoly maintained the economic distinctions, and such wealth played a vital role in Osage spiritual life.

Wealth was required to purchase entry into each of the seven degrees of ceremonial knowledge that were necessary in order to become a Non-hon-zhin-ga. One had to purchase ritual knowledge that included the lengthy wi-gi-e, the ceremonial presentation, and copies of specific sacred objects. In addition, initiation ceremonies were grand events; the initiate and his family had to feed and care for the large crowds of people participating in the ritual for the duration of the ceremony. Such wealth requirements limited the membership to a small elite, and the small membership provided additional status and prestige to the sacred positions.

The distribution of cash annuities of equal amounts to each individual Osage brought about a dramatic end to the economic advantages of the leader class. Earlier annuity payments, often in the form of trade goods but occasionally in the form of cash or trade tokens, were always given to the band leaders, who never distributed them equally. They passed them out according to their wishes, keeping the best and handing out enough to provide for their people. Some received more payment as a reward for their loyalty and support, while others who might have challenged the leaders received less. This new system had not only brought an end to Osage starvation and poverty, it brought about important social changes that would eventually inspire another set of "moves to a new country."

The annuities would increase a bit, for the land sales continued and the interest grew. In 1884 the pasture lease money, which was $17,500 the first year, was added to the annuity payments. The land payments, combined with pasture revenues, made the Osage a prosperous people with the prosperity divided equally.

With such widespread prosperity, former commoners could now purchase ritual positions. They could buy the surviving rituals, learn the wi-gi-e, and participate in the ceremonies. They could also buy the sacred wa-xo-be, and as owners of wa-xo-be could participate in even more rituals. This privilege caused a curious change in the Osage's spiritual and ceremonial life. While there was a decline in the number both of ceremonies and of fully initiated surviving participants, those ceremonies that survived and were still conducted became crowded with participants who had purchased their way into the rituals. With the increasing number of participants, combined with the decreasing number of ceremonies, the status and prestige of the ceremonial positions declined dramatically.[28]

Thus, in the 1880s, the Osage again confronted Ga-ni-tha. Some of their ceremonies no longer had a place in their lives, for certain ceremonies provided protection and sanction for activities the Osage no longer conducted. Much of the Osage ritual had involved war and conflict. When the Osage had been driven from the eastern forests and had established their homes on the prairie-plains, their expansion of control over the central and southern prairie-plains in the eighteenth century had involved conflicts and war, and the Osage had shaped their lives around their successful military exploits. This was no longer necessary, for they were no longer able to go to war.

They had also shaped their spiritual lives to provide support and reward for warfare. With the forced peace of the late nineteenth century they had less need for such rituals. The Wa-sha-be A-thin Wa-tsi was no longer necessary. They also no longer needed to conduct the *Ni´-ki Non-k'on* (Hearing of the Sayings of the Ancient Men) or the *Wa´-wa-thon* (peace ceremony), both elements of the tribe's war rites.

Other rituals survived, but the new realities of reservation life made them impossible to perform in their old traditional forms. The Osage had commemorated death with a mourning ritual that obligated families to kill an enemy to provide a soul to accompany their dead, and they decorated the graves of their families with the scalps of their dead enemies. In the 1880s the Osage could no longer go out and kill a Pawnee or a Wichita to accompany their kin to the other side. They had to create a compromise ritual that provided enough of the old familiar form to honor the dead by providing comfort and solace, but without the requisite slaying.

The Non-hon-zhin-ga and Ga-hi-ga confronted this spiritual crisis and made the necessary moves to a new country, winnowing through their rituals and ceremonies and discarding the irrelevant portions. The leadership would adapt and create compromises consistent with their culture that were familiar in form. They would move to a new country and modify the mourning ritual to stop the revenge killings. Mourning relatives would still go out and seek an enemy scalp, but instead of killing and scalping him, they would purchase a lock of his hair, which they took back to the grave as a symbol of the scalp to accompany their dead.[29] "Mourning parties, who committed depredations occasionally of a serious character, have been so modified in their object that no harm has been done by any of them known to us."[30]

With no opportunities for their war rituals, and no means to honor their warriors and respected leaders, the Osage leaders accepted and adapted a plains dance they got from the Kansa and Ponca. The plains Grass Dance was welcomed into their villages in the mid-1880s by Black Dog and Claremore, and it soon became incorporated into their culture. They gave the dance an Osage name, *I'n-Lon-Schka*, incorporated the use of Osage wa-xo-be, cedar, tobacco, and other elements of their ceremonial culture, and made it a part of Osage life.[31] The Osage would use the I'n-Lon-Schka to honor their warriors and defenders of the tribe. Despite all of the chaos and changes, the Osage therefore found a way for their Osage leaders to retain enough status, prestige, and power in the conservative Con-dseu-gthin and Pa-ciu-gthin communities to shape the spiritual consciousness of the Osage people, and the people would come to accept and perform this new dance, the I'n-Lon-Schka.[32]

While the Osage were confronting dramatic changes in their lives and seeking new spiritual rituals and forms to confront their new realities, they still remained selective, embracing only those rituals that provided spiritual relevance for their lives. They did not accept every new ritual that passed through Indian Territory. In 1890 the Ghost Dance arrived in Indian Territory, and many of the tribes begin dancing it in hopes of improving their lives. A Caddo-Delaware spiritual leader, John Wilson, who would later return to the Osage with another spiritual message, brought the Ghost Dance to the Pa-ciu-gthin villages along Salt Creek in 1890. The Pa-ciu-gthin people danced it once, but it held no attraction for them, and they never danced it again. The nearby Con-dseu-gthin people on Hominy Creek also danced it once that year, but quickly dismissed it.[33] The Osage were not interested in the Ghost Dance. By 1890, the Osage were no longer in desperate straits, and perhaps, as James Mooney suggested, they had no need for a redeemer.[34] Ghost Dance prophets found little welcome among the Osage, for they were not interested in moving to that new country.[35]

The 1890s were filled with Ga-ni-tha, for Osage prosperity had a price, and that price was crime, fraud, disorder, and disarray. Their quarterly payments were made at Pawhuska, and payment days became carnivals as peddlers, gamblers, whiskey sellers, and swindlers flocked to Pawhuska to extract as much money as they could from the Osage. Traders anticipating the quarterly payments advanced their customers enormous amounts of credit and arrived to take it before it reached the hands of the Osage. "The large amount paid to the Osages (about $90,000 quarterly) attracts a swarm of persons who seek by hook or crook to divert the money into their pockets."[36] Some, returning home with their cash, were attacked and robbed along the way.

The annuity payments and pasture rents had also attracted a crowd of would-be Osage. Mixed-bloods who had left years ago returned to the reservation to get a share of the newly available Osage money. White men were attracted to the reservation, for if they secured an Osage wife they could get a share of the Osage assets. The mixed-bloods population increased from 263 in 1879 to 800 in 1896.[37]

Outsiders flocked to an Indian Territory that the federal government was racing to transform into the state of Oklahoma. Any lands in the territory that had not been assigned to a specific tribe were opened up to white settlement, and in the spring of 1889, when the federal government opened two million acres of land to settlement, fifty thousand white settlers rushed into the region to seize the land. With allotment being forced on all the territory tribes save the Osage, Cherokee, Choctaw, Chickasaw, Seminole, and Creek, millions of acres of land were made available for white settlers. In a series of land rushes in the early 1890s, white homeseekers flooded Indian Territory. In a single rush in September 1893 more than one hundred thousand settlers invaded the Cherokee Outlet, just west of the Osage reservation, and seized six million acres of land.[38]

Another element causing change would arrive largely unnoticed in 1895 but have enormous impact later: the beginning of oil exploration on the Osage reservation. The Osage would grant a ten-year lease to Edwin Foster in 1896, and his lease would lead to the discovery of oil on Osage land. By the 1920s oil would make them the richest Indians in North America and bring about incredible changes among the Osage.[39]

By the 1890s the Osage reservation was surrounded by hundreds of thousands of white settlers who hungered for Osage land. Federal commissioners made repeated visits to the Osage to persuade them to accept allotment. Political factionalism on the reservation was tearing the people apart. Their Non-hon-zhin-ga were dying; preparation of wi-gi-e for successful war campaigns, securing Wa-kon-da's blessing for the winter and summer buffalo hunt, and saying their ritual prayers had little relevance and seemed thin and hollow in the chaos of the Indian Territory of the 1890s. In this looming spiritual crisis of Ga-ni-tha, some of the surviving Non-hon-zhin-ga found an avenue for spiritual relief. They would again make the necessary and effective moves to a new country. This move would be to Peyotism.[40]

Peyote had been used by the Mescalero Apache in the 1870s, and by the 1880s its use had spread to the Comanche and Kiowa. Native peoples forced together in Indian Territory were looking for spiritual help. They found their traditional faiths had not saved them from defeat, and like that of the Osage, often had little relevance for their newly created reservation lives. Many had temporarily embraced the Ghost Dance, but when it failed to provide the promised relief it was rejected. This left an opening for a new spiritual path, and Peyotism became very popular and widespread in the late 1880s.[41]

Around 1890 the Caddo, Delaware, and Quapaw became practitioners of Peyotism; sometime in the early 1890s Black Wolf, a Caddo practitioner of Peyotism, brought Little Moon Peyotism to the Osage. He came to one of the Con-dseu-gthin camps where Claremore was the Ga-hi-ge. Claremore's daughter was very ill, and Black Wolf tried to cure the girl with his peyote prayers and rituals. Black Wolf failed to save Claremore's daughter, and although it was claimed that Claremore saw value in the ritual, Peyotism did not spread at that time.[42]

Peyotism returned, however, to the Osage in 1898, when a Caddo-Delaware, John Wilson, also known as Moonhead, came to build a peyote altar for Tall Chief, a Quapaw living near the Upland Forest camps.[43] Tall Chief had invited John Wilson to his camp to construct an altar and to conduct the Big Moon rituals. Wilson was a spiritual leader among the Caddo and Delaware and had been deeply involved in the Ghost Dance religion. He was introduced to Peyotism by the Comanche, and after a series of divine revelations created his own version of peyote worship, known as Big Moon Peyotism. Wilson claimed that peyote had come to him as a person and taught him the proper way to worship for salvation. Moonhead's Big Moon Peyotism contained Christian, Caddo, and Delaware religious symbols and linked the taking of peyote with Caddo and Delaware rituals. He claimed all of the elements combined in his Big Moon Peyotism would reveal the proper path to heaven. Wilson's Big Moon Peyotism became very popular, and he criss-crossed Indian Territory constructing Big Moon altars and conducting Big Moon ceremonies.

Osage from the nearby Con-dseu-gthin camps began visiting Tall Chief's camp and began practicing Wilson's variety of Peyotism. Francis Claremore brought Wilson to his camp and had him construct a Big Moon altar. It was at Francis Claremore's camp that two prominent Osage leaders, Black Dog and Claremore, witnessed the Big Moon Peyotism that eventually led to their conversion to Peyotism.

Their conversion was important because these two men were Ga-hi-ge of the Upland Forest People and were also prominent leaders of the entire tribe. They had helped reorganize the tribe politically in 1881 and had served as representatives from the Upland Forest district in the tribal council. Claremore had been one of the tribal leaders who met and challenged the Jerome Commission who came to the reservation to force the Osage to allot their reservation, and Black Dog was elected principal chief in 1899. These two Osage leaders were also spiritual leaders and had been deeply involved in reshaping Osage religion to meet the new reservation realities. They had introduced and spread the I´n-Lon-schka in the 1880s and were still engaged in seeking effective compromises when they met John Wilson in 1898.

In 1898 their old religion was still being practiced, but by 1898 it was drastically changed from its pre-reservation self. Most of the ceremonies had little meaning in their 1890s lives. Their traditional religion provided little direction regarding the dilemmas created by their newfound wealth. They were bitterly divided over issues of leadership and direction for the tribe. Some sought allotment while others fought to keep their land and tribal sovereignty. Their old faith simply did not provide relevant answers for their new questions nor the palliative rituals to soothe and calm the madness of the 1890s and bring order to their universe.

For Black Dog and Claremore, their old tribal religion no longer provided any relevance or meaning. Ga-ni-tha continued, but their Non-hon-zhin-ga could make no more meaningful "moves to a new country." The spiritual itinerary of their old faith was exhausted, and when this new, simpler, and pleasant religion arrived they were willing to abandon their old faith and adopt the new path.[44] Their old religion did, however, provide the context and means for change. The Osage tribal religion, with its ability to confront Ga-ni-tha and permit moves to a new country, still contained enough significance in Osage life to permit its own demise. It permitted Black Dog and Claremore to move beyond familiar country and create a new religion for their people. Black Dog and Claremore followed old traditional patterns to this new religion. They consulted with their band's Non-hon-zhin-ga and band kinsmen and decided to pursue this new faith. Their people, consistent with their traditions, followed these Ga-hi-ge as they led them to Peyotism.

In 1898 when Black Dog and Claremore began practicing Big Moon Peyotism, it would be the last move they made to a new country. In true Osage fashion, they placed their mark on Wilson's Big Moon Peyotism. Black Dog redesigned and redirected Wilson's peyote altar to meet Osage demands. He turned the altar to face the west, unlike all other peyote altars that faced east. Black Dog insisted that an Osage could not look east for spiritual direction, but must look west where the sun was leading, not where it had been. Black Dog also convinced Wilson to place Osage symbols of the morning star on the mound at the opening of the altar, and to draw lightning symbols on the altar's apron.[45]

Big Moon Peyotism required the Osage to completely abandon their old religion. Wilson claimed that Peyotism focused on heaven and eternal life, and that their old religion only focused on earth, and that its limited, narrow focus interfered and prevented them from reaching heaven. The old tribal religion had become irrelevant and cumbersome. Wilson's admonitions, combined with Black Dog's, Claremore's, and other respected Ga-hige's directives, soon convinced full-bloods to abandon their old religion and embrace Peyotism. Within a few years almost all full-blood Osage had converted to Peyotism and abandoned their traditional religion.[46]

What Protestants and Roman Catholics had been trying to bring about for eighty years was accomplished in only a few years. The Osage finally abandoned their old tribal religion and converted, but not to white Christianity—instead to a religion inspired, created, and directed by Native people.

Fig. 9. Osage Indians (Pawhuska, Oklahoma). This is a photograph of a
group of Osage dancing around a wa-xo-be (Hawk Bundle) in
Pawhuska, Indian Territory, ca. 1890s. (M. C. Murray, Denver Public
Library, between 1880 and 1910?, copyright © 1995–2003 Denver
Public Library, Colorado Historical Society, and Denver Art
Museum.)

10

Epilogue

The ways that they had, they were still working pretty
strong. They still lived by it, they adhered to those things.
Then somebody come in and tell them something and
make them change that. I can't see, the only way that I
can see that, is that it must be so. Otherwise them people
wouldn't have done that because even back to the beginning of recorded times, Osage history, we know the
things they went through. Even the Priests [Catholic]
came, and like that, and they didn't have no impact on
them whatsoever, on the way they were. And now here,
this man [Wilson] came and when he told them and
showed them and give them those Peyote and said you
find out for yourself. Then they took it and they put all
that they had, they put that aside.

—Leroy Logan, Interview[1]

Political factionalism shaped and limited the expansion
of West Moon Peyotism. The critical political issues
involving allotment and tribal rolls divided the Osage,
and the political opponents of Black Dog and Claremore were unwilling to convert to a religion touted by their rivals. They would, however, in time abandon their old religion, and Peyotism would
eventually spread to the Non-dse-wa-cpe, Wa-xa-ga-u-gthin, and Iu-
dse-ta, but they converted to Moonhead Wilson's East Moon Peyotism
instead of Black Dog's West Moon version.[2]

The last public performance of a major traditional Osage ritual was
a mourning dance conducted at Gray Horse in 1911.[3] By then the Osage
had largely abandoned their old tribal religion, and almost all full-bloods

had become Peyotists. There were a few full-bloods, notably James Bigheart, and some mixed-bloods who were Roman Catholics; and a few others who had joined various Protestant faiths. Although many Osage of different faiths continued to celebrate the I´n-Lon-schka, it had lost its religious character and had become just a social event, an opportunity for the Osage to come together and visit with friends and family, to celebrate their culture.

While it seems somewhat clear why they abandoned their old religion, we will never be certain why they adopted Peyotism. Perhaps it was because it promised a pathway to an afterlife that was more attractive than that of the Catholics and Protestants. Perhaps it was syncretic enough to offer comfort missing in those other faiths. Its songs, drums, and tobacco were all familiar, and the mild hallucinations provided happiness and promises of heaven. Although the hallucinations were only temporary, they were a welcomed relief from the constant stress and unpleasantness that would only continue to grow in twentieth-century Indian Territory, which become the state of Oklahoma in 1907.

Perhaps the reasons why they adopted Peyotism should concern only the Osage. What is important to us is not the reasons they chose it, but the fact that they made the choice. The Osage themselves made the decision, chose their own spiritual path. Granted, it was a choice shaped by outsiders, but they rejected the Euro-American religions that the missionaries attempted to force upon them. They successfully resisted years of cultural attacks by well-educated, well-funded, committed zealots who had the support of large churches and the U.S. government. The Osage successfully resisted their incursions and chose a religion created, not by Protestants or Roman Catholics, but by Native peoples and shaped by the Osage, to fit their needs, themselves.

The Osage in nineteenth-century Kansas and Oklahoma became neither Protestants nor Roman Catholics. They remained Osage. Despite the differences in Roman Catholic and Protestant theologies and religious practices, both were Christian faiths that shared a common European-inspired worldview of a theological construct with a dominant Christian God and his son, Jesus.

The Osage, however, believed that humans were only one of many spiritual creatures sharing the universe. Their shared place within the universe's space was maintained by acts of reciprocity with all others. Religious ritual was required to maintain the reciprocal relationship between humans and non-humans for the required balance of the universe. This view was in striking contrast to that of both Catholics and Protestants, who never saw themselves as merely another set of participants in the world.

Europeans believed that only humans possessed spiritual value, and they arranged their universe according to a linear hierarchical construct with their God reigning supreme over the universe he had created. Christians did not believe in an equality of existence and a sharing of space with the elements of nature. They insisted in seizing, controlling, and consuming nature. Native Americans did not understand the European ideologies of domination and submission, for the Indians' ethos was one in which the social, natural, and supernatural worlds were defined and shaped by sharing.

Christians focused on sin and guilt, and while the Catholics provided a means of forgiveness, notions of sin and guilt were alien to the Osage. Wrongdoing by individuals could be assuaged by acts of contrition. Young men could apologize to the individual they wronged and make amends with gifts, and the crime would be forgotten without guilt. If individuals refused to make amends, they would be publicly shamed and ostracized by the community until they behaved, but no Osage was ever condemned to hell for his behavior on earth.

Christians preached that the followers of Christ made individual decisions of belief and chose Christian moral behaviors, and thus at death were separated from the sinners by a judgmental God. Notions of heaven, hell, and purgatory were the very antithesis of Osage beliefs, which maintained that all Osage were certain to reach the other world after death, regardless of their earthly behavior. The Osage paid little attention to the afterlife, but they believed that it was much like the present life on the prairies, only with ample game and bountiful gardens.

The Osage prayed, but not to be saved from eternal damnation; they prayed to find bison, deer, and other game to feed their people. They prayed for successful raids against their enemies, not for salvation. The Christian faith was simply too alien, and neither Catholicism with all its seeming similarities, nor Protestantism with its sharp contradictions, was attractive or acceptable to the Osage. As long as the Osage were able to hunt and raid on the plains and farm on the prairies, they held fast to their faith that provided order to their world and met their basic needs.

When their situation changed in the late 1800s and they were no longer able to hunt and raid, but could only farm and ranch, they sought a new faith. With this new faith in their midst, they still rejected Christianity, for it still remained too foreign; instead the Osage turned to a Native American religion that they could embrace with enthusiasm. The Osage were never unaffected by their own gospel, only by the gospel of the Euro-American strangers.

Notes

Chapter 1

1. Rev. Nathaniel Dodge, "Osages: Extracts from a Letter of Mr. Dodge, dated Boudinot, Osage Nation, March 12, 1832," *Missionary Herald* 28 (September 1832): 290.

2. Gilbert J. Garraghan, S.J., *The Jesuits of the Middle United States* (New York: J. J. Little and Ives, n.d.; reprint, Chicago: Loyola University Press, 1983–84), 2:534.

3. See Colin G. Calloway, *New Worlds for All: Indians, Europeans, and the Remaking of Early America* (Baltimore: Johns Hopkins University Press, 1997).

4. See Willard H. Rollings, *The Osage: An Ethnohistorical Study of Hegemony on the Prairie-Plains* (Columbia: University of Missouri Press, 1992); and Gilbert C. Din and Abraham P. Nasatir, *The Imperial Osages: Spanish-Indian Diplomacy in the Mississippi Valley* (Norman: University of Oklahoma Press, 1983).

5. See Rollings, *The Osage*, 1–14, 95–212; Jeremy Adelman and Stephen Aron, "From Borderlands to Borders: Empires, Nation-States, and the Peoples in Between in North American History," *American Historical Review* 104 (June 1999): 814ç41.

6. See Gary Clayton Anderson, *The Indian Southwest, 1580–1830: Ethnogenesis and Reinvention* (Norman: University of Oklahoma Press, 1999); Elizabeth A. H. John, *Storms Brewed in Other Men's Worlds: The Confrontation of Indians, Spanish, and French in the Southwest, 1540–1795* (College Station: Texas A&M University Press, 1975; reprint, Lincoln: University of Nebraska Press, 1981); Thomas W. Kavanagh, *Comanche Political History: An Ethnohistorical Perspective, 1706–1875* (Lincoln: University of Nebraska Press, 1996).

7. See Robert F. Berkhofer, *Salvation and the Savage: An Analysis of Protestant Missions and American Indian Response, 1787–1862* (Lexington: University of Kentucky Press, 1965). "The object of your Mission is not merely to improve the temporal state of the Indians, but to save their souls; not merely, therefore, to civilize, but also to christianize them." Rev. Philip Milledoler, "Address, delivered to the Union Mission Family, in the Dutch Church in Nassau-street, on Monday evening, April 17, 1820," *American Missionary Register* 1 (September 1820): 98.

8. See William W. Graves, *The First Protestant Osage Missions, 1820–1837* (Oswego, Kans.: Carpenter Press, 1949); see Father Paul Mary Ponziglione, "The Annals of the Mission of Saint Francis of Hieronymus, by the Fathers of the Society of the Jesuits Among the Indians of North America called the Osage," Midwest Jesuit Archives, St. Louis, Missouri. I tend to agree with the sentiments of noted Borderlands scholar John Kessell, who wrote in his review of Cynthia Raddings' *Wandering Peoples* that too many scholars are fooled by Jesuit propaganda (*Ethnohistory* 45 [fall 1998]: 817–19).

9. Col. T. L. McKenney, and other correspondents, "Second Mission Family," *American Missionary Register* 1 (July 1820): 29–33.

10. "A call to come over for their help, like that from Macedonia to the apostle, has since reached us from another tribe of our savages, still more remote in the American desert, and we are pledged, through the organ of our Society, to send them relief." Philip Milledoler, Alexr. Proudfit, and Gardiner Spring, "Postscript: United Foreign Missionary Society, Second Mission Family," *American Missionary Register* 1 (December 1820): 238; Rev. Dr. Milledoler, Mr. Z. Lewis, and William Wilson, "Fourth Report of the United Foreign Missionary Society," *American Missionary Register* 1 (May 1821): 420–21.

11. Mr. Jones to the Editor of the Recorder, "United Foreign Missionary Society: Home Proceedings," *American Missionary Register* 2 (December 1821): 225–26; Rev. Dr. Milledoler and Mr. Z. Lewis, "Reports of Societies: Fifth Report of the United Foreign Missionary Society, Union Mission," *American Missionary Register* 2 (June 1822): 471.

12. Board of Managers of the United Foreign Missionary Society, "Instructions to the Members of the Mission Family, Designated for the Harmony Station, Among the Great Osages of the Missouri," *American Missionary Register* 1 (February 1821): 325; Mr. Sprague, "[Letter] to his Brother in Brooklyn," *American Missionary Register* 2 (January 1822): 275.

13. William Clark, "Papers Relating to Benton Pixley," February 18, 1829, *Letters Received by the Office of Indian Affairs, 1824–81*, Osage Agency 1824–1880, Record Group 75, M234 (Washington, D.C.: National Archives, 1958); Graves, *Osage Missions*, 192–93.

14. Rev. John Rothensteiner, "Early Missionary Efforts among the Indians in the Diocese of St. Louis," *St. Louis Catholic Historical Review* 2 (April–July 1920): 66.

15. Rothensteiner, "Early Missionary Efforts," 66; Garraghan, *Jesuits of the Middle United States*, 1:180–81.

16. Rothensteiner, "Early Missionary Efforts," 71.

17. Ibid., 72.

18. Ibid., 73.

19. Ibid., 86.

20. Garraghan, *Jesuits of the Middle United States,* 1:395, 2:194.

21. The school became St. Francis Institution for boys and St. Ann's Academy for girls. Garraghan, *Jesuits of the Middle United States,* 3:450.

22. William C. Requa, "Mission to the Osages," *Missionary Herald* 33 (January 1837): 22–23.

23. Graves, *Osage Missions,* 174.

24. Louis F. Burns, *Osage Mission Baptisms, Marriages, and Interments, 1820–1886* (Fallbrook, Calif.: Ciga Press, 1986).

25. Garrick A. Bailey, ed., *The Osage and the Invisible World: From the Works of Francis La Flesche* (Norman: University of Oklahoma Press, 1995), 54–57.

26. Clark, "Papers Relating to Pixley."

27. Clifton Jackson Phillips, *Protestant America and the Pagan World: The First Half Century of the American Board of Commissioners for Foreign Missions, 1810–1860* (Cambridge, Mass.: Harvard University Press, East Asian Research Center, 1969), 18, 22–24.

28. "Fifth Report of the United Foreign Missionary Society," *American Missionary Register* 2 (June 1822): 467.

29. Kevin Orlin Johnson, *Why Do Catholics Do That? A Guide to the Teachings and Practices of the Catholic Church* (New York: Ballantine Books, 1995), originally entitled *Expressions of the Catholic Faith* (New York: Ballantine Books, 1994), 214–15; James Axtell, *The Invasion Within: The Contest of Cultures in Colonial North America* (New York: Oxford University Press, 1985), 91–127, 271–86.

30. It is extremely difficult to prove the nonexistence of something. There are continuous references made about their mission mills and not one reference to any crosses erected at any of the Protestant mission sites. There indeed may have been crosses erected at the Protestant missions, but there is no evidence of their existence, unlike the Catholic missionaries who repeatedly remarked upon the erection of a variety of spiritual monuments.

31. The instructions given to the UFMS missionaries included the following: "As soon as any are instructed in the great truths of our holy religion, are brought to embrace the faith, and give good hope of steadfastness in their profession, you will publicly admit them to the ordinance of baptism, and afterward their children. You will appoint regular periods for the administration of the ordinance of the Lord's Supper, to the members of the Mission family, and the baptized adults among the Indians. You will be careful to admit none to these seals of the covenant, without frequent conversation, and sufficient interval for trial. An hasty admission will be injurious to the persons themselves; and they may, by their apostacy [*sic*],

deeply wound the cause of Christ." Board of Managers, "Instructions to the Members," 325.

32. The Mission family, having been invited to take Communion with the Presbyterian Churches in Pittsburgh, wrote: "We approached the table of the Lord with a lively impression that this will probably be our last season of communion with the Christian Church. We have been strengthened and encouraged, especially with the hope that soon we shall behold this table spread in the wilderness, surrounded by many of the long lost children of darkness, redeemed by Christ's blood, the fruits of this Mission." William F. Vaill and Epaphras Chapman, "Extracts from the Journal of the Union Mission," *American Missionary Register* 1 (September 1820): 91.

33. Johnson, *Why Do Catholics Do That?*, 215.

34. Harold L. Harrod, *Mission among the Blackfeet* (Norman: University of Oklahoma Press, 1971), 187.

35. Neal Salisbury, *Manitou and Providence: Indians, Europeans, and the Making of New England, 1500–1643* (1982; reprint, New York: Oxford University Press, 1984.) 38, 56.

Chapter 2

1. Din and Nasatir, *Imperial Osages*, 235–36.

2. "Their [Osage] history is unknown—their ancestry is lost. The enthusiasm of a scholar wandering among the ruined cities of Greece—the sensibilities of a Christian travelling through the land where the Son of God was born—lived—died and rose again, and from whence he ascended on high, will not be awakened from local associations in that country to which you are going. You go to settle among strangers, not merely to yourselves, but to your God and Saviour." Rev. Dr. Romeyn, "Charge to the Great Osage Mission," *American Missionary Register* 1 (April 1821): 398.

3. Richard White, *The Middle Ground: Indians, Empires, and Republics in the Great Lakes Region, 1650–1815* (1991; reprint, Cambridge, UK: Cambridge University Press, 1995), 1–49; Daniel K. Richter, *The Ordeal of the Longhouse: The Peoples of the Iroquois League in the Era of European Colonization* (Chapel Hill: University of North Carolina Press; Williamsburg: Institute of Early American History and Culture, 1992), 50–74.

4. Michael J. O'Brien and W. Raymond Wood, *The Prehistory of Missouri* (Columbia: University of Missouri Press, 1998), 347.

5. F. Todd Smith, *The Wichita Indians: Traders of Texas and the Southern Plains, 1540–1845* (College Station: Texas A&M University Press, 2000), 8, 28; John, Storms Brewed, 215.

6. Pierre Margry, ed., *Découvertes et Établissements des Français dans l'Ouest et dans le Sud de l'Amérique Septentrionale, 1614–1754*, vol. 1, *Voyages*

*des Français sur les Grands lacs et découverte de l'Ohio et du Mississipi,
1614–1684* (Paris: n.p., 1888; reprint, New York: AMS Press, 1974), 595.

7. Margry, *Voyages des Français*, 595.

8. Ibid.

9. Eighteenth-century French records contain accounts of Osage
attacks along the Arkansas, Red, and Missouri Rivers. See Margry,
Découvertes et Établissements; see also Archives des Colonies, série C13A:
Correspondance générale, Louisiana, and série C11A: Correspondence
générale. Archives Nationales, Paris, France.

10. Eighteenth-century Spanish records from Natchitoches, Arkansas,
and St. Louis are filled with accounts of Osage attacks on foreign traders.
See Nasatir, *Before Lewis and Clark*; see also Din and Nasatir, *Imperial
Osages*.

11. Lettre de DuTisné à M. de Bienville, le 22 Novembre 1719, in Pierre
Margry, ed., *Découvertes et Établissements des Français dans l'Ouest et dans
le Sud de l'Amérique Septentrionale, 1614–1754*, vol. 6, *Exploration des
Affluents du Mississipi et Découverte des Montagnes Rocheuses, 1679–1754*
(Paris: n.p., 1888; reprint New York: AMS Press, 1974), 313-15.

12. Lettre de DuTisné à M. de Bienville, le 22 Novembre 1719, in
Margry, ed., *Explorations des Affluents*, 313-15.

13. John, *Storms Brewed*, 305.

14. Richard White, "The Winning of the West: The Expansion of the
Western Sioux in the Eighteenth and Nineteenth Centuries," *Journal of
American History* 65 (September 1978): 337.

15. John, *Storms Brewed*, 318.

16. John, *Storms Brewed*, 213–21; Mildred Mott Wedel, "J.-B. Bénard,
Sieur de la Harpe: Visitor to the Wichitas in 1719," *Great Plains Journal* 10
(spring 1971): 37–70.

17. John, *Storms Brewed*, 305.

18. Margry, *Exploration des Affluents*, 311; Lewis A. Houck, ed., *The
Spanish Régime in Missouri* (Chicago: R. R. Donnelley and Sons, 1909), 1:140.

19. Rollings, *The Osage*, 56-59.

20. W. J. Eccles, "The Fur Trade and Eighteenth-Century
Imperialism," *William and Mary Quarterly*, 3d ser., 40 (July 1983): 342–46.

21. Din and Nasatir, *Imperial Osages*, 110; John, Storms Brewed, 379.

22. Din and Nasatir, *Imperial Osages*, 152–53.

23. White, "Winning of the West"; John C. Ewers, *Plains Indian
History and Culture: Essays on Continuity and Change*, foreword by
William T. Hagan (1997; reprint, Norman: University of Oklahoma Press,
1999), 222–36.

24. Bourgmont to Directors of the Company of the Indies, January
2, 1794, *Archives des Colonies*, C13A, C4, fols. 117–25; Frank Norall,

Bourgmont, *Explorer of the Missouri, 1698–1725* (Lincoln: University of Nebraska Press, 1988), 133.

25. Donald Jackson, ed., *The Journals of Zebulon Montgomery Pike: With Letters and Related Documents* (Norman: University of Oklahoma Press, 1966), 2:128; Henry Conway to Secretary of War, Lewis Cass, September 25, 1832, *Letters Received by the Office of Indian Affairs,* Osage Agency, 1824–1880. Record Group 75. M234 Washington, D.C.: National Archives, 1958).

26. Nasatir, *Before Lewis and Clark,* 52.

27. Rollings, *The Osage,* 149.

28. John, *Storms Brewed,* 254–55, 265.

29. Ibid., 317–18.

30. Ibid., 317–18. This trading post was called the Spanish Fort, although the Spanish had nothing to do with the fort save a failed attack on it by Colonel Diego Ortiz Parilla in 1759.

31. Ibid., 318.

32. John, *Storms Brewed,* 316–17; Smith, *Wichita Indians,* 26.

33. John, *Storms Brewed,* 388.

34. Mildred P. Mayhall, *The Kiowas,* 2d ed. (Norman: University of Oklahoma Press, 1971), 15.

35. For an excellent description of the peace "process," see Kavanagh, *Comanche Political History,* 146–48.

36. Ibid., 110–21.

37. Ibid., 148.

38. Din and Nasatir, *Imperial Osages,* 249.

39. See Dan L. Flores, ed., *Journal of an Indian Trader: Anthony Glass and the Texas Trading Frontier, 1790–1810* (College Station: Texas A&M University Press, 1985).

40. See Herbert E. Bolton, ed., *Athanase de Mézières and the Louisiana-Texas Frontier, 1768–1780,* 2 vols. (Cleveland: Arthur H. Clark Co., 1914); Nasatir, *Before Lewis and Clark;* Din and Nasatir, *Imperial Osages.*

41. Bolton, *Athanase de Mézières,* 1:167.

42. R. David Edmunds, *The Potawatomis: Keepers of the Fire* (Norman: University of Oklahoma Press, 1978), 157; James A. Clifton, *The Prairie People: Continuity and Change in Potawatomi Indian Culture, 1665–1965* (Lawrence: Regents Press of Kansas, 1977), 190.

43. See Edmunds, *Keepers of the Fire;* Clifton, *Prairie People;* Arrell M. Gibson, *The Kickapoos: Lords of the Middle Border* (Norman: University of Oklahoma Press, 1963); Clinton Alfred Weslager, *The Delaware Indians: A History* (New Brunswick, N.J.: Rutgers University Press, 1972).

44. Din and Nasatir, *Imperial Osages,* 234.

45. Ibid., 234.

46. William G. McLoughlin, *Cherokee Renascence in the New Republic* (1986; Princeton, N.J.: Princeton University Press, 1992), 56.

47. Din and Nasatir, *Imperial Osages*, 190, 234, 240.

48. In 1794 French trader Jean Baptiste Truteau wrote that attacks by the Mississippi tribes had driven the Little Osage from the Missouri River. Jean Baptiste Truteau, "Journal of Jean Baptiste Truteau on the Upper Missouri, 'Premier Partie,' June 7, 1794–March 26, 1795," *American Historical Review* 19 (January 1914): 303.

49. Jackson, *Journals of Zebulon Pike*, 2:32.

50. See Anthony F. C. Wallace, *Jefferson and the Indians: The Tragic Fate of the First Americans* (Cambridge, Mass.: Belknap Press of Harvard University Press, 1999), 206–40.

51. James P. Ronda, *Lewis and Clark among the Indians* (Lincoln: University of Nebraska Press, 1984), 6. Lewis wrote from the winter camp among the Mandans: "I think two villages on the Osage river might be prevailed on to move to the Arkansas, and the Kansas, higher up the Missouri, and thus leave a sufficient scope of country for the Shawnees, Delawares, Miamies and Kickapos." *American State Papers: Indian Affairs* (Washington, D.C.: Gales and Seaton, 1832), 1:707; Wallace, *Jefferson and the Indians*, 100.

52. Stephen E. Ambrose, *Undaunted Courage: Meriwether Lewis, Thomas Jefferson, and the Opening of the American West* (New York: Simon and Schuster for Touchstone Books, 1997), 133, 136–38.

53. Donald Jackson, ed., *Letters of the Lewis and Clark Expedition: With Related Documents, 1783–1854*, 2d ed. (Urbana: University of Illinois Press, 1978), 1:200.

54. Ora Brooks Peake, *A History of the United States Indian Factory System, 1795–1822* (Denver: Sage Books, 1954); Francis Paul Prucha, *The Great Father: The United States Government and the American Indians*, 2 vols. (1984; reprint, Lincoln: University of Nebraska Press, 1995), 123–34.

55. Jefferson to Harrison, February 27, 1803, *Jefferson's Works*, by Thomas Jefferson (Princeton, N.J.: Princeton University Press, 1950), 10:370.

56. Wilkinson to Dearborn, July 27, 1805, in *The Territorial Papers of the United States*, ed. Clarence E. Carter (Washington, D.C.: Government Printing Office, 1934–62), 13:170.

57. Meriwether Lewis, St. Louis, to Secretary of War Henry Dearborn, Washington, D.C., July 1, 1808, *Letters Received by the Secretary of War, Main Series;* Wallace, *Jefferson and the Indians*, 268–73; Kate L. Gregg, ed., *Westward with Dragoons: The Journal of William Clark on His Expedition to Establish Fort Osage, August 25 to September 22, 1808, a Description of the Wilderness, an Account of the Building of the Fort, Treaty-making with the Osages and Clark's Return to St. Louis* (Fulton, Mo.: Ovid Bell Press,

1937); "Treaty with the Osage, 1808," 7 Stat. 107 (1810), in *Indian Treaties, 1778–1883,* ed. Charles J. Kappler (Washington, D.C.: Government Printing Office, 1903; reprint, New York: Interland Publishing Inc., 1972), 1:95–99. This covered 32 million acres and constituted much of present-day Missouri and Arkansas.

58. McLoughlin, *Cherokee Renascence,* 152, 164.

59. "Treaty with the Osage, 1808," 1:95–99; "Treaty with the Osage, 1818," 7 Stat. 183 (1819), 1:167–68; "Treaty with the Osage, 1825," 7 Stat. 240 (1825), 1:217–21; "Treaty with the Osage, 1839," 7 Stat. 576 (1839), 1:525–27; all in Kappler, *Indian Treaties.*

60. Prucha, *Great Father,* 243–69.

61. "Treaty with the Cherokee, 1817," 7 Stat. 156 (1817), 1:140–44, Kappler, *Indian Treaties.*

62. Prucha, *Great Father,* 235.

63. Ed Bearss and Arrell M. Gibson, *Fort Smith: Little Gibraltar on the Arkansas* (Norman: University of Oklahoma Press, 1969), 13–14.

64. Ibid., 21–22.

65. See Thomas D. Hall, *Social Change in the Southwest, 1350–1880* (Lawrence: University Press of Kansas, 1989).

66. Kavanagh, *Comanche Political History,* 211; Thomas James, *Three Years among the Indians and Mexicans,* with an introduction by A. P. Nasatir (n.p., 1846; reprint, Lincoln: University of Nebraska Press, 1984), 85.

67. Kavanagh, *Comanche Political History,* 199; Grant Foreman, *Indians and Pioneers: The Story of the American Southwest before 1830,* rev. ed. (1936; reprint, Norman: University of Oklahoma Press, 1967), 188.

68. Kavanagh, *Comanche Political History,* 198, 215; Donald J. Berthrong, *The Southern Cheyennes* (1963; reprint, Norman: University of Oklahoma Press, 1986); Virginia Cole Trenholm, *The Arapahoes, Our People* (Norman: University of Oklahoma Press, 1970).

69. Brad Agnew, *Fort Gibson: Terminal on the Trail of Tears* (1980; reprint, Norman: University of Oklahoma Press, 1981), 20, 25.

Chapter 3

1. Milledoler, "Address, delivered to the Union Mission Family," 98.

2. Board of Managers, "Instructions to the Missionaries who are about proceeding to the Station on the Grand River, to be denominated Union," *American Missionary Register* 1 (July 1820): 23–24.

3. Berkhofer, *Salvation and the Savage,* 1.

4. Roger Finke and Rodney Stark, *The Churching of America, 1776–1990: Winners and Losers in our Religious Economy* (New Brunswick, N.J.: Rutgers University Press, 1992), 92–96.

5. Ibid., 99.

6. Phillips, *Protestant America*, 10.

7. Ibid., 15–16.

8. Berkhofer, *Salvation and the Savage*, 3.

9. Phillips, *Protestant America*, 20–21, 49–50.

10. Berkhofer, *Salvation and the Savage*, 4–6; Axtell, *Invasion Within*, 272.

11. Robert F. Berkhofer Jr., *The White Man's Indian: Images of the American Indian from Columbus to the Present* (New York: Alfred A. Knopf, 1978), 143–45.

12. Prucha, *Great Father*, 151.

13. "Address of the Board of Managers of the United Foreign Missionary Society, July 28, 1817," United Foreign Missionary Society Papers, August 1817, 6; Hope Holway, "Union Mission, 1826–1837," *Chronicles of Oklahoma* 40 (winter 1962–63): 355.

14. Rev. Philip Milledoler, "Annual Report, May 10, 1820," United Foreign Missionary Society Papers, May 1820, 131–45; Epaphras Chapman and Job P. Vinall, "Third Report of the United Foreign Missionary Society," *American Missionary Register* 1 (July 1820): 16.

15. Chapman and Vinall, "Third Report," 17.

16. Ibid., 18.

17. Ibid.

18. William G. McLoughlin, *Cherokees and Missionaries, 1789–1839* (New Haven, Conn.: Yale University Press, 1984), 327.

19. Vinall would later die at Fort Smith. Chapman and Vinall, "Third Report," 18.

20. Milledoler, "Annual Report," 131–45; Chapman and Vinall, "Third Report," 19.

21. Milledoler, "Annual Report," 150.

22. Milledoler, "Annual Report," 125; Chapman and Vinall, "Third Report," 20.

23. Milledoler, "Address, delivered to the Union Mission Family," 95–101.

24. "[Letter to] Hon. J. C. Calhoun, March 14, 1821," United Foreign Missionary Society Papers, April 1821, 246.

25. Vaill and Chapman, "Extracts from the Journal of the Union Mission," 91.

26. McKenney, "Second Mission Family," 30.

27. Pierre Chouteau to Secretary of War, May 20, 1813; Frederick Bates, Governor, to Secretary of War, March 4, 1813; Benjamin Howard, Governor, to Secretary of War, March 1813, all in *Letters Received by the Secretary of War, Unregistered Series, 1789–1861*.

28. Robert Lenox, Peter Wilson, Philip Milledoler, Z. Lewis, Pascal N. Strong, and William Wilson, "[Talk delivered] To the Chief, the Counsellor,

and the principal Warrior of the Osages of the Missouri, now at Washington," *American Missionary Register* 1 (July 1820): 30.

29. Philip Milledoler and Sans Nerf, "Interview [Talk] with Indian Chiefs," *American Missionary Register* 1 (July 1820): 32–33.

30. Ibid., 31.

31. Ibid.

32. Dolly E. Hoyt, "Extracts from the Journal of the Union Mission," *American Missionary Register* 1 (May 1821): 434–36.

33. "Extracts from the Journal of the Union Mission," *American Missionary Register* 1 (June 1821): 473.

34. "Extracts from the Journal of the Union Mission," 475–76; Epaphras Chapman, "Extract from Mr. Chapman's Journal," *American Missionary Register* 2 (November 1821): 182.

35. Mr. Redfield, "Extracts of Private Letters from Members of the Union, Mission," *American Missionary Register* 1 (May 1821): 437.

36. Dr. Palmer, "Union Mission [Correspondence]: Doctor Palmer to his Brother," *American Missionary Register* 2 (August 1821): 59.

37. Ibid.

38. Milledoler, Lewis, and Wilson, "Fourth Report," 420.

39. Ibid., 421.

40. Ibid.

41. Ibid.

42. Board of Managers, "Instructions to the Members of the Mission Family," 324.

43. William E. Foley and C. David Rice, *The First Chouteaus: River Barons of Early St. Louis* (Urbana: University of Illinois Press, 1983), 45, 67.

44. "Journal of the Great Osage Mission," *American Missionary Register* 2 (April 1822): 402–6.

45. "Journal of the [Great Osage] Mission," *American Missionary Register* 2 (June 1822): 492–93.

Chapter 4

1. Mr. Dodge, "Osages: Report of the Station at Harmony, June 1st, 1830," *Missionary Herald* 27 (February 1831): 46.

2. *American State Papers: Indian Affairs*, 4:707–8.

3. Carl H. Chapman and Eleanor F. Chapman, *Indians and Archaeology of Missouri*, rev. ed. (Columbia: University of Missouri Press, 1983), 90–92.

4. William Redfield to "his friend," September 26, 1821: "I was awakened in the morning by cries of the Osages, in every direction to the Great Spirit. . . . I was informed that they always pray for that which concerns

them most at the time. In the midst of their prayers, they black their faces, but wash again before they eat." "United Foreign Missionary Society [Letters]," *American Missionary Register* 2 (December 1821): 223.

5. Francis La Flesche, *War Ceremony and Peace Ceremony of the Osage Indians,* Smithsonian Institution, Bureau of American Ethnology Bulletin 101 (Washington, D.C.: Government Printing Office, 1939), 3–6.

6. Francis La Flesche, "The Osage Tribe: Rite of the Chiefs; Sayings of the Ancient Men," Bureau of American Ethnology, *Thirty-sixth Annual Report, 1914–1915* (Washington, D.C.: Government Printing Office, 1921), 66; John Joseph Mathews, *The Osages: Children of the Middle Waters* (1961; reprint, Norman: University of Oklahoma Press, 1982), 76.

7. Mathews, *Osages,* 144–47.

8. James Mooney, "Myths of the Cherokee and Sacred Formulas of the Cherokee," Bureau of American Ethnology, *Nineteenth Annual Report, 1897–1898* (Washington, D.C.: Government Printing Office, 1900), 390–91.

9. John Phillip Reid, *A Better Kind of Hatchet: Law, Trade, and Diplomacy in the Cherokee Nation during the Early Years of European Contact* (University Park: Pennsylvania State University Press, 1976), 8–9. Cherokee notions of blood revenge were especially strong among the more conservative and traditional Cherokee, and these were the Cherokee who were moving to the Ozarks in the late eighteenth and early nineteenth centuries.

10. William Clark to George Sibley, factor at Fort Osage Factory, November 11, 1817, Sibley Papers (St. Louis: Missouri Historical Society); Foreman, *Indians and Pioneers,* 51–52.

11. "Extracts from the Journal: Visit from the Principal Chief, April 4, 1821," *American Missionary Register* 2 (October 1821): 147.

12. "Journal of the [Union] Mission: Indian Murder, June 24, 1821," *American Missionary Register* 2 (January 1822): 269–70.

13. Osage Agent Richard Graham, St. Louis, to Secretary of War John C. Calhoun, Washington, D.C., December 28, 1821, Richard Graham Papers, Missouri Historical Society, St. Louis; "Union Mission: Journal for the Month of October 1821," *American Missionary Register* 2 (March 1822): 349–50.

14. Bradford to Calhoun, November 18, 1821, Carter, *Territorial Papers,* 19:355–56.

15. James H. Merrell, *Into the American Woods: Negotiators on the Pennsylvania Frontier* (New York: W. W. Norton and Co., 1999), 57.

16. "Union Mission: Extracts from the Journal, February 23, 1821," *American Missionary Register* 2 (September 1821): 114.

17. "Union Mission: Extracts from the Journal, March 7, 1821," 114.

18. "[UFMS] Board Meeting, May 5, 1823: Great Osage Mission," United Foreign Missionary Society Papers, May 1823, 153.

19. "Union Mission: Journal for the Months of April and May, 1822, April 15, 1822," *American Missionary Register* 3 (October 1822): 139.

20. Mr. Otis Sprague, "[Letter] to his Brother in Brooklyn, August 20, 1821," *American Missionary Register* 2 (January 1822): 276; Rev. Mr. Montgomery, "Great Osage Mission: Extracts of Letters, December 3, 1821," *American Missionary Register* 2 (March 1822): 353; Rev. E. Chapman, "Union Mission: [Letter] to the Domestic Secretary, March 4, 1822," *American Missionary Register* 2 (June 1822): 489; Graves, *Osage Missions,* 23.

21. "An attempt has been made by Mr [sic] Williams, the interpreter, to translate a few chapters of Scripture into the Osage. With how much success and correctness, we are scarcely prepared to determine. We would hope, however, it is good." "Great Osage Mission: Journal for June and July, 1823; June 14, 1823," *American Missionary Register* 4 (December 1823): 372.

22. "Extracts from the Journal: Want of labourers, April 4, 1821," *American Missionary Register* 2 (October 1821): 147–48.

23. "Annual Report to the Secretary of War: Union, Osage Nation, October 1, 1823," *American Missionary Register* 5 (March 1824): 79.

24. Montgomery, "Extracts of Letters, December 3, 1821," 351.

25. Mr. Z. Lewis, "Sixth Report of the United Foreign Missionary Society: Resources, and Conclusion," *American Missionary Register* 4 (June 1823): 175.

26. McLoughlin, *Cherokees and Missionaries,* 27.

27. "George Sibley to Thomas L. McKenney, October 1, 1820," *Missouri Historical Review* 9 (October 1914–July 1915): 48.

28. La Flesche, *War Ceremony,* 28.

29. "Rev. Mr. Pixley's Journal: Indian Worship," *American Missionary Register* 5 (April 1824): 112.

Chapter 5

1. William B. Montgomery, "Osages: Extract from a Letter of Mr. Montgomery, Dated Union, December 27, 1831," *Missionary Herald* 28 (August 1832): 258.

2. Foreman, *Indians and Pioneers,* 47–48.

3. Lovely's Purchase was made in 1816, but since it was an unauthorized acquisition the federal government had to renegotiate the cession in 1818. Claremore insisted that he had only consented to give a small parcel of land, and that the Osage intended to give it to whites, not Cherokee. Crawford to Clark et al., September 17, 1816, Carter, *Territorial Papers* 15:173; Clark to Calhoun, October 1818, Carter, *Territorial Papers,* 15:454–55.

4. W. Edwin Hemphill, ed., *The Papers of John C. Calhoun,* vol. 5, 1820–21 (Columbia: University of South Carolina Press, South Carolina Department of Archives and History, and South Caroliniana Society, 1971), 167–68.

5. Montgomery, "Extracts of Letters, December 3, 1821," 351–52.

6. "Journal of the [Harmony] Mission: For the Month of February; February 12, 1822," *American Missionary Register* 3 (August 1822): 49.

7. Rev. Nathaniel Dodge, Superintendent of the Harmony Mission, to Secretary of the United Foreign Missionary Society, November 4, 1822: "The Indians have left their village in our neighbourhood, and it is expected they will settle at a distance of about seventy miles from our establishment." "Great Osage Mission: Extracts of Letters," *American Missionary Register* 4 (February 1823): 43.

8. Montgomery, "Osages: Extract from a Letter," 258.

9. Ibid.

10. "Union Mission: Extracts of Letters, March 31, 1823," *American Missionary Register* 4 (August 1823): 237.

11. Berkhofer, *Salvation and the Savage,* 70–83.

12. "Journal of the [Great Osage] Mission: Arrival of Indian Chiefs, August 11–12, 1821," *American Missionary Register* 2 (June 1822): 492–93.

13. Claremore said, "I wish that the war was over, that I might send my children there also." William Vaill, "Union Mission: Extract of Letters, December 26, 1821," *American Missionary Register* 2 (April 1822): 399–400.

14. Milledoler and Lewis, "Fifth Report of the United Foreign Missionary Society," 466.

15. "Union Mission: Journal of the Mission; Arrival of Indian Children, August 27, 1821," *American Missionary Register* 2 (January 1822): 273.

16. Osage Agent Richard Graham, St. Louis, to Secretary of War John C. Calhoun, Washington, D.C., December 28, 1821, Graham Papers.

17. Bradford to Calhoun, November 18, 1821, Carter, *Territorial Papers,* 19:355–56.

18. Milledoler and Lewis, "Fifth Report of the United Foreign Missionary Society," 473–74.

19. Milledoler and Lewis, "Fifth Report of the United Foreign Missionary Society," 474; Benton Pixley, "Great Osage Mission: Extracts of Letters, January 17, 1822," *American Missionary Register* 2 (May 1822): 434–35.

20. Nathaniel Dodge, "Great Osage Mission: Extracts of Letters, February 1, 1822," *American Missionary Register* 2 (May 1822): 433.

21. "Union Mission: Journal for the Months of January and February, 1823, Increase of the School, February 14, 1823," *American Missionary Register* 4 (July 1823): 203.

22. McLoughlin, *Cherokees and Missionaries,* 132.

23. "To stimulate our boys to exertion, we have this day introduced the use of tickets, which we intend to redeem with small books and other articles." "Extracts from the Journal for the Month of September, 1822: Affecting Interview, September 11, 1822," *American Missionary Register* 4

(February 1823): 41; Miss [Susan] Comstock, "Great Osage Mission: Extracts of Letters, January 17, 1822," *American Missionary Register* 2 (May 1822): 437; Berkhofer, *Salvation and the Savage*, 24–25.

24. Note that her working was mentioned before her reading. "Union Mission: Journal for the Months of January and February 1823, Spirit of religious inquiry among the Indians, January, 31, 1823," *American Missionary Register* 4 (July 1823): 203.

25. "Great Osage Mission: Extract of Letters, Regulations for the Indian Children, March 26, 1822," *American Missionary Register* 3 (September 1822): 94.

26. "Union Mission: Journal for the Months of April and May, 1822," *American Missionary Register* 3 (October 1822): 142.

27. "Union Mission: Journal for the Months of October and November, 1822, Indian Mourning, October 23, 1822," *American Missionary Register* 4 (May 1823): 136.

28. "The girl [one who had fled the school], in order to excuse herself, said she had been whipped." "Union Mission [Journal]: Desertion of the Indian woman and one of the children, September 17, 1821," *American Missionary Register* 2 (February 1822): 328; "Thomas Montgomery, one of our Indian boys, went off this evening, having been reproved in consequence of misconduct in school." "Great Osage Mission: Journal for the Month of March, 1822, First Marriage among the Osages, March 21, 1822," *American Missionary Register* 3 (September 1822): 94.

29. See the following tables: "Record of Heathen Youth, in the Mission School at Harmony, April 12, 1824," *American Missionary Register* 5 (July 1824): 212; "Report of the School at Union Mission, Osage Nation, September 21, 1824," *American Missionary Register* 6 (February 1825): 47; "Harmony Mission [Table]," *American Missionary Register* 6 (September 1825): 273–74; "Table of Missions, Stations, Missionaries, Schools and Churches," *Missionary Herald* 29 (January 1833): 14; "Table of Stations, Missionaries, Churches, and Schools," *Missionary Herald* 31 (January 1835): 31.

30. See Charles Hudson, *The Southeastern Indians* (Knoxville: University of Tennessee Press, 1976), 260. Although Hudson is writing about the Cherokee, the division of labor is almost identical to that of the early Osage.

31. See "Invoice of Boat and Cargo forwarded by the Board of Agency at Cincinnati, on the 30th of March, 1824, to the Union Mission," *American Missionary Register* 5 (June 1824): 183.

32. Otis Sprague, "Great Osage Mission: Mr. Sprague to his Brother, no date," *American Missionary Register* 2 (February 1822): 330; Mr. Newton, "Great Osage Mission: [Letter] to his friend, January 20, 1822," *American Missionary Register* 2 (June 1822): 492.

33. "Union Mission: Journal for the Month of April, 1823, Indian Farmer, no date," *American Missionary Register* 4 (September 1823): 274.

34. "Union Mission: Journal of the Mission for the Month of May, Indian Labourers, May 5, 1823," *American Missionary Register* 4 (December 1823): 369.

35. "Union Mission: Extract of Letters," *American Missionary Register* 5 (July 1824): 206–9.

36. "Union Mission: Journal for June and July, 1824, Various Notices, July 31, 1824," *American Missionary Journal* 5 (November 1824): 332.

37. Rev. William F. Vaill, "Journal for August, 1824, State and Progress of the Indian Settlement," *American Missionary Register* 5 (December 1824): 363.

38. See Daniel C. Swan, "Locality as a Factor in the Band Organization of the Osage Indians: A Quantitative Analysis," *Occasional Papers Series* 8 (Chicago, Ill.: Newberry Library, Center for the History of the American Indian, 1987), 1–21; Rollings, *The Osage*, 258–59.

39. "Union Mission: Journal for the Month of April, 1823, Indian Farmer, April 25, 1823," *American Missionary Register* 4 (September 1823): 274; "Union Mission: Civil Government established at Hopefield, May 13, 1825," *American Missionary Register* 6 (September 1825): 271–72; "Meineh Per-she is evidently listening to our advice, and is decidedly doing better than any Chief with whom we are acquainted." "Union Mission: Journal for July and August, 1825, Lord's Day, August 14, 1825," *American Missionary Register* 6 (November 1825): 336.

40. During meeting at Fort Gibson, "Claremore made bold to state some grievances against the mission, particularly in reference to the settlement of the Indians at Hopefields." "Journal of the Union Mission, for January and February, 1825, Great National Council.—Indians consent to Remove, January 29, 1825," *American Missionary Register* 6 (July 1825): 215.

41. Rev. Mr. Chapman, "Missionary Intelligence: Union Mission, Hopefield, July 2, 1824," *American Missionary Register* 6 (January 1825): 23–24.

42. Dr. Marcus Palmer, "Union Branch of the Mission," *Missionary Herald* 23 (May 1827): 149. "During the month of April [1826], the school continued to increase, notwithstanding that the Indians were most of the time in great fear. The settlers at Hopefield were several times put to flight at a mere shadow." Palmer, "Union Branch," 148.

43. "Much of their corn, during the last winter, has either been stolen or eaten up by the crowd of wild Indians, that have thronged about them, to live on the fruit of their industry." "Journal of the Union Mission, Gov. M'Nair's Visit to Hopefields, February 3, 1825," *American Missionary Register* 6 (July 1825): 216.

44. Chapman, "Missionary Intelligence," 24.

45. Agnew, *Fort Gibson*, 52.

46. See Carter, *Territorial Papers*, vols. 13–21.

47. Kavanagh, *Comanche Political History*, 198, 215; Berthrong, *Southern Cheyennes;* Trenholm, *Arapahoes.*

48. Foreman, *Indians and Pioneers*, 188.

49. See Hall, *Social Change in the Southwest.*

50. "The Osage came in crowds, bringing their most important stuffs to deposit with us while they go on their summer hunt." "Great Osage [Journal]: The Indians prepare for their Summer Hunt, May 15, 1822," *American Missionary Register* 3 (October 1822): 147.

51. "Union Mission: Journal for the Month of April, 1823, Indian Medical Remedy, no date," *American Missionary Register* 4 (September 1823): 273.

52. Miss Woolley, "Great Osage Mission: Extract of a letter to her mother, September 23, 1822," *American Missionary Register* 3 (December 1822): 211.

53. "[N]ow the Osages bring forward great numbers of their axes, guns, &c. to be mended." "Union Mission: Journal for the Months of April and May, 1822, The Indians manufacturing Salt, April 26, 1822," *American Missionary Register* 3 (October 1822): 140.

54. "The Indians flock around us in crowds to-day, begging for something to eat. We cannot support them, and to deny them wholly would probably destroy our object among them." "Great Osage [Journal]: Day of Fasting, May 10, 1822," *American Missionary Register* 3 (October 1822): 147.

55. Nathaniel Philbrook was found drowned and shot near the mouth of the Neosho River in May 1824. Foreman, *Indians and Pioneers*, 167–68.

56. Rollings, *The Osage*, 244–53.

57. "Union Mission: Journal for the Months of January and February, 1823, Various Notices, January 14, 1823," *American Missionary Register* 4 (July 1823): 202.

58. Agnew, *Fort Gibson*, 29.

59. "The Chiefs having requested me to be present on the occasion, I went with cheerfulness, yet with doubts and fears respecting any good result of the interview." Rev. William F. Vaill, "Union: Extracts of Letters, June 11, 1824," *American Missionary Register* 5 (October 1824): 301; "Union Mission: Journal for June and July, 1824, The Great Indian, 10 June 1824," *American Missionary Register* 5 (November 1824): 330.

60. Skitok was known to whites as Mad Buffalo. He was taken to Little Rock, where he was tried and convicted of murder. He was sentenced to death, but a last-minute pardon by President Adams stopped his execution. He was released in May 1825 and returned to his father's village. See Vaill,

"Extracts of Letters, June 11, 1824," 304; *Little Rock Arkansas Gazette,* October 19, 1824; October 26, 1824; December 21, 1824; December 28, 1824; April 5, 1825; May 3, 1825.

61. "Indians consent to Remove, January 29, 1825," 215.

62. "[T]here is a culpable want of economy in the management of their concerns.—After a comfortable outfit and the expenditure of $14,847 upon the establishment of Harmony . . . ." "[UFMS] Committee Meeting, July 4, 1825," United Foreign Missionary Society Papers, July 1825, 128.

63. Jeremiah Evarts, Boston, to Nathaniel Dodge, Harmony Mission, September 6, 1828, "American Board of Commissioners for Foreign Missions Letterbook," 549, American Board of Commissioners for Foreign Missions Papers, Houghton Library, Harvard University, Cambridge, Mass.

64. "Union Mission: Journal for April [1825], April 9, 1825," *American Missionary Register* 6 (August 1825): 243.

65. McLoughlin, *Cherokees and Missionaries,* 240; Agnew, *Fort Gibson,* 61.

66. Prucha, *Great Father,* 186–213.

67. Ibid.

68. In June 1831 there were sixty-five students at the Union school; thirteen Osage, twenty-five Creek, sixteen Cherokee, and eleven white. "Osages: Report of the Station at Union, June 1, 1831," *Missionary Herald* 27 (October 1831): 321.

69. Benton Pixley, Osage Country, to James Barbour, Secretary of War, Washington, D.C., April 7, 1828; Benton Pixley, Osage Country, to Thomas McKenney, Superintendent of Indian Affairs, Washington, D.C., August 20, 1828; John Hamtramck, Osage Agency, to William Clark, Superintendent of Indian Affairs, St. Louis, February 18, 1829, all in *Letters Received by the Office of Indian Affairs, 1824–1881.*

70. See Robert A. Glenn, "The Osage War," *Missouri Historical Review* 14 (January 1920): 201–10; see also Roy Godsey, "The Osage War, 1837," *Missouri Historical Review* 20 (October 1925): 96–100.

71. Evarts to Dodge, September 6, 1828, "American Board of Commissioners for Foreign Missions Letterbook," 548–52.

72. Conway to Cass, September 4, 1832; September 25, 1832, *Letters Received by the Office of Indian Affairs, 1824–1881.* Conway explained that it was impossible to collect all the Osage in August, and that he was only able to vaccinate 2,177 Osage.

73. Alfred W. Crosby Jr., "Virgin Soil Epidemics as a Factor in the Aboriginal Depopulation in America," *William and Mary Quarterly,* 3d ser., 33 (April 1976): 289–99.

74. Mr. Redfield, "Osages: Obituary Notice of the Rev. William B. Montgomery and his Wife," *Missionary Herald* 30 (December 1834): 452;

"Mission to the Osages," *Missionary Herald* 32 (January 1836): 24; John Francis McDermott, ed., *Tixier's Travels on the Osage Prairies*, trans. Albert J. Salvan (1940; reprint, Norman: University of Oklahoma Press, 1968), 140; Grant Foreman, *Advancing the Frontier, 1830–1860* (1933; reprint, Norman: University of Oklahoma Press, 1968), 121, 133, 143.

75. "Mission to the Osage," 24.

76. "Mission to the Osage," 24; Foreman, *Advancing the Frontier*, 133, 143.

77. Graves, *Osage Missions*, 206.

78. A. Redfield, "Osages: August 25, 1834," *Missionary Herald* 30 (December 1834): 452–53; "Annual Report: Mission to the Osages," *Missionary Herald* 32 (January 1836): 24.

79. Conway to Cass, September 4, 1832; September 25, 1832, *Letters Received by the Office of Indian Affairs, 1824–1881*.

80. Graves, *Osage Missions*, 197–210; Carolyn Thomas Foreman, "Hopefield Mission in Osage Nation, 1823–1837," *Chronicles of Oklahoma* 28 (summer 1950): 203–4.

81. Graves, *Osage Missions*, 201–6; "Annual Report: Mission to the Osages," 25.

82. Mr. Dodge, "Extracts from a Communication of Mr. Dodge, Osage Nation, June 18, 1832: View of the Last Quarter, Wednesday, [June] 25," *Missionary Herald* 28 (September 1832): 291.

83. "Osages: Journal of Mr. Vaill; Indian Scalp-Dance, May 15," *Missionary Herald* 29 (October 1833): 370.

84. "Journal for April [1825], April 9, 1825," 243.

85. "Journal of the Union Mission, Idolatry of the Osages," *American Missionary Register* 6 (July 1825): 216.

86. James Mooney, "Calendar History of the Kiowa Indians," Bureau of American Ethnology, *Seventeenth Annual Report, 1895–1896* (Washington, D.C.: Government Printing Office, 1898): 169–70, 257–63; Mayhall, *Kiowas*, 69, 169–70.

87. Vaill was mistaken about the attack being on the Pawnee. The Osage were celebrating their victory over an undefended Kiowa village at Cut Throat Gap. "Osages: Journal of Mr. Vaill; Excultation occasioned by the Slaughter of the Pawnees," *Missionary Herald* 29 (October 1833): 367.

88. "Idolatry of the Osages," 217.

89. "Osages: Extract from a Letter of Mr. Montgomery, dated Union, Dec. 27, 1831," *Missionary Herald* 28 (August 1832): 257.

90. Mr. Vaill, "Osages: Preaching Tour among the Osage Villages," *Missionary Herald* 27 (September 1831): 288.

91. "Idolatry of the Osages," 217.

92. Berkhofer, *Salvation and the Savage*, 32.

93. "Annual Report: Mission to the Osages," *Missionary Herald* 31 (January 1835): 26.

94. David Greene, Boston, to William C. Requa, Hopefield, March 25, 1836, "American Board of Commissioners for Foreign Missions Letterbook," 497–98.

95. "Great Osage Mission," *American Missionary Register* 4 (June 1823): 164; Graves, *Osage Missions,* 130.

96. Graves, *Osage Missions,* 209.

97. "Osages: Extracts from the Report of the Union Station for the Year Ending June 1, 1832," *Missionary Herald* 28 (November 1832): 360.

Chapter 6

1. Graves, *Osage Missions,* 174.

2. La Flesche, *War Ceremony,* 3–143.

3. Rev. William B. Montgomery was told about it by one of the elders: "They relate that a great while ago, an Osage boy killed a bird with an arrow, and after picking off the feathers, showed it to some old men, and inquired whether it was a good thing to kill birds. The old men approved of what he had done and encouraged him to proceed. They further told him, there were men whom they should kill in like manner, and advised that the young men should adopt the disposition of the voracious birds and animals, and carry their skins with them when they went to war." "Mr. Montgomery's Journal, from Union to Harmony: Interview with an intelligent Osage, May 11, 1824," *American Missionary Register* 5 (September 1824): 274.

4. "Idolatry of the Osages," 216–17.

5. La Flesche, *War Ceremony,* 3–6; Rollings, *The Osage,* 30.

6. See McDermott, *Tixier's Travels.* While Tixier's descriptions are detailed, one must be careful with his interpretations of events and details.

7. La Flesche, *War Ceremony,* 53–57.

8. McDermott, *Tixier's Travels,* 216–18.

9. Mooney, "Calendar History of the Kiowa," 169–70, 257–63; Mayhall, *Kiowas,* 169–70.

10. McDermott, *Tixier's Travels,* 150–54; Kavanagh, *Comanche Political History,* 281, 317.

11. In 1833, in an attempt to establish peace in Indian Territory, Congress created a regiment of dragoons and sent them to Fort Gibson in the winter of 1833–34. In June 1834 the dragoons, under the command of General Henry Leavenworth, left Fort Gibson and marched west to meet and make peace with the Southern Plains tribes. The expedition had several individuals who would later assume vital roles in the history of

the United States: Colonel Henry Dodge, Colonel Stephen Watts Kearny, and Lieutenant Jefferson Davis. Famed western artist George Catlin also traveled with the dragoons and painted some of the first paintings of the Comanche, Wichita, and Kiowa people. This first dragoon expedition, although it established friendly contact with the Southern Plaines tribes, was plagued with illness, and many, including General Leavenworth, died in the course of that summer's expedition. Grant Foreman, *Pioneer Days in the Early Southwest* (Cleveland: Arthur H. Clark, 1926; reprint, Lincoln: University of Nebraska Press, 1994), 125.

12. "Treaty with the Comanche, etc., 1835," 7 Stat. 474 (1836), Kappler, *Indian Treaties,* 1:435–39.

13. David La Vere, *Contrary Neighbors: Southern Plains and Removed Indians in Indian Territory* (Norman: University of Oklahoma Press, 2000), 80–83.

14. See La Vere, *Contrary Neighbors.*

15. Foreman, *Advancing the Frontier,* 205–16; Grant Foreman, ed., *A Traveler in Indian Territory: The Journal of Ethan Allen Hitchcock, Late Major-General in the United States Army,* foreword by Michael D. Green (Cedar Rapids, Iowa: Torch Press, 1930; reprint, Norman: University of Oklahoma Press, 1996), 38.

16. Foreman, *Advancing the Frontier,* 229.

17. John M. Richardson to Commissioner of Indian Affairs, February 25, 1848, in Foreman, *Advancing the Frontier,* 242, n. 9.

18. James R. Christianson, "A Study of Osage History prior to 1876," (Ph.D. diss., University of Kansas, 1968), 203.

19. Report of Commissioner of Indian Affairs for 1854, in Foreman, *Advancing the Frontier,* 90, 279, n. 13.

20. Berthrong, *Southern Cheyennes,* 359–60.

21. Ibid.

22. Clifton, *Prairie People,* 361; Kavanagh, *Comanche Political History,* 351.

23. Clifton, *Prairie People,* 361.

24. McDermott, *Tixier's Travels,* 128–29; Bailey, *Osage and the Invisible World,* 65; Rollings, *The Osage,* 36.

25. Thomas L. McKenney, "Letter from the Superintendent of Indian Trade," *American Missionary Register* 1 (August 1820): 56.

26. Col. T. L. McKenney, "Second Mission Family, July 5, 1820," *American Missionary Register* 1 (July 1820): 29–30.

27. Christianson, "Study of Osage History," 165.

28. Ibid., 167.

29. James Miller, "Miscellanies: The Arkansas Territory, September 2, 1820," *American Missionary Register* 1 (January 1821): 287.

30. Rev. William F. Vaill, "Union Mission: Extract of Letters, June 11, 1821," *American Missionary Register* 2 (September 1821): 107.

31. Rev. William F. Vaill, "Osage Indians: Name and Character," *Missionary Herald* 22 (September 1826): 268.

32. Requa, "Mission to the Osages," 23.

33. Robert Calloway, Osage Sub-agency, to T. Hartley Crawford, Washington, D.C., May 2, 1842, *Letters Received by the Office of Indian Affairs, 1824–1881.*

34. Christianson, "Study of Osage History," 150.

35. Ibid., 194.

Chapter 7

1. Rev. Father Eugene Michaud, à grand-vicaire du diocèse de Chambéry, juillet 1823, *Annales de la Propagation de la Foi* 5 (March 1825): 56.

2. Gilbert J. Garraghan, *Chapters in Frontier History: Research Studies in the Making of the West* (Milwaukee, Wisc.: Bruce Publishing Co., 1934), 58.

3. Norall, *Bourgmont,* 42, 47, 108; Gilbert Garraghan, "Fort Orleans of the Missoury," *Missouri Historical Review* 35 (April 1941): 373–84; Garraghan, *Chapters in Frontier History,* 67; Henri Folmer, "Etienne Veniard de Bourgmond in the Missouri Country," *Missouri Historical Review* 36 (April 1942): 279–98.

4. Garraghan, *Chapters in Frontier History,* 66–67.

5. Richard N. Ellis and Charlie R. Steen, eds., "An Indian Delegation in France, 1725," trans. Charlie R. Steen, *Journal of Illinois State Historical Society* 67 (September 1974): 401.

6. Garraghan, *Chapters in Frontier History,* 66–67.

7. Morris Arnold, *Unequal Laws unto a Savage Race: European Legal Traditions in Arkansas, 1686–1836* (Fayetteville: University of Arkansas Press, 1985), 5.

8. Garraghan, *Jesuits of the Middle United States,* 3:7.

9. Ibid., 1:43.

10. "[Q]u'il y ferait beaucoup de bien, et qu'il jetterait de l'eau sur la tête de plusieurs." Rev. Eugene Michaud, à grand-vicaire du diocèse de Chambéry, juillet 1823, *Annales de la Propagation de la Foi* 5 (March 1825): 55–59.

11. Ibid.

12. "La vue du crucifix les frappa d'étonnement; ils regardaient avec des yeux avides et attendris." Ibid., 56.

13. Ibid.

14. For the remainder of this chapter, numbers in parentheses in the text, unless otherwise indicated, will refer to the cited volume and page number in Garraghan, *Jesuits of the Middle United States*.

15. "Treaty with the Osage, 1822," 7 Stat., 222 (1823), Kappler, *Indian Treaties*, 1:201–2.

16. The records do not include any surnames for the slaves. Garraghan, *Jesuits of the Middle United States*, 1:79.

17. Rothensteiner, "Early Missionary Efforts," 86.

18. Ibid.

19. Joseph B. Herring, "Kenekuk, the Kickapoo Prophet: Acculturation without Assimilation," *American Indian Quarterly* 9 (summer 1985): 295–307.

20. Garraghan, *Jesuits of the Middle United States*, 1:389; see Tanis C. Thorne, *The Many Hands of My Relations: French and Indians on the Lower Missouri* (Columbia: University of Missouri Press, 1996).

21. Pahusca, Ticho-honga, Cho-ne-ksais, Wa-ma-ka Wachis, Haraita, Osage Sub-Agency, to John Tyler, President of the United States, Washington, D.C., June 14, 1843, *Letters Received by the Office of Indian Affairs, 1824–1881*.

22. Felix L. Verreydt, "Memoirs of Felix L. Verreydt, S.J. (1874)," transcription, Midwest Jesuit Archives, St. Louis, Missouri, 73–75.

23. "Osage Petition," August 30, 1842, *Letters Received by the Office of Indian Affairs, 1824–1881*. This letter contains the remarks of the chiefs recounting their feelings in 1839, and while it seems they maintain those feelings about the missionaries, they are brought up in the context of praising the agent for not pressing them on the issue of establishing a school in 1842.

Chapter 8

1. Father Paul Mary Ponziglione, "Origin of the Osage Mission," *Woodstock Letters* 6 (1877): 141–47.

2. Father Paul Mary Ponziglione, "Western Missions Journal No. 2," Midwest Jesuit Archives, St. Louis, Missouri, III Osage Mission, 165, March 14, 1870, 19–27.

3. Ponziglione, "Western Missions Journals No. 2," 26.

4. Father Paul M. Ponziglione, "Western Missions Journal No. 3," Midwest Jesuit Archives, St. Louis, Missouri, III Osage Mission, 166, January 16, 1871, 1.

5. Ponziglione, "Western Missions Journal No. 3," 37.

6. Ponziglione, "Father John Schoenmakers," *Woodstock Letters* 12 (1883): 339–40.

7. Isaac T. Gibson, Osage Agency I.T., to Edward P. Smith, Commissioner of Indian Affairs, Washington, D.C., April 30, 1875, *Letters Received by the Office of Indian Affairs, 1824–1881.*

8. Augustin C. Wand, *The Jesuits in Territorial Kansas, 1827–1861* (St. Marys, Kans.: St. Marys Star, 1962), 37; 1875 Statistical Report, *Letters Received by the Office of Indian Affairs, 1824–1881.* Father Ponziglione's earlier count of seven thousand Osage is incorrect.

9. Father Paul Mary Ponziglione, "The Annals of the Mission of Saint Francis of Hieronymus, by the Fathers of the Society of the Jesuits Among the Indians of North America Called the Osage," trans. Gussie Tanenhaus, Midwest Jesuit Archives, St. Louis, Missouri, 184.

10. Ponziglione, "Kansas: Letter from Father Ponziglione, July 2, 1883," *Woodstock Letters* 12 (1883): 297.

11. Ibid.

12. Ibid.

13. Ibid.

14. "The Brothers of the church agreed to hold communion once in two months . . . and to attend the lecture preparatory to communion on the Friday preceding." "Union Mission: Journal for the Month of Oct. 1821, October 21, 1821," *American Missionary Register* 2 (March 1822): 350.

15. See Johnson, *Why Do Catholics Do That?*, xiii.

16. La Flesche, *War Ceremony*, 22; Bailey, *Osage and the Invisible World*, 111–12.

17. La Flesche, *War Ceremony*, 204; Bailey, *Osage and the Invisible World*, 53–54.

18. Johnson, *Why Do Catholics Do That?*, 214–15.

19. Ponziglione, "Kansas: Letter from Father Ponziglione, July 1, 1882," *Woodstock Letters* 11 (1882): 283.

20. Ibid., 283–85.

21. Ibid., 285.

22. Ibid., 285.

23. La Flesche, *War Ceremony*, 213.

24. Robert L. Hall, *An Archaeology of the Soul: North American Indian Belief and Ritual* (Urbana: University of Illinois Press, 1997), 14, 15, 29.

25. Ponziglione, "*Western Missions Journal No. 3*," 16, 33.

26. Clifton, *Prairie People*, 361; Kavanagh, *Comanche Political History*, 351.

27. "Treaty with the Comanche, Kiowa, and Apache, 1853," 10 Stats. 1013 (1854), Kappler, *Indian Treaties*, 2:600–602.

28. Foreman, *Advancing the Frontier*, 279.

29. Christianson, "Study of Osage History," 203, 205.

30. John Mathews was the grandfather of the noted Osage scholar John Joseph Mathews. Ponziglione, "Annals of the Mission of Saint Francis," 109–13; Albert E. Castel, *A Frontier State at War: Kansas, 1861–1865* (Ithaca, N.Y.: Cornell University Press, 1958; reprint, Westport, Conn.: Greenwood Press, 1979), 54.

31. Ponziglione, "Annals of the Mission of Saint Francis," 116–17.

32. Christianson, "Study of Osage History," 219–20; Ponziglione, "Annals of the Mission of Saint Francis," 126–27.

33. Christianson, "Study of Osage History," 227.

34. Douglas C. Jones, *The Treaty of Medicine Lodge: The Story of the Great Treaty Council as Told by Eyewitnesses* (Norman: University of Oklahoma Press, 1966).

35. G. C. Snow, July 24, 1869, *Annual Report of the Commissioner of Indian Affairs for the Year 1869* (Washington, D.C.: Government Printing Office, 1870): 380–81.

36. Christianson, "Study of Osage History," 252–55.

37. Ibid., 262.

38. *Indian Appropriation Act,* Statutes at Large, sec. 12, 362 (1870).

39. Christianson, "Study of Osage History," 269.

40. Ibid., 275.

41. "But Since the Consulters of the province do not favor the establishment of this New Mission among the Osage, our Superior must reject any further offered propositions." Ponziglione, "Annals of the Mission of Saint Francis," 172, 175, 178.

42. "Treaty with the Osage, 1865," 14 Stat. 687 (1866), Kappler, *Indian Treaties,* 2:879–83. Article 14 provided that a limited-number of Osage "half-breeds" could acquire patents to eighty-acre plots of land in Kansas.

43. Christianson, "Study of Osage History," 279, 282.

44. "Since the Osage now are separated from us by great distance it follows that the number of their Adolescents among us diminishes daily; but in their place the White ones come anew, and thus our schools flourish." Ponziglione, "Annals of the Mission of Saint Francis," 178, 183.

Chapter 9

1. James Mooney, *The Ghost-Dance Religion and the Sioux Outbreak of 1890* (1965; reprint, Chicago: University of Chicago Press, Phoenix edition, 1976), 159, originally published as part 2 of the *Fourteenth Annual Report of the Bureau of Ethnology to the Secretary of the Smithsonian Institution, 1892–93* (Washington, D.C.: Government Printing Office, 1896).

2. Testimony of Chief Black Dog before a Committee of House of Representatives of the State of Oklahoma, January 21, 1908, Guthrie, Oklahoma, in Daniel Charles Swan, "West Moon—East Moon: An

Ethnohistory of the Peyote Religion among the Osage Indians, 1898–1930"
(Ph.D. diss., University of Oklahoma, 1990), 530.

3. Christianson, "Study of Osage History," 282.

4. Charles Ewing, Catholic Commissioner of Indian Missions to
Acting Commissioner of Indian Affairs, Washington, D.C., October 4,
1876, *Letters Received by the Office of Indian Affairs, 1824–1881*, 635:157;
Christianson, "Study of Osage History," 279.

5. Father Paul Mary Ponziglione, "Western Missions Journal No. 5,"
III Osage Mission, 168, July 13, 1875, 16, 19–20. "The School Superintendent,
an old-fashioned-Quaker some 6 feet high whom They call uncle Ben, and
his evangelical woman, a small crafty looking lady, whom people call Aunt
Annie—seem to be moved by good deal of spirit and zeal especially when
I go to visit the children, and more than once calling me aside requested
me with great politeness not to tell the Children that one must be baptized, and that out of the Catholic Church there is no salvation, these
words, say they, create great disturbance, and when we try to teach them
Christianity they do not want to listen to us! You may easy imagine what
answer I can give to the entreaties, of people who claim to teach
Christianity, and at the same time deny the necessity of Baptism."

6. Isaac Gibson, *Report of the Commissioner of Indian Affairs for the
Year 1873* (Washington, D.C.: Government Printing Office, 1874), 279.

7. Agent Gibson writes that the "Government school at the agency,
which is not sectarian . . ." *Report of the Commissioner of Indian Affairs for
the Year 1873*, 279.

8. Laban J. Miles, September 1, 1884, *Report of the Commissioner of
Indian Affairs for the Year 1843* (Washington, D.C.: Government Printing
Office, 1884), 82.

9. Ponziglione, "Western Missions Journal No. 2," 7, 16.

10. Garrick Alan Bailey, "Changes in Osage Social Organization:
1673–1969" (Ph.D. diss., University of Oregon, 1970), 138.

11. William Nicolson, Superintendent, Lawrence, Kans., to J. Q. Smith,
Commissioner of Indian Affairs, Washington, D.C., May 22, 1876, *Letters
Received by the Office of Indian Affairs, 1824–1881*, 635:941.

12. Nicholson to Smith, May 22, 1876, *Letters Received by the Office of
Indian Affairs*, 635:941.

13. Ewing to Acting Commissioner of Indian Affairs, October 4, 1876,
Letters Received by the Office of Indian Affairs, 635:157.

14. Terry P. Wilson, *The Underground Reservation: Osage Oil* (Lincoln:
University of Nebraska Press, 1985), 25; Bailey, "Changes in Osage Social
Organization," 139.

15. Agent Isaac Gibson, September 1, 1875, *Report of the Commissioner
of Indian Affairs for the Year 1873*, 280.

16. Bailey, "Changes in Osage Social Organization," 141.

17. Wilson, *Underground Reservation,* 29.

18. Wilson, *Underground Reservation,* 35; see Robert M. Burrill, "The Establishment of Ranching on the Osage Indian Reservation," *Geographical Review* 62 (October 1972): 542; Robert M. Burrill, "The Osage Pasture Map," *Chronicles of Oklahoma* 53 (summer 1975): 204–11.

19. Bailey, "Changes in Osage Social Organization," 143.

20. *Report of the Commissioner of Indian Affairs for the Year 1889* (Washington, D.C.: Government Printing Office, 1889): 55; C. A. Dempsey to Commissioner of Indian Affairs, Washington, D.C., September 5, 1893, *Report of the Commissioner of Indian Affairs for the Year 1993–94* (Washington, D.C.: Government Printing Office, 1895): 256; Bailey, "Changes in Osage Social Organization," 145.

21. Prucha, *Great Father,* 667. In 1890 the land allotments were all changed to equal allotments of 160 acres.

22. Laban J. Miles, October 31, 1889, *Report of the Commissioner of Indian Affairs for the Year 1889* (Washington, D.C.: Government Printing Office, 1889), 193.

23. La Flesche, *War Ceremony,* 47; Swan, "West Moon—East Moon," 113.

24. Laban J. Miles, Osage Agency to Commissioner of Indian Affairs, Washington, D.C., September 12, 1882, *Report of the Commissioner of Indian Affairs for the Year 1882* (Washington, D.C.: Government Printing Office, 1882), 72.

25. Bailey, "Changes in Osage Social Organization," 152.

26. The amount $160 is deceptive: $160 in 1879 dollars is equal to $2,857 in 2002 dollars, according to the *Columbia Journalism Review* inflation calculator.

27. Ponziglione, "Kansas: Letter July 2, 1883," 297.

28. Swan, "West Moon—East Moon," 206.

29. Mathews, *Osages,* 739.

30. Isaac Gibson, September 1, 1874, *Report of the Commissioner of Indian Affairs for the Year 1874* (Washington, D.C.: Government Printing Office, 1874): 226.

31. Swan, "West Moon—East Moon," 292–94.

32. Although modified from its 1880 form, the I′n-Lon-Schka is still an honored ritual among the Osage people, and it is still performed today in Osage communities. See Alice Anne Callahan, *The Osage Ceremonial Dance I′n-Lon-Schka* (1990; reprint, Norman: University of Oklahoma Press, 1993); Daniel C. Swan, "100 Years of Dancing: The Osages of Pawhuska District Observe an Anniversary," *Chronicles of Oklahoma* 63 (spring 1985): 90–97.

33. Bailey, "Changes in Osage Social Organization," 155.

34. Mooney, *Ghost-Dance,* 159.

35. Their agent, Laban Miles, wrote in fall 1892: "There has never been a "ghost dance" at the agency, nor are they [Osage] much inclined to such superstitions." *Report of the Commissioner of Indian Affairs, 1892* (Washington, D.C.: Government Printing Office, 1893): 391.

36. H. B. Freeman, Acting Agent, Osage Agency, to Commissioner of Indian Affairs, Washington, D.C., October 2, 1896, *Report of the Commissioner of Indian Affairs for the Year 1896* (Washington, D.C.: Government Printing Office, 1896): 261.

37. Freeman to Commissioner of Indian Affairs, October 2, 1896, 261; Bailey, "Changes in Osage Social Organization," 149.

38. Tom Wikle, ed., *Atlas of Oklahoma: Classroom Edition* (Stillwater: Oklahoma State University for Department of Geography, Computer Cartography Laboratory, 1991), 103–4; Arrell M. Gibson, *Oklahoma: A History of Five Centuries* (Norman: Harlow Publishing Corp., 1965), 300–304.

39. See Wilson, *Underground Reservation.*

40. For an excellent account and analysis of Osage Peyotism, see Daniel C. Swan's concise and excellent "Early Osage Peyotism," *Plains Anthropologist* 43 (1998): 51–71; see also Swan, "West Moon—East Moon."

41. See Omer C. Stewart, *Peyote Religion: A History* (Norman: University of Oklahoma Press, 1987); Weston La Barre, *The Peyote Cult,* 4th ed. (Hamden, Conn.: Shoe String Press, 1959; reprint, n.p.: Archon Books, 1975).

42. Swan, "West Moon—East Moon," 231–32.

43. The Quapaw, another Dhegian Siouan group, had lived on the Osage Reservation from 1874 to 1889, and several, like Tall Chief, had married Osage women and remained on the reservation after the Quapaw left for their reservation. Swan, "West Moon—East Moon," 236.

44. Swan, "Early Osage Peyotism," 63–64.

45. Swan, "West Moon—East Moon," 271–80.

46. Bailey, *Osage and the Invisible World,* 19.

Chapter 10

1. Leroy Logan interview in Swan, "Early Osage Peyotism," 63–64.

2. Swan, "West Moon—East Moon," 362.

3. Bailey, *Osage and the Invisible World,* 19.

References

Manuscript Collections and Archives

American Board of Commissioners for Foreign Missions. Papers, Houghton Library, Harvard University, Cambridge, Massachusetts.

Archives des Colonies, Archives Nationales, Paris, France.

Graham, Richard. Papers. Missouri Historical Society, St. Louis, Missouri.

Midwest Jesuit Archives, St. Louis, Missouri.

National Archives, Washington, D.C.

Ponziglione, Father Paul Mary, S.J. Annales Missionis S. Francisei de Hieronymo A Patribus Societalis Jesu institutae Apud Indos Americae Septemtrionalis Osagios dictos. Translated by Gussie Tanenhaus. "The Annals of the Mission of Saint Francis of Hieronymus, by the Fathers of the Society of the Jesuits Among the Indian of North America Called the Osage." Midwest Jesuit Archives, St. Louis, Missouri.

———. "The Osages and Father John Schoenmakers, S.J.: Interesting Memoirs Collected from Legends, Traditions and Historical Documents." III Osage Mission, 158 and 159. Midwest Jesuit Archives, St. Louis, Missouri.

———. "Western Missions Journals," Father Ponziglione's handwritten journals covering August 11, 1867, to February 20, 1898. Midwest Jesuit Archives, St. Louis, Missouri.

Sibley, George C. Papers. Missouri Historical Society, St. Louis, Missouri.

United Foreign Missionary Society Papers, 1817 to 1825, Houghton Library, Harvard University, Cambridge, Massachusetts.

Verreydt, Felix L. "Memoirs of Felix L. Verreydt, S.J. (1874)." Transcription in Midwest Jesuit Archives, St. Louis, Missouri.

Newspapers and Religious Periodicals

American Missionary Register, New York.

Annales de la Propagation de la Foi: Des lettres des Évéques et des Missionnaires des Missions des Deux Mondes, et de Tous les Documents Relatifs Aux Missions et a L´oeuvre de la Propagation de la Foi, Lyon, France, 1842.

Little Rock Arkansas Gazette, 1820–1839.

Missionary Herald, Boston.

Woodstock Letters: A Record of Current Events and Historical Notes Connected with the Colleges and Missions of the Society of Jesus in North and South America. N.p.: Woodstock College, 1872–1901.

Books and Other Sources

Adelman, Jeremy, and Stephen Aron. "From Borderlands to Borders: Empires, Nation-States, and the Peoples in Between in North American History." *American Historical Review* 104 (June 1999): 814–41.

Agnew, Brad. *Fort Gibson: Terminal of the Trail of Tears.* 1980. Reprint, Norman: University of Oklahoma Press, 1981.

Ambrose, Stephen E. *Undaunted Courage: Meriwether Lewis, Thomas Jefferson, and the Opening of the American West.* New York: Simon and Schuster for Touchstone Books, 1997.

"American Board of Commissioners for Foreign Missions Letterbook." American Board of Commissioners for Foreign Missions Papers. Houghton Library, Harvard University, Cambridge, Massachusetts.

American State Papers: Indian Affairs. Vols. 1 and 4. Washington, D.C.: Gales and Seaton, 1832–34.

Anderson, Gary Clayton. *The Indian Southwest, 1580–1830: Ethnogenesis and Reinvention.* Norman: University of Oklahoma Press, 1999.

"Annual Report: Mission to the Osages." *Missionary Herald* 31 (January 1835): 26.

"Annual Report to the Secretary of War: Union, Osage Nation, October 1, 1823." *American Missionary Register* 5 (March 1824): 79.

Arnold, Morris S. *Unequal Laws unto a Savage Race: European Legal Traditions in Arkansas, 1686–1836.* Fayetteville: University of Arkansas Press, 1985.

Axtell, James. *The Invasion Within: The Contest of Cultures in Colonial North America.* New York: Oxford University Press, 1985.

Bailey, Garrick Alan. "Changes in Osage Social Organization: 1673–1969." Ph.D. diss. University of Oregon, 1970.

———., ed. *The Osage and the Invisible World: From the Works of Francis La Flesche.* Norman: University of Oklahoma Press, 1995.

Bearss, Ed, and Arrell M. Gibson, *Fort Smith: Little Gibraltar on the Arkansas.* Norman: University of Oklahoma Press, 1969.

Berkhofer, Robert F. Jr. *The White Man's Indian: Images of the American Indian from Columbus to the Present.* New York: Alfred A. Knopf, 1978.

———. *Salvation and the Savage: An Analysis of Protestant Missions and American Indian Response, 1787–1862.* Lexington: University of Kentucky Press, 1965.

Berthrong, Donald J. *The Southern Cheyennes.* 1963. Reprint, Norman: University of Oklahoma Press, 1986.

Board of Managers of the United Foreign Missionary Society. "Instructions to the Members of the Mission Family, Designated for the Harmony Station, Among the Great Osages of the Missouri." *American Missionary Register* 1 (February 1821): 325.

———. "Instructions to the Missionaries who are about proceeding to the Station on the Grand River, to be denominated Union." *American Missionary Register* 1 (July 1820): 23–24.

Bolton, Herbert E., ed. *Athanase de Mézières and the Louisiana-Texas Frontier, 1768–1780.* 2 vols. Cleveland: Arthur H. Clark Company, 1914.

Burns, Louis F. *Osage Mission Baptisms, Marriages, and Interments, 1820–1886.* Fallbrook, Calif.: Ciga Press, 1986.

Burrill, Robert M. "The Establishment of Ranching on the Osage Indian Reservation." *Geographical Review* 62 (October 1972): 524–43.

———. "The Osage Pasture Map." *Chronicles of Oklahoma* 53 (summer 1975): 204–11.

Callahan, Alice Anne. *The Osage Ceremonial Dance I'n-Lon-Schka.* 1990. Reprint, Norman: University of Oklahoma Press, 1993.

Calloway, Colin G. *New Worlds for All: Indians, Europeans, and the Remaking of Early America.* Baltimore: Johns Hopkins University Press, 1997.

Calloway, Robert. Osage Sub-agency, to T. Hartley Crawford, Washington, D.C. May 2, 1842. *Letters Received by the Office of Indian Affairs, 1824–1881.* Osage Agency, 1824–1880. Record Group 75, M234. National Archives, Washington, D.C.

Carter, Clarence E., ed. *The Territorial Papers of the United States.* 26 vols. Washington, D.C.: Government Printing Office, 1934–62.

Castel, Albert E. *A Frontier State at War: Kansas, 1861–1865.* Ithaca, N.Y.: Cornell University Press, 1958. Reprint, Westport, Conn.: Greenwood Press, 1979.

Chapman, Carl H., and Eleanor F. Chapman. *Indians and Archaeology of Missouri.* Rev. ed. Columbia: University of Missouri Press, 1983.

Chapman, E. "Union Mission: to the Domestic Secretary, March 4, 1822." *American Missionary Register* 2 (June 1822): 489.

Chapman, Rev. Mr. "Missionary Intelligence: Union Mission, Hopefield, July 2, 1824." *American Missionary Register* 6 (January 1825): 23–24.

Chapman, Epaphras, and Job P. Vinall. "Third Report of the United Foreign Missionary Society." *American Missionary Register* 1 (July 1820): 16.

Christianson, James R. "A Study of Osage History prior to 1876." Ph.D. diss., University of Kansas, 1968.

Clark, William, to George Sibley, factor at Fort Osage Factory. November 11, 1817. Sibley Papers, St. Louis: Missouri Historical Society.

————. "Papers Relating to Benton Pixley." February 18, 1829. *Letters Received by the Office of Indian Affairs, 1824–81.* Osage Agency 1824–1880. Record Group 75, M234. Washington, D.C.: National Archives, 1958.

Clifton, James A. *The Prairie People: Continuity and Change in Potawatomi Indian Culture, 1665–1965.* Lawrence: Regents Press of Kansas, 1977.

Conway to Cass. September 4, 1832; September 25, 1832. *Letters Received by the Office of Indian Affairs, 1824–1881.* Osage Agency 1824–1880. Record Group 75, M234. Washington, D.C.: National Archives, 1958.

Crosby, Alfred W. Jr. "Virgin Soil Epidemics as a Factor in the Aboriginal Depopulation in America." *William and Mary Quarterly,* 3d ser., 33 (April 1976): 289–99.

Dempsey, C. A., to Commissioner of Indian Affairs, Washington, D.C. September 5, 1893. *Report of the Commissioner of Indian Affairs for the Year 1993–94.* Washington, D.C.: Government Printing Office, 1895.

Denton, Doris. "Harmony Mission, 1821–1837." M.A. thesis, University of Missouri, 1929.

Din, Gilbert C., and Abraham P. Nasatir. *The Imperial Osages: Spanish-Indian Diplomacy in the Mississippi Valley.* Norman: University of Oklahoma Press, 1983.

Dodge, Mr. "Extracts from a Communication of Mr. Dodge, Osage Nation, June 18, 1832: View of the Last Quarter, Wednesday, [June] 25." Missionary Herald 28 (September 1832): 291.

————. "Osages: Report of the Station at Harmony, June 1st, 1830." *Missionary Herald* 27 (February 1831): 46.

Dodge, Nathaniel. "Great Osage Mission: Extracts of Letters, February 1, 1822." *American Missionary Register,* May 1822, 433.

————. "Osages: Extracts from a Letter of Mr. Dodge, dated Boudinot, Osage Nation, March 12, 1832." *Missionary Herald* 28 (September 1832): 290.

Eccles, W. J., "The Fur Trade and Eighteenth-Century Imperialism." *William and Mary Quarterly,* 3d ser., 40 (July 1983): 341–62.

Edmunds, R. David. *The Potawatomis: Keepers of the Fire.* Norman: University of Oklahoma Press, 1978.

Ellis, Richard N., and Charlie R. Steen, eds. "An Indian Delegation in France, 1725." Translated by Charlie R. Steen. *Journal of Illinois State Historical Society* 67 (September 1974): 385–405.

Evarts, Jeremiah, Boston, to Nathaniel Dodge, Harmony Mission. September 6, 1828. "American Board of Commissioners for Foreign Missions Letterbook," 549. American Board of Commissioners for Foreign Missions Papers, Houghton Library, Harvard University, Cambridge, Massachusetts.

Ewers, John C. *Plains Indian History and Culture: Essays on Continuity and Change.* Foreword by William T. Hagan. 1997. Reprint, Norman: University of Oklahoma Press, 1999.

Ewing, Charles, Catholic Commissioner of Indian Missions, to Acting Commissioner of Indian Affairs, Washington, D.C. October 4, 1876. *Letters Received by the Office of Indian Affairs, 1824–1881,* 635:157. Osage Agency, 1824–1880. Record Group 75, M234. National Archives, Washington, D.C.

"Extracts from the Journal for the Month of September, 1822: Affecting Interview, September 11, 1822." *American Missionary Register* 4 (February 1823): 41.

"Extracts from the Journal: Visit from the Principal Chief, April 4, 1821." *American Missionary Register* 2 (October 1821): 147.

"Extracts from the Journal: Want of labourers, April 4, 1821." *American Missionary Register* 2 (October 1821): 147–48.

"Extract from Mr. Chapman's Journal." *American Missionary Register* 2 (November 1821): 182.

Finke, Roger, and Rodney Stark. *The Churching of America, 1776–1990: Winners and Losers in Our Religious Economy.* New Brunswick, N.J.: Rutgers University Press, 1992.

Flores, Dan L., ed. *Journal of an Indian Trader: Anthony Glass and the Texas Trading Frontier, 1790–1810.* College Station: Texas A&M University Press, 1985.

Foley, William E., and C. David Rice. *The First Chouteaus: River Barons of Early St. Louis.* Urbana: University of Illinois Press, 1983.

Folmer, Henri. "Etienne Veniard de Bourgmond in the Missouri Country." *Missouri Historical Review* 36 (April 1942): 279–98.

Foreman, Carolyn Thomas. "Hopefield Mission in Osage Nation, 1823–1837." *Chronicles of Oklahoma* 28 (summer 1950): 193–205.

Foreman, Grant. *Pioneer Days in the Early Southwest.* Cleveland: Arthur H. Clark Company, 1926. Reprint, Lincoln: University of Nebraska Press, 1994.

————, ed. *A Traveler in Indian Territory: The Journal of Ethan Allen Hitchcock, Late Major-General in the United States Army.* Foreword by Michael D. Green. Cedar Rapids, Iowa: Torch Press, 1930. Reprint, Norman: University of Oklahoma Press, 1996.

————. *Advancing the Frontier, 1830–1860.* 1933. Reprint, Norman: University of Oklahoma Press, 1968.

————. *Indians and Pioneers: The Story of the American Southwest before 1830.* Rev. ed. 1936. Reprint, Norman: University of Oklahoma Press, 1967.

Freeman, H. B., Acting Agent, Osage Agency, to Commissioner of Indian Affairs, Washington, D.C. October 2, 1896. *Report of the Commissioner of Indian Affairs for the Year 1896.* Washington, D.C.: Government Printing Office, 1896.

Garraghan, Gilbert J. *Chapters in Frontier History: Research Studies in the Making of the West.* Milwaukee: Bruce Publishing Company, 1934.

————. "Fort Orleans of the Missoury." *Missouri Historical Review* 35 (April 1941): 373–84.

————. *The Jesuits of the Middle United States.* 3 vols. New York: J. J. Little and Ives Company, n.d. Reprint, Chicago: Loyola Press, 1983–84.

"George Sibley to Thomas L. McKenney, October 1, 1820." *Missouri Historical Review* 9 (October 1914–July 1915): 48.

Gibson, Arrell M. *The Kickapoos: Lords of the Middle Border.* Norman: University of Oklahoma Press, 1963.

————. *Oklahoma: A History of Five Centuries.* Norman: Harlow Publishing, 1965.

Gibson, Isaac T., Osage Agency I.T., to Edward P. Smith, Commissioner of Indian Affairs, Washington, D.C. April 30, 1875. *Letters Received by the Office of Indian Affairs, 1824–1881,* 634:94–96. Osage Agency, 1824–1880. Record Group 75, M234. National Archives, Washington, D.C.

Gibson, Isaac. *Report of the Commissioner of Indian Affairs for the Year 1873*. Washington, D.C.: Government Printing Office, 1874.

——. *Report of the Commissioner of Indian Affairs for the Year 1874*. Washington, D.C.: Government Printing Office, 1874.

Glenn, Robert A. "The Osage War." *Missouri Historical Review* 14 (January 1920): 201–10.

Godsey, Roy. "The Osage War, 1837." *Missouri Historical Review* 20 (October 1925): 96–100.

Graham, Richard, Osage Agent, St. Louis, to Secretary of War John C. Calhoun, Washington, D.C. December 28, 1821. Richard Graham Papers, Missouri Historical Society, St. Louis.

Graves, William W. *The First Protestant Osage Missions, 1820–1837.* Oswego, Kans.: Carpenter Press, 1949.

"Great Osage [Journal]: Day of Fasting, May 10, 1822." *American Missionary Register* 3 (October 1822): 147.

"Great Osage [Journal]: The Indians prepare for their Summer Hunt, May 15, 1822." *American Missionary Register* 3 (October 1822): 147.

"Great Osage Mission." *American Missionary Register* 4 (June 1823): 164.

"Great Osage Mission: Extract of Letters, Regulations for the Indian Children, March 26, 1822." *American Missionary Register* 3 (September 1822): 94.

"Great Osage Mission: Journal for June and July, 1823; June 14, 1823." *American Missionary Register* 4 (December 1823): 372.

"Great Osage Mission: Journal for the Month of March, 1822, First Marriage among the Osages, March 21, 1822." *American Missionary Register* 3 (September 1822): 94.

Greene, David, Boston, to William C. Requa, Hopefield. March 25, 1836. "American Board of Commissioners for Foreign Missions Letterbook," 497–98. American Board of Commissioners for Foreign Missions Papers, Houghton Library, Harvard University, Cambridge, Massachusetts.

Gregg, Kate L., ed. *Westward with Dragoons: The Journal of William Clark on His Expedition to Establish Fort Osage, August 25 to September 22, 1808, a Description of the Wilderness, an Account of the Building of the Fort, Treaty-making with the Osages and Clark's Return to St. Louis.* Fulton, Mo.: Ovid Bell Press, 1937.

Hall, Robert L. *An Archaeology of the Soul: North American Indian Belief and Ritual.* Urbana: University of Illinois Press, 1997.

Hall, Thomas D. *Social Change in the Southwest, 1350–1880.* Lawrence: University Press of Kansas, 1989.

Hamtramck, John, Osage Agency, to William Clark, Superintendent of Indian Affairs, St. Louis. February 18, 1829. *Letters Received by the Office of Indian Affairs, 1824–1881.* Osage Agency, 1824–1880. Record Group 75, M234. National Archives, Washington, D.C.

"Harmony Mission." *American Missionary Register* 6 (September 1825): 273–74.

Harrod, Harold L. *Mission among the Blackfeet.* Norman: University of Oklahoma Press, 1971.

Hemphill, W. Edwin, ed. *The Papers of John C. Calhoun.* Volume 5, 1820–1821. Columbia: University of South Carolina Press for the South Carolina Department of Archives and History and South Caroliniana Society, 1971.

Herring, Joseph B. "Kenekuk, The Kickapoo Prophet: Acculturation without Assimilation." *American Indian Quarterly* 9 (summer 1985): 295–307.

Holway, Hope. "Union Mission, 1826–1837." *Chronicles of Oklahoma* 40 (winter 1962–63): 355–78.

Houck, Lewis A., ed. *The Spanish Régime in Missouri.* 2 vols. Chicago: R. R. Donnelley and Sons, 1909.

Hoyt, Dolly E. "Extracts from the Journal of the Union Mission." *American Missionary Register* 1 (May 1821): 434–36.

Hudson, Charles. *The Southeastern Indians.* Knoxville: University of Tennessee Press, 1976.

"Invoice of Boat and Cargo forwarded by the Board of Agency at Cincinnati, on the 30th of March, 1824, to the Union Mission." *American Missionary Register* 5 (June 1824): 183.

Jackson, Donald, ed. *The Journals of Zebulon Montgomery Pike: With Letters and Related Documents.* 2 vols. Norman: University of Oklahoma Press, 1966.

———, ed. *Letters of the Lewis and Clark Expedition: With Related Documents, 1783–1854.* 2d ed. 2 vols. Urbana: University of Illinois Press, 1978.

James, Thomas. *Three Years among the Indians and Mexicans.* With an introduction by A. P. Nasatir. N.p., 1846. Reprint, Lincoln: University of Nebraska Press, 1984.

Jefferson, Thomas. *The Papers of Thomas Jefferson.* Edited by Julian P. Boyd et al. 10 vols. Princeton, N.J.: Princeton University Press, 1950.

John, Elizabeth A. H. *Storms Brewed in Other Men's Worlds: The Confrontation of Indians, Spanish, and French in the Southwest, 1540–1795.* College Station: Texas A&M University Press, 1975. Reprint, Lincoln: University of Nebraska Press, 1981.

Johnson, Kevin Orlin. *Why Do Catholics Do That? A Guide to the Teachings and Practices of the Catholic Church.* New York: Ballantine Books, 1995. Originally entitled Expressions of the Catholic Faith. New York: Ballantine Books, 1994.

Jones, Douglas C. *The Treaty of Medicine Lodge: The Story of the Great Treaty Council as Told by Eyewitnesses.* Norman: University of Oklahoma Press, 1966.

Jones, Mr., to the Editor of the Recorder. "United Foreign Missionary Society: Home Proceedings." *American Missionary Register* 2 (December 1821): 225–26.

"Journal of the Great Osage Mission." *American Missionary Register* 2 (April 1822): 402–6; (June 1822): 492–93.

"Journal of the [Great Osage] Mission: Arrival of Indian Chiefs, August 11–12, 1821." *American Missionary Register* 2 (June 1822): 492–93.

"Journal of the [Harmony] Mission: For the Month of February; February 12, 1822." *American Missionary Register* 3 (August 1822): 49.

"Journal of the Union Mission, for January and February, 1825, Great National Council.—Indians consent to Remove, January 29, 1825." *American Missionary Register* 6 (July 1825): 215.

"Journal of the Union Mission, Gov. M'Nair's Visit to Hopefields, February 3, 1825." *American Missionary Register* 6 (July 1825): 216.

"Journal of the Union Mission, Idolatry of the Osages." *American Missionary Register* 6 (July 1825): 216.

"Journal of the [Union] Mission: Indian Murder, June 24, 1821." *American Missionary Register* 2 (January 1822): 269–70.

Kappler, Charles J., ed. *Indian Treaties, 1778–1883.* 2 vols. Washington, D.C.: Government Printing Office, 1903. Reprint, New York: Interland Publishing Inc., 1972.

Kavanagh, Thomas W. *Comanche Political History: An Ethnohistorical Perspective, 1706–1875.* Lincoln: University of Nebraska Press, 1996.

Kessell, John. "Review of Cynthia Raddings' Wandering Peoples." *Ethnohistory* 45 (fall 1998): 817–19.

La Barre, Weston. *The Peyote Cult.* 4th ed. Hamden, Conn.: Shoe String Press, 1959. Reprint, n.p.: Archon Books, 1975.

La Flesche, Francis. "The Osage Tribe: Rite of the Chiefs; Sayings of the Ancient Men." *Bureau of American Ethnology Thirty-sixth Annual Report, 1914–1915,* 37–601. Washington, D.C.: Government Printing Office, 1921.

————. *War Ceremony and Peace Ceremony of the Osage Indians.* Smithsonian Institution, Bureau of American Ethnology Bulletin 101. Washington, D.C.: Government Printing Office, 1939.

La Vere, David. *Contrary Neighbors: Southern Plains and Removed Indians in Indian Territory.* Norman: University of Oklahoma Press, 2000.

Lenox, Robert, et al. "To the Chief, the Counsellor, and the principal Warrior of the Osages of the Missouri, now at Washington." *American Missionary Register* 1 (July 1820): 30.

Letters Received by the Office of Indian Affairs, 1824–1881. Osage Agency, 1824–1880. Record Group 75, M234. National Archives, Washington, D.C.

Letters Received by the Secretary of War, Main Series, 1801–1870. Record Group 107, M221. National Archives, Washington, D.C.

Letters Received by the Secretary of War, Unregistered Series, 1789–1861. Record Group 107, M222. National Archives, Washington, D.C.

Lewis, Z. "Sixth Report of the United Foreign Missionary Society: Resources, and Conclusion." *American Missionary Register* 4 (June 1823): 175.

McDermott, John Francis, ed. *Tixier's Travels on the Osage Prairies.* Translated by Albert J. Salvan. 1940. Reprint, Norman: University of Oklahoma Press, 1968.

McKenney, Thomas L. "Letter from the Superintendent of Indian Trade." *American Missionary Register* 1 (August 1820): 56.

McKenney, T. L., et al. "Second Mission Family." *American Missionary Register* 1 (July 1820): 29–33.

McLoughlin, William G. *Cherokee Renascence in the New Republic.* 1986. Reprint, Princeton, N.J.: Princeton University Press, 1992.

————. *Cherokees and Missionaries, 1789–1839.* New Haven, Conn.: Yale University Press, 1984.

Margry, Pierre, ed. *Découvertes et Établissements des Français dans l'Ouest et dans le Sud de l'Amérique Septentrionale, 1614–1754.* Vol. 1, *Voyages des Français sur les Grands lacs et découverte de l'Ohio et du Mississipi, 1614–1684.* Paris: n.p., 1888. Reprint, New York: AMS Press, 1974.

————, ed. *Découvertes et Établissements des Français dans l'Ouest et dans le Sud de l'Amérique Septentrionale, 1614-1754.* Vol. 6, *Exploration des*

Affluents du Mississipi et Découverte des Montagnes Rocheuses, 1679–1754. Paris: n.p., 1888. Reprint, New York: AMS Press, 1974.

Mathews, John Joseph. *The Osages: Children of the Middle Waters*. 1961. Reprint, Norman: University of Oklahoma Press, 1982.

Mayhall, Mildred P. *The Kiowas*. 2d ed. Norman: University of Oklahoma Press, 1971.

Merrell, James H. *Into the American Woods: Negotiators on the Pennsylvania Frontier*. New York: W.W. Norton and Company, 1999.

Michaud, Eugene, à grand-vicaire du diocèse de Chambéry. Juillet 1823. *Annales de la Propagation de la Foi* 5 (March 1825): 55–59.

Miles, Laban J., Osage Agency, to Commissioner of Indian Affairs, Washington, D.C. September 12, 1882. *Report of the Commissioner of Indian Affairs for the Year 1882*. Washington, D.C.: Government Printing Office, 1882.

———. *Report of the Commissioner of Indian Affairs for the Year 1843*. Washington, D.C.: Government Printing Office, 1884.

———. *Report of the Commissioner of Indian Affairs for the Year 1889*. Washington, D.C.: Government Printing Office, 1889.

———. *Report of the Commissioner of Indian Affairs, 1892*. Washington, D.C.: Government Printing Office, 1893.

Milledoler, Philip. "Address, delivered to the Union Mission Family, in the Dutch Church in Nassau-street, on Monday evening, April 17, 1820." *American Missionary Register* 1 (September 1820): 98.

———. "Annual Report, May 10, 1820." United Foreign Missionary Society Papers.

Milledoler, Philip, and Z. Lewis. "Reports of Societies: Fifth Report of the United Foreign Missionary Society, Union Mission." *American Missionary Register* 2 (June 1822): 471.

Milledoler, Philip, Z. Lewis, and William Wilson. "Fourth Report of the United Foreign Missionary Society." *American Missionary Register* 1 (May 1821): 420–21.

Milledoler, Philip, Alexr. Proudfit, and Gardiner Spring. "Postscript: United Foreign Missionary Society, Second Mission Family." *American Missionary Register* 1 (December 1820): 238.

Milledoler, Philip, and Sans Nerf. "Interview [Talk] with Indian Chiefs." *American Missionary Register* 1 (July 1820): 32–33.

Miller, James. "Miscellanies: The Arkansas Territory, September 2, 1820." *American Missionary Register* 1 (January 1821): 287.

"Mission to the Osages." *Missionary Herald* 32 (January 1836): 24.

Montgomery, Mr. "Great Osage Mission: Extracts of Letters, December 3, 1821." *American Missionary Register* 2 (March 1822): 353.

Montgomery, William B. "Osages: Extract from a Letter of Mr. Montgomery, Dated Union, December 27, 1831." *Missionary Herald* 28 (August 1832): 258.

Mooney, James. "Calendar History of the Kiowa Indians." Bureau of American Ethnology, *Seventeenth Annual Report, 1895–1896*. Washington, D.C.: Government Printing Office, 1898.

———. "Calendar History of the Kiowa Indians." Bureau of American Ethnology *Seventeenth Annual Report, 1895–1896*, 141–444. Washington, D.C.: Government Printing Office, 1898.

———. *The Ghost-Dance Religion and the Sioux Outbreak of 1890*. 1965. Reprint, Chicago: University of Chicago Press, Phoenix edition, 1976. Originally published as part 2 of the *Fourteenth Annual Report of the Bureau of Ethnology to the Secretary of the Smithsonian Institution, 1892–93*. Washington, D.C.: Government Printing Office, 1896.

———. "Myths of the Cherokee and Sacred Formulas of the Cherokee." Bureau of American Ethnology, *Nineteenth Annual Report, 1897–1898*. Washington, D.C.: Government Printing Office, 1900.

"Mr. Montgomery's Journal, from Union to Harmony: Interview with an intelligent Osage, May 11, 1824." *American Missionary Register* 5 (September 1824): 274.

Nasatir, A. P., ed. *Before Lewis and Clark: Documents Illustrating the History of the Missouri, 1785–1804*. 2 vols. With an introduction by James P. Ronda. St. Louis: St. Louis Historical Documents Foundation, 1952. Reprint, Lincoln: University of Nebraska Press, 1990.

Newton, Mr. "Great Osage Mission: [Letter] to his friend, January 20, 1822." *American Missionary Register* 2 (June 1822): 492.

Nicolson, William, Superintendent, Lawrence, Kans., to J. Q. Smith, Commissioner of Indian Affairs, Washington, D.C. May 22, 1876. *Letters Received by the Office of Indian Affairs, 1824–1881*, 635:941. Osage Agency, 1824–1880. Record Group 75, M234. National Archives, Washington, D.C.

Norall, Frank. *Bourgmont, Explorer of the Missouri, 1698–1725*. Lincoln: University of Nebraska Press, 1988.

O'Brien, Michael J., and W. Raymond Wood. *The Prehistory of Missouri*. Columbia: University of Missouri Press, 1998.

"Osage Petition." August 30, 1842. *Letters Received by the Office of Indian*

Affairs, 1824–1881. Osage Agency, 1824–1880. Record Group 75, M234. National Archives, Washington, D.C.

"Osages: Extract from a Letter of Mr. Montgomery, dated Union, Dec. 27, 1831." *Missionary Herald* 28 (August 1832): 257.

"Osages: Extracts from the Report of the Union Station for the Year Ending June 1, 1832." *Missionary Herald* 28 (November 1832): 360.

"Osages: Journal of Mr. Vaill; Excultation occasioned by the Slaughter of the Pawnees." *Missionary Herald* 29 (October 1833): 367.

"Osages: Journal of Mr. Vaill; Indian Scalp-Dance, May 15." *Missionary Herald* 29 (October 1833): 370.

"Osages: Report of the Station at Union, June 1, 1831." *Missionary Herald* 27 (October 1831): 321.

Pahusca, Ticho-honga, Cho-ne-ksais, Wa-ma-ka Wachis, Haraita, Osage Sub-Agency, to John Tyler, President of the United States, Washington, D.C. June 14, 1843. *Letters Received by the Office of Indian Affairs, 1824–1881.* Osage Agency, 1824–1880. Record Group 75, M234. National Archives, Washington, D.C.

Palmer, Marcus. "Union Branch of the Mission." *Missionary Herald* 23 (May 1827): 149.

Palmer, Dr. "Union Mission: Doctor Palmer to his Brother." *American Missionary Register* 2 (August 1821): 59.

Peake, Ora Brooks. *A History of the United States Indian Factory System, 1795–1822.* Denver: Sage Books, 1954.

Phillips, Clifton Jackson. *Protestant America and the Pagan World: The First Half Century of the American Board of Commissioners for Foreign Missions, 1810–1860.* Cambridge, Mass.: Harvard University Press, East Asian Research Center, 1969.

Pixley, Benton, Osage Country, to James Barbour, Secretary of War, Washington, D.C. April 7, 1828. *Letters Received by the Office of Indian Affairs, 1824–1881.* Osage Agency, 1824–1880. Record Group 75, M234. National Archives, Washington, D.C.

———, Osage Country, to Thomas McKenney, Superintendent of Indian Affairs, Washington, D.C. August 20, 1828. *Letters Received by the Office of Indian Affairs, 1824–1881.* Osage Agency, 1824–1880. Record Group 75, M234. National Archives, Washington, D.C.

Ponziglione, Paul Mary. "Father John Schoenmakers." *Woodstock Letters* 12 (1883): 339–40.

———. "Kansas: Letter from Father Ponziglione, July 2, 1883." *Woodstock Letters* 12 (1883): 297.

————. "Origin of the Osage Mission." *Woodstock Letters* 6 (1877): 141–47.

————. "Western Missions Journal No. 2." Midwest Jesuit Archives, St. Louis, Missouri, III Osage Mission, 165, March 14, 1870, 19–27.

————. "Western Missions Journal No. 3." Midwest Jesuit Archives, St. Louis, Missouri, III Osage Mission, 166, January 16, 1871, 1.

————. "Western Missions Journal No. 5." Midwest Jesuit Archives, St. Louis, Missouri, III Osage Mission, 168, July 13, 1875, 16, 19–20.

Prucha, Francis Paul. *The Great Father: The United States Government and the American Indians.* 2 vols. 1984. Reprint, Lincoln: University of Nebraska Press, 1995.

"Record of Heathen Youth, in the Mission School at Harmony, April 12, 1824." *American Missionary Register* 5 (July 1824): 212.

Redfield, A. "Osages: August 25, 1834." *Missionary Herald* 30 (December 1834): 452–53.

Redfield, Mr. "Extracts of Private Letters from Members of the Union, Mission." *American Missionary Register* 1 (May 1821): 437.

————. "Osages: Obituary Notice of the Rev. William B. Montgomery and his Wife." *Missionary Herald* 30 (December 1834): 452.

Redfield, William. "United Foreign Missionary Society." *American Missionary Register* 2 (December 1821): 223.

Reid, John Phillip. *A Better Kind of Hatchet: Law, Trade, and Diplomacy in the Cherokee Nation during the Early Years of European Contact.* University Park: Pennsylvania State University Press, 1976.

Requa, William C. "Mission to the Osages." *Missionary Herald* 33 (January 1837): 22–23.

Report of the Commissioner of Indian Affairs, 1858–1897. Washington, D.C.: Government Printing Office, 1858–1897.

"Report of the School at Union Mission, Osage Nation, September 21, 1824." *American Missionary Register* 6 (February 1825): 47.

"Rev. Mr. Pixley's Journal: Indian Worship." *American Missionary Register* 5 (April 1824): 112.

Richter, Daniel K. *The Ordeal of the Longhouse: The Peoples of the Iroquois League in the Era of European Colonization.* Chapel Hill: University of North Carolina Press; Williamsburg: Institute of Early American History and Culture, 1992.

Rollings, Willard H. *The Osage: An Ethnohistorical Study of Hegemony on the Prairie-Plains.* Columbia: University of Missouri Press, 1992.

————. "Osages' Oil and Allotment, 1887–1906." Paper presented at the annual meeting of the Western Social Science Association Conference, Albuquerque, New Mexico, April 1983.

Romeyn, Rev. Dr. "Charge to the Great Osage Mission." *American Missionary Register* 1 (April 1821): 398.

Ronda, James P. *Lewis and Clark among the Indians.* Lincoln: University of Nebraska Press, 1984.

Rothensteiner, John. "Early Missionary Efforts among the Indians in the Diocese of St. Louis." *St. Louis Catholic Historical Review* 2 (1919): 66.

Salisbury, Neal. *Manitou and Providence: Indians, Europeans, and the Making of New England, 1500–1643.* 1982. Reprint, New York: Oxford University Press, 1984.

Smith, F. Todd. *The Wichita Indians: Traders of Texas and the Southern Plains, 1540-1845.* College Station: Texas A&M University Press, 2000.

Snow, G. C. *Annual Report of the Commissioner of Indian Affairs for the Year 1869.* Washington, D.C.: Government Printing Office, 1870.

Sprague, Mr. Otis. "[Letter] to his Brother in Brooklyn." *American Missionary Register* 2 (January 1822): 275, 276.

————. "Great Osage Mission: Mr. Sprague to his Brother, no date." *American Missionary Register* 2 (February 1822): 330.

Stewart, Omer C. *Peyote Religion: A History.* Norman: University of Oklahoma Press, 1987.

Swan, Daniel C. "100 Years of Dancing: The Osages of Pawhuska District Observe an Anniversary." *Chronicles of Oklahoma* 63 (spring 1985): 90–97.

————. "West Moon—East Moon: An Ethnohistory of the Peyote Religion among the Osage Indians, 1898–1930." Ph.D. diss., University of Oklahoma, 1990.

————. "Early Osage Peyotism." *Plains Anthropologist* 43 (1998): 51–71.

————. "Locality as a Factor in the Band Organization of the Osage Indians: A Quantitative Analysis." *Occasional Papers Series* 8, 1–21. Chicago: Newberry Library, Center for the History of the American Indian, 1987.

"Table of Missions, Stations, Missionaries, Schools and Churches." *Missionary Herald* 29 (January 1833): 14.

"Table of Stations, Missionaries, Churches, and Schools." *Missionary Herald* 31 (January 1835): 31.

Thorne, Tanis C. *The Many Hands of My Relations: French and Indians on the Lower Missouri*. Columbia: University of Missouri Press, 1996.

Trenholm, Virginia Cole. *The Arapahoes, Our People*. Norman: University of Oklahoma Press, 1970.

Truteau, Jean Baptiste. "Journal of Jean Baptiste Truteau on the Upper Missouri, 'Premier Partei,' June 7, 1794–March 26, 1795." *American Historical Review* 19 (January 1914): 299–333.

"[UFMS] Board Meeting, May 5, 1823: Great Osage Mission." United Foreign Missionary Society Papers, May 1823, 153.

"[UFMS] Committee Meeting, July 4, 1825." United Foreign Missionary Society Papers, July 1825, 128.

"Union Mission: Civil Government established at Hopefield, May 13, 1825." *American Missionary Register* 6 (September 1825): 271–72.

"Union Mission: Desertion of the Indian woman and one of the children, September 17, 1821." *American Missionary Register* 2 (February 1822): 328.

"Union Mission: Extract of Letters." *American Missionary Register* 5 (July 1824): 206–9.

"Union Mission: Extracts of Letters, March 31, 1823." *American Missionary Register* 4 (August 1823): 237.

"Union Mission: Extracts from the Journal, February 23, 1821." *American Missionary Register* 2 (September 1821): 114.

"Union Mission: Journal for April, April 9, 1825." *American Missionary Register* 6 (August 1825): 243.

"Union Mission: Journal for June and July, 1824, The Great Indian, 10 June 1824." *American Missionary Register* 5 (November 1824): 330.

"Union Mission: Journal for June and July, 1824, Various Notices, July 31, 1824." American Missionary Journal 5 (November 1824): 332.

"Union Mission: Journal for July and August, 1825, Lord's Day, August 14, 1825." *American Missionary Register* 6 (November 1825): 336.

"Union Mission: Journal for the Month of April, 1823, Indian Farmer, no date." *American Missionary Register* 4 (September 1823): 274.

"Union Mission: Journal for the Month of April, 1823, Indian Medical Remedy, no date." *American Missionary Register* 4 (September 1823): 273.

"Union Mission: Journal for the Months of April and May, 1822, The Indians manufacturing Salt, April 26, 1822." *American Missionary Register* 3 (October 1822): 140.

"Union Mission: Journal of the Mission for the Month of May, Indian Labourers, May 5, 1823." *American Missionary Register* 4 (December 1823): 369.

"Union Mission: Journal for the Months of January and February, 1823, Various Notices, January 14, 1823." *American Missionary Register* 4 (July 1823): 202.

"Union Mission: Journal for the Month of October 1821." *American Missionary Register* 2 (March 1822): 349–50.

"Union Mission: Journal for the Months of April and May, 1822." *American Missionary Register* 3 (October 1822): 139, 142.

"Union Mission: Journal for the Month of April, 1823, Indian Farmer, no date." *American Missionary Register* 4 (September 1823): 274.

"Union Mission: Journal for the Months of January and February, 1823, Increase of the School, February 14, 1823" and "Spirit of religious inquiry among the Indians, January, 31, 1823." *American Missionary Register* 4 (July 1823): 203.

"Union Mission: Journal for the Months of October and November, 1822, Indian Mourning, October 23, 1822. "*American Missionary Register* 4 (May 1823): 136.

"Union Mission: Journal of the Mission; Arrival of Indian Children, August 27, 1821." *American Missionary Register* 2 (January 1822): 273.

———. "Union Mission: Extract of Letters, December 26, 1821." *American Missionary Register* 2 (April 1822): 399–400.

———. "Union Mission: Extract of Letters, June 11, 1821." *American Missionary Register* 2 (September 1821): 107.

———. "Union: Extracts of Letters, June 11, 1824." *American Missionary Register* 5 (October 1824): 301

———. "Journal for August, 1824, State and Progress of the Indian Settlement." *American Missionary Register* 5 (December 1824): 363.

Vaill, Mr. "Osages: Preaching Tour among the Osage Villages." *Missionary Herald* 27 (September 1831): 288.

Vaill, William. "Osage Indians: Name and Character." *Missionary Herald* 22 (September 1826): 268.

Vaill, William F., and Epaphras Chapman. "Extracts from the Journal of the Union Mission." *American Missionary Register* 1 (September 1820): 91.

Wallace, Anthony F. C. *Jefferson and the Indians: The Tragic Fate of the First Americans.* Cambridge, Mass: Belknap Press of Harvard University Press, 1999.

Wand, Augustin C. *The Jesuits in Territorial Kansas, 1827–1861.* St. Marys, Kans.: St. Marys Star, 1962.

Wedel, Mildred Mott, "J.-B. Bénard, Sieur de la Harpe: Visitor to the Wichitas in 1719." *Great Plains Journal* 10 (spring 1971): 37–70.

Weslager, Clinton Alfred. *The Delaware Indians: A History.* New Brunswick, N.J.: Rutgers University Press, 1972.

White, Richard. *The Middle Ground: Indians, Empires, and Republics in the Great Lakes Region, 1650–1815.* 1991. Reprint, Cambridge, UK: Cambridge University Press, 1995.

———. "The Winning of the West: The Expansion of the Western Sioux in the Eighteenth and Nineteenth Centuries." *Journal of American History* 65 (September 1978): 319–43.

Wikle, Tom, ed. *Atlas of Oklahoma: Classroom Edition.* Stillwater: Oklahoma State University for Department of Geography, Computer Cartography Laboratory, 1991.

Wilkinson to Dearborn. July 27, 1805. *The Territorial Papers of the United States,* ed. Clarence E. Carter, 13:170. Washington, D.C.: Government Printing Office, 1934–62.

Wilson, Terry P. *The Underground Reservation: Osage Oil.* Lincoln: University of Nebraska Press, 1985.

Woolley, Miss. "Great Osage Mission: Extract of a letter to her mother, September 23, 1822." *American Missionary Register* 3 (December 1822): 211.

Index